PRATT WARE

English and Scottish relief decorated and
underglaze coloured earthenware
1780 – 1840

Frontispiece. The Sailor's Return and Farewell jug c.1790-1800
Impressed mark PRATT on the base and made at the Pratt pottery at Lane Delph.
Private Collection.

The other side of this jug is shown on page 19.

PRATT WARE

English and Scottish relief decorated and
underglaze coloured earthenware
1780-1840

John and Griselda Lewis

with an introduction by
Michael Archer

Antique Collectors' Club
in association with
Leo Kaplan Ltd.

ISBN 1 85149 191 0

British Library Cataloguing-in-Publication data
A catalogue record for this book is available from the British Library

Leo Kaplan Ltd.
967 Madison Avenue, New York, New York 10021
Phone 212 249 6766 Fax 212 861 2674
Specialist dealers in Pratt Ware and other English ceramics

Designed by John and Griselda Lewis

Printed in England by the Antique Collectors' Club, Woodbridge, Suffolk
on Consort Royal Satin paper supplied by the Donside Paper Company,
Aberdeen, Scotland

Antique Collectors' Club

The Antique Collectors' Club was formed in 1966 and now has a five figure membership spread throughout the world. It publishes the only independently run monthly antiques magazine *Antique Collecting* which caters for those collectors who are interested in widening their knowledge of antiques, both by greater awareness of quality and by discussion of the factors which influence the price that is likely to be asked. The Antique Collectors' Club pioneered the provision of information on prices for collectors and the magazine still leads in the provision of detailed articles on a variety of subjects.

It was in response to the enormous demand for information on 'what to pay' that the price guide series was introduced in 1968 with the first edition of *The Price Guide to Antique Furniture* (completely revised, 1978 and 1989), a book which broke new ground by illustrating the more common types of antique furniture, the sort that collectors could buy in shops and at auctions rather than the rare museum pieces which had previously been used (and still to a large extent are used) to make up the limited amount of illustrations in books published by commercial publishers. Many other price guides have followed, all copiously illustrated, and greatly appreciated by collectors for the valuable information they contain, quite apart from prices. The Antique Collectors' Club also publishes other books on antiques, including horology and art reference works, and a full book list is available.

Club membership, which is open to all collectors, costs £19.50 per annum. Members receive free of charge *Antique Collecting,* the Club's magazine (published ten times a year), which contains well-illustrated articles dealing with the practical aspects of collecting not normally dealt with by magazines. Prices, features of value, investment potential, fakes and forgeries are all given prominence in the magazine.

Among other facilities available to members are private buying and selling facilities, the longest list of 'For Sales' of any antiques magazine, an annual ceramics conference and the opportunity to meet other collectors at their local antique collectors' clubs. There are over eighty in Britain and more than a dozen overseas. Members may also buy the Club's publications at special pre-publication prices.

As its motto implies, the Club is an organisation designed to help collectors get the most out of their hobby: it is informal and friendly and gives enormous enjoyment to all concerned.

For Collectors — By Collectors — About Collecting

The Antique Collectors' Club, 5 Church Street, Woodbridge, Suffolk

Acknowledgements

Working on this book has been a most heartwarming experience. Museum Directors and Keepers of Departments of Ceramics have, almost without exception, treated us with the utmost consideration and generosity, as have the dealers in pottery and the private collectors who have allowed us to photograph their pieces. As well as these kind people, we are much indebted to friends, potters, historians, scientists and doctors who have consented to read various parts of the book and have given us valuable help, advice and encouragement.

Among all these, we would particularly like to thank:

Anne and Roy Aldridge	John Hadfield	Mark Pemberton
Robert Allbrook	Reginald Haggar	Julia Poole
Michael Archer	Catherine Haill	Rina Prentice
G.F. Arnold	Pat Halfpenny	Gerard Quail
John C. Austin	John Hall	Robin Reilly
Michael Beard	Peter Hall	Sheila and Edwin Rideout
Harold Blakey	Rodney and Aileen Hampson	Jessica Rutherford
Gaye Blake Roberts	Charlotte Haw	Leonard Russell
Julia Brant	P.K. Hill	Wynn A. Sayman
Jim Briggs	Jonathan Horne	David Scarratt
Mary Brook-Hart	Tristan Jones	John Smith
Lionel Burman	Pamela Judkins	Edward Smyth, FRCS
Jackie and David Clark	Peter Kaellgren	Messrs. Sotheby & Co.
Timothy Clifford	Heather Lawrence	Constance Stobo
Robert Copeland	Maureen Leese	Terence Suthers
Simon Cottle	Peter Leigh	Ross E. Taggart
Michael Cross	Terence Manby	W.N. Terry
Graeme Cruickshank	Pearl and Peter Manheim	Richard Talbot
George Dalgleish	John May	Beaumont Varcoe
Diana Darlington	David Mayer	Alex Walker
Aileen Dawson	Patrick McVeigh	R.J.B. Walker
M. Mellanay Delhom	John Morley	Sadia Walsh
Roger Edmundson	Corinne Miller	Peter Walton
Gordon Elliot	Lynn Miller	Geoffrey Warrington
Robin Emerson	Margaret Morris	Rose Watban
D. Fernyhough	John Munday	Josiah Wedgwood & Sons Ltd.
Alan Garlick	Revel Oddy	Reginald Williams
Cherry and Richard Gray	Simon Olding	Eleanor Winyard
Nancy Gunson	Molly Pearce	

We would like to express our gratitude to Mr. Alan Kaplan, the most prestigious of American dealers in old English ceramics and particularly in Pratt Ware, for making possible this new edition of our book.

Leo Kaplan Ltd. at 967 Madison Avenue, New York, has for long been the haunt of collectors of this ware. It was Alan Kaplan who put us right about the date of the so-called 'Waterloo' jug, with a cavalryman running down a gun crew. We had erroneously dated it 1815 (see page 171); Mr. Kaplan had found a jug with the same decoration inscribed and dated 1795, some twenty years earlier than the famous battle.

We would also like to thank Robert Alcock and his team at the Buttermarket Studio, Ipswich, who have so quickly and efficiently processed all our photographs.

Contents

List of Colour Plates

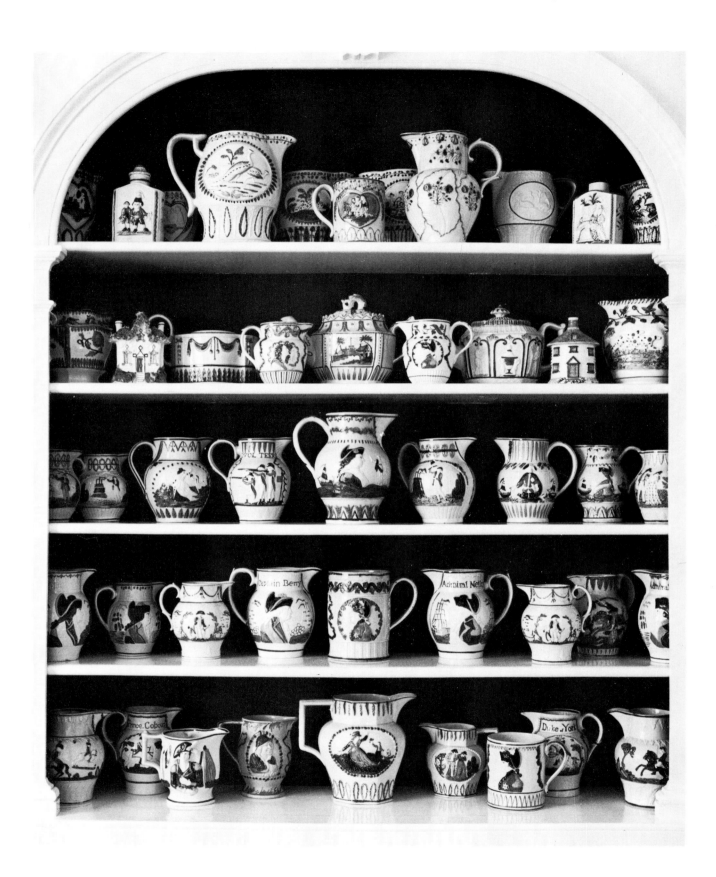

Introduction

When John and Griselda Lewis first started collecting Pratt ware over forty years ago nobody had yet made a serious study of the subject and even now this book is the first ever to do so. Collectors and students of English ceramics have long been accustomed to using terms such as 'Whieldon' or 'Astbury' to identify particular categories of object and unlike 'Oriental Lowestoft' they are not entirely misleading even if they do not express the whole truth. 'Pratt ware' is just such a term, used to describe what the authors define as 'relief decorated, high temperature fired, underglaze coloured cream and pearlware made from about 1780 to 1840'. While explaining that it is strictly speaking a misnomer, the Lewises wisely recommend the continuing use of a convenient and concise name which immediately brings to mind a readily identifiable type of pottery.

The mark 'Pratt' appears on only two pieces and the authors can now show that numerous other potters made the ware, over twenty of whom marked with their names. This book which makes use of a large number of original sources begins by concentrating on the marked pieces and goes on to associate with them others which from their moulded details or the style in which they are painted can be similarly attributed. Such attribution is extremely difficult since a number of potters made very similar wares and figures but with their sharp eye for minute differences in moulding the Lewises skilfully build up groups of associated pieces. They make use too of the evidence both of excavated shards and of closely related fine stoneware decorated in relief. They have also gone to considerable trouble to find out just how these pots were manufactured, taking into account the technological limitations of the time.

Until further excavation takes place there is bound to be much Pratt ware which eludes attribution and all this material has been grouped here according to subject matter. Commemorative pieces, rural and sporting scenes and classical subjects were all extremely popular and through the authors' meticulous research we are shown the extraordinary richness of source material on which the potters drew for their decoration. Unlike the cool and elegant neo-classical motifs on the products of Wedgwood and Turner which were meant for a more educated market, subjects such as 'Coriolanus with his wife and mother' probably meant little either to the makers or the purchasers of Pratt ware. The image was what mattered and the potters translated whatever subjects came to hand into vigorous works of art with a directness which is as appealing now as it must have been then.

John and Griselda Lewis have brought to their writing a similar blend of vigour, elegance and humour, as well as exemplary scholarship and an infectious enthusiasm. The fact that they have also designed the book themselves and taken many of the excellent photographs makes this invaluable and beautiful work an unusually personal achievement.

Michael Archer
DEPUTY KEEPER OF CERAMICS DEPARTMENT
VICTORIA AND ALBERT MUSEUM

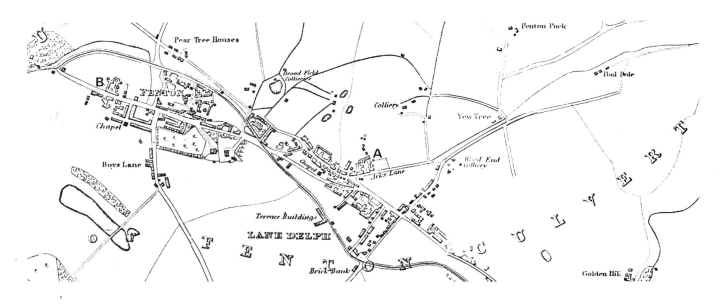

Detail from Thomas Hargreaves' map of the Potteries of 1832
William Pratt's pottery in Arks Lane is marked with an A and
F.& R.Pratt's pottery in Fenton is marked with a B. *Courtesy
Staffordshire County Library.*

Pratt mark
The impressed mark that appears on 'The
Sailor's Farewell' (see frontispiece).

Transfer printed mug c.1850
The subtle multi-coloured transfer prints on each side are set
against a vivid tomato red background, enriched with gold lines
top and bottom and on the handle. Produced at the Fenton
pottery by F. & R.Pratt. 103mm high. *Private Collection.*

Pratt mark
Transfer printed mark in brown that appears on
the base of the F. & R.Pratt mug.

12

1. The Pratt family and the reason for their name being associated with this ware.

The association of the name Pratt with relief decorated, high temperature fired, underglaze coloured cream and pearlware made from about 1785 to 1840, seems to rest solely on the evidence of two marked pieces; a creamware jug decorated with the seated figure of Britannia on one side and 'The Sailor's Return' on the other, and a pearlware jug with the latter subject on one side and 'The Sailor's Farewell' on the other, both impressed PRATT in capital letters on their bases.

The name Pratt belonged to a family of potters who were working at Lane Delph in the late eighteenth century and also at Fenton after 1807. Fenton and Lane Delph were situated on the borders of the two townships of Fenton Vivian to the north and Fenton Culvert to the south.

The potteries, shops and other buildings of the two Fentons mainly stood on or near the main road from Stoke to Longton, a distance of some two miles. This road formed the boundary between the two townships. At the end of the eighteenth century and in the early years of the nineteenth century, Church Fenton (formerly called Lower Lane), Lane Delph and the Foley were three separate villages. Church Fenton was the nearest to Stoke.

The districts of Fenton Vivian and Fenton Culvert were later amalgamated, about 1827, under the name of Fenton and Lane Delph became Middle Fenton. Lane Delph had long been a centre for earthenware manufacture. The word 'delph' is derived from ' 'delve', that is anything such as a pit or quarry (or in Holland a canal) which is delved or dug. In 'Lane Delph' it no doubt referred to the clay workings.

It was at Fenton in the middle of the nineteenth century that the firm of F. & R. Pratt did a considerable trade in underglaze coloured transfer printed pot lids and table ware, which is sometimes referred to as 'Pratt Ware'. Here inevitably is the cause of some confusion, for 'Pratt Ware' is a term that has long been used by collectors, dealers and by some museums for jugs, teapots, figures and other pieces of cream or pearlware, relief modelled and coloured in the restrained but distinctive palette that high temperature firing imposes, when the glaze is put on over the colouring.

Over seventy years ago there was a mention in Chaffers'[1] monumental work of 'Pratt Ware' referring to relief decorated, underglaze coloured ware, but three years before that, in 1909, a practical potter called G. Woolliscroft Rhead, writing in *The Connoisseur*[2] had already entitled his article 'Pratt Ware', so he may well have coined the term.

In 1910 Arthur Hayden, a rival author on ceramic subjects, also writing in *The Connoisseur*[3] said: 'Pratt jugs have come as a new nomenclature in Staffordshire; but there were other potters than Pratt who made jugs with the

---

1. William Chaffers, *Marks and Monograms on Pottery and Porcelain*, London, 13th edn., 1912.
2. G. W. Rhead, 'Pratt Ware', *The Connoisseur*, Vol. XXV, September 1909.
3. Arthur Hayden, 'Colonel Herbert Brock's Collection of Earthenware jugs', *The Connoisseur*, Vol. XXVI.

The three jugs referred to in Arthur Hayden's article. For full descriptions see pages 185, 51 and 181.

peculiar decoration which it is sought to attribute solely to him...' He illustrates his article with three jugs, a Gretna Green jug with curved flutes, a jug with a scene of men drinking and a large hunting jug, and says of them: 'They are in Pratt style with yellow, blue and green decorations and the acanthus ornamentation at the base; the smaller one in the middle (the men drinking) has the WEDGWOOD mark impressed. This is an important fact and should prevent collectors from too hastily assigning this type of jug to Pratt...' Arthur Hayden concludes his article '...the Pratt period from 1775 to 1810 coincides with much fine pottery by other Staffordshire potteries. The leading characteristic of the zigzag or pointed borders at top and bottom is not, as we have shown, confined to Pratt'. (Nor is it confined to Staffordshire and the ware continued to be made by at least one or two potters until the end of the 1830s.)

It would look as if Hayden's remarks were aimed at Woolliscroft Rhead; however, in spite of his cautions, the term has stuck. Rhead later expanded his 1909 article in his book,[4] calling a chapter 'Pratt Ware'. It is a convenient term, admirable in its brevity and is certainly simpler than calling these pots every time one mentions them 'relief decorated, high-temperature fired, underglaze coloured pearl or cream coloured earthenware'. If one can use the term 'Delft' to describe decorated tin-glazed earthenware made in Bristol or Southwark long before it was ever made in the Dutch town of Delft, there is at least as good a justification for using 'Pratt ware' as a generic term. Had Woolliscroft Rhead first found similar jugs with the impressed mark of HAWLEY, FERRYBRIDGE or DANIEL, as he might well have done, no doubt he might have called them after one of these potters or potteries, for these names and many others are to be found on so-called Pratt ware.

There is not much evidence to support Hayden's claim that Pratt ware was made as early as 1775. The earliest dated piece we have yet seen is a Rodney head mug, inscribed 1785, and that was a transitional piece, part coloured glaze. Most of the dated pieces we have found belong to the 1790s, though

---

4. G. Woolliscroft Rhead, *The Earthenware Collector,* London, 1920.

there are some plaques bearing dates as late as 1818 and a clock money-box is incised 1838.

Rhead had served his time at Mintons and had also been a student at the Royal College of Art. In his book he records a visit he had made to the Pratt pottery at Fenton, some time before 1909. There he interviewed a representative of the firm. He wrote: 'Although little is known of the earlier Pratts, the family possessing no records beyond the grandfather, (Felix Pratt 1780-1859) of the present members of the firm, we elicited two or three interesting items of information, such as there have been six generations of Pratts, potters. A Felix Pratt, presumably the first, married one of the daughters of Thomas Heath, who was potting at Lane Delph (now Middle Fenton) in 1710. The two other daughters became the wives of the potters Palmer and Neale... the present factory was built on the site of that occupied by Thomas Heath.[5] The Felix Pratt of the pieces under review considered himself a better potter than Josiah Wedgwood and that he was an excellent colour maker; an important piece of information, since there can be no doubt that colour is the most valuable quality of these pieces'.

This brings us to the first of many confusions in the Pratt saga. The Felix Pratt that Rhead mentions was only born in 1780. He was fifteen when Josiah Wedgwood died, so it is hardly likely that he would have compared his talents as an apprentice potter with those of the great Josiah Wedgwood. It is almost certainly his father William Pratt (1753-99) a master potter of Lane Delph, to whom the Pratt's representative must have been referring. So, if this supposition is correct, it was William Pratt who was the first of his family to make this distinctive ware, but whether he was the first potter to make it is by no means certain.

Apart from the cream and pearlware jugs, and of course the transfer printed wares, the only other piece of marked Pratt pottery that we have found is a buff coloured jasper ware pot-pourri vase with a perforated lid and blue applied

---

5. The Thomas Heath factory was actually on the site of the original Pratt pottery at Lane Delph and not the one at Fenton which Rhead visited.

Pot-pourri Vase and cover c.1785-90
This putty coloured stoneware vase with a pierced lid is decorated with sprigged on decorative borders of grapes and vine leaves in a contrasting grey blue colour. The medallions enclose reliefs of a seated shepherdess with a dog and a lady playing a lyre. It is marked underneath the base 'Pratt' in impressed upper and lower case lettering. 159mm high. *Fitzwilliam Museum, Cambridge. C 11. 1983.*

There is a similar vase in the Victoria and Albert Museum, which lacks the lid. *2545.1906.* These are the only stoneware pieces marked 'Pratt' that we have ever seen.

decorative borders of vines and classical medallions. This is marked 'Pratt' in impressed upper and lower case letters on the base. It was recently acquired by the Fitzwilliam Museum at Cambridge. There is a similar piece lacking the lid, in the Victoria and Albert Museum, also marked in the same way. What other wares the Pratt potteries made, with our present state of knowledge it is impossible to say.

The Staffordshire Parish Registers that deal with the Parish of Stoke-on-Trent give us some bare facts about the Pratt family. William Pratt, son of Thomas and Elizabeth Pratt of Lane End, was born in 1753. He was christened on December 19th of that year. On April 15th 1776 he married Ellen Edwards, with Thomas Pratt (probably his father) as a witness. They had seven children. The eldest boy William must have been born about 1778 (we have been unable to find any record of his birth or christening). William became a successful maltster and grocer in Lane Delph. We have no means of knowing why he did not carry on his father's pottery. This duty fell to three of the sons, Felix, John and Richard, the other son Samuel became a plumber and a glazier. Felix was born in 1780 and his christening was on March 24th. John, Samuel and Richard and his two sisters Myra and Mary Heath followed at approximately two yearly intervals.

In the 1780s William Pratt was working as a master potter at Lane Delph[6] at a pottery in Arks Lane on the site of Thomas Heath's old factory. Our assumptions are that the marked Pratt jugs were made during William's lifetime, though no doubt they continued to be made by the potteries directed by his widow and his sons after his death. By 1791 William Pratt had become a master potter of some consequence. In company with Richard and John Astbury, Samuel Spode, William and John Turner and others he had signed a Resolution, published as a Handbill in answer to a 'maliciously circulated' bill from some of Mr Spode's journeymen potters at the Foley, complaining about the alteration in the time of their Dinner Hour (from midday to one o'clock).

The *Staffordshire Advertiser* of February 9th 1799 announced that 'William Pratt, Lane Delph, manufacturer died Friday sennight'. He was only forty-six years old. William Pratt had made his will in 1794. He chose his 'dear and loving wife Ellen Pratt', James Caird of Newcastle under Lyme and Charles Simpson of Lane End as his executors, to hold his estate in trust until his youngest surviving child reached the age of twenty-one, when the estate was to be divided equally between his children, with the exception of the capital sum of £600, which was to be put aside to provide an income for his widow. She was also to have any household effects that she needed 'to furnish a convenient dwelling house'. (If she married again, the £600 went back into the estate and she was to be given a lump sum of £300).[7]

On William Pratt's death in 1799, James Caird and Charles Simpson renounced their executorships in favour of Ellen Pratt, who then had sole charge of the estate. In 1805 *Holden's Triennial Directory* listed Ellin (*sic*) Pratt as an earthenware manufacturer in Lane Delph and also John Pratt as an earthenware manufacturer in Lane Delph. Her son Felix must also have been helping his mother to run the Lane Delph works. In 1806 Felix married a spinster called Ann Poulson, by whom he eventually had three sons and three daughters, the eldest child being christened Felix Edwards. He was called Felix

---

6.   *Bailey's Northern Directory*, 1781.
7.   Appendix I, William Pratt's Will.

after his father and Edwards after his grandmother Ellen's maiden name.

In the local Rate Books Ellen Pratt is shown in 1807 (the transcriptions only date from that year)[8] as owner of a pottery in Fenton Vivian which she had let to Pratt and Coomer. The Pratt referred to is Ellen's newly married son Felix and his partner was probably William Coomer who had been a master potter at Lane End from 1799 to 1805. This pottery had belonged to Harrison and Hyatt, (George Harrison was a potter and William Hyatt a well-to-do solicitor in Meir) they had been trying to let this newly-built potworks since 1801. George Harrison died in 1806 so it looks as if Ellen Pratt bought it up in 1807 and installed Felix there in that year. The pottery was situated near the railway and within a mile of Stoke Wharf. The railway was in fact a horse-drawn tramway from the Whieldon Basin on the Trent and Mersey Canal. Parts of this narrow gauge line can still be seen.

By 1810 William Coomer's name had disappeared from the Rate Books and Felix Pratt had become Ellen's sole tenant for the part of the property described in the rate book as 'late Coomer and Pratt'. The remainder of the property was let to a potter called William Cartwright. Meanwhile John Pratt is listed as owner-occupier of a house and potworks in Fenton Culvert, which of course was his father's old Lane Delph works.

Though Felix was running the Fenton pottery with Coomer, he must also have been helping John at the Lane Delph works. *The Victoria County History* states that Felix and John were running the Lane Delph Works until 1812, when Felix moved to Fenton, but John continued at the Lane Delph pottery. In fact Felix must also have been working at Fenton for the previous five years.

1811 or 1812 must have been the year when Mary Heath, William Pratt's youngest child, reached the age of twenty-one and when Felix, John and Richard, the potting members of the family and the other children came into their patrimony.

During and immediately after the Napoleonic wars, times were very difficult for the potters. Bankruptcies were common and properties frequently changed hands or remained unsold or unlet. On several occasions the Pratt potteries were advertised for sale or to let during those years.

On January 7th 1815 the *Staffordshire Advertiser* announced the death of Ellen Pratt, with these words: 'On Monday last, at an advanced age, Mrs Pratt of Lane Delph in the Potteries'. So Ellen Pratt, mother of a family of potters expired on January 3rd 1815. She had nominated her youngest son Richard and Thomas Harley, potter of Lane End and the husband of her elder daughter Myra, as executors. William Pratt had left half of his estate for her disposal. She left various properties in Lane End and her half share in the potworks and other premises in Lane Delph to be divided equally among her children. In addition she left £100 to her unmarried daughter Mary Heath.[9]

In 1816 Ellen Pratt is still shown as the owner of the property at Fenton Vivian, with Felix as her lessee, subletting to his brother John. The Rate Books were clearly behind the times. In the same year Felix Pratt took over Charles Bourne's pottery at Lane Delph. This property belonged to one John Smith, a wealthy landowner who lived near Lichfield. In 1815 Ellen Pratt is also listed in the Rate Books as having as tenants of a potworks at Fenton Vivian, the

---

8. Transcriptions by Alfred Meigh (1940) from the 1807/8 Rate Books. Res. Local Collection, NK 4987.S7.M3, Keele University Archives.
9. Appendix II, Ellen Pratt's Will.

Plaque with the bust of a hussar c.1800-15

This portrait plaque is coloured in green, blue and manganese only. It is inscribed 'Daniel Goostry' in dark blue on the front. 153mm high. *The Royal Pavilion Art Gallery and Museums, Brighton. HW 343.*

There were several Daniel Goostreys listed in the Stoke-on-Trent Parish Registers kept during the eighteenth and early nineteenth centuries; as a Daniel Goostry was a tenant of Ellen Pratt's, it would be nice to think that one of the Pratts had made this plaque, but there is not a shred of evidence to justify such a speculation.

1 & 2. Britannia jug c.1790-1800 *opposite*

This jug is found in at least three sizes (127, 155 and 178mm high). The body is usually of a warm cream-coloured earthenware and the glaze has a greenish hue. Among the usual colouring of cobalt, ochre and manganese brown there is a distinctive rather pale greyish green. The slightly raised footrim is flat and varies from 50mm to 80mm in width. It is slightly ovoid in shape, and pointed at front and back where the sides of the mould have met. The shape of the handles varies from a plain loop to an ear-shape, to a loop with a thumb-rest at the top.

The design shows on one side Britannia seated against a circular shield, holding an olive branch in her right hand and a trident in her left. At her feet is a seated lion, a ship of the line is in the background. On the other side is a scene of the 'Sailor's Return' with a single figure of a sailor waving a swagger stick, his ship in the background with rocks on either side. The handle and the top of the jug are banded in brown and a green and ochre anthemion repeat pattern surrounds the neck of the jug, these motifs are mirrored and divided by a blue line. A casually painted chain of brush strokes forming husks runs from the base of the spout to the uncoloured fluted border at the bottom of the jug. An identical jug to this is impressed PRATT in capital letters on the base. Made at the Pratt pottery in Lane Delph. 127mm high. *Private Collection.*

Pratt jug footrim and mark

A noticeable feature of these marked PRATT jugs is the flat raised footrim, which goes to a slight point at the front and back, producing a semi-ovoid, almost lemon shape where the two halves of the mould have met, yet the jugs are intrinsically round in shape. On no other Pratt type jug is this exact type of footrim featured. On some other jugs the footrim is circular inside, though the outside of it goes to a slight point.

partnership of Goostrey and Simkin. For the next nine years Ellen Pratt continued to be listed as their landlord even though she had died in 1815. She is actually listed in the Rate Books as the owner of a property at Fenton Vivian until October 1825.[10]

In 1815 an auction of a house and potworks on the main road at Lane Delph occupied by Felix Pratt and a 'China Manufactory' occupied by Goostrey and

10. Rodney Hampson, in a letter to the authors July 17th 1983 wrote: 'Ellen Pratt's life after death owning the Fenton Vivian Pottery, could be explained by the failure of the Rate Book clerks to amend their information, or perhaps because her executors owned it for some time on behalf of her legatees'.

There is a marked version of the Britannia jug in the British Museum *1920 6-17 1.* Unmarked, but very similar specimens can be seen at the Merseyside County Museum, Liverpool *5.4.171.836,* the Royal Pavilion Art Gallery and Museums, Brighton *HW271* and the Castle Museum, Norwich *29.158.23.* In the last mentioned version the colouring is rather more intense.

3. The Sailor's Return and Farewell jug c.1790-1800

One of a set of pearlware jugs with a marked bluish tint to the glaze. It is decorated with two scenes of a sailor and his lass, with on one side, a man in a rowing boat in the background. These scenes are set within a semicircular border made up of two sizes of small leaves, the larger ones alternately coloured blue and orange, the smaller leaves in pairs in between are left uncoloured. There is a border of stiff green acanthus leaves around the bottom of the jug while the top is banded in brown, below which there is a wider border of leaves tapering to a point, alternated with pendant olive twigs with two leaves and two fruits. The handle, which terminates at the lower end in a leaf shape, is banded in brown, its top end is fixed within a blue and green leaf decoration, which pattern is repeated round the base of the spout. A blue band encircles the lower neck of the jug and blue lines are painted in pairs down the front and back. This jug has exactly the same kind of footrim as the Britannia jug and it is also impressed PRATT in capital letters. Made at the Pratt factory at Lane Delph. 155mm high. *Private Collection.*
See frontispiece for the other side of this jug.

Another of these marked jugs is in the Victoria and Albert Museum *C.45.1940.* There are two small versions 127mm high of it in the Royal Pavilion Art Gallery and Museum at Brighton *HW 292 & A.*

Simkin was announced in the *Staffordshire Advertiser*. Auctions in those days frequently resulted in no sale and this was no exception. Though the Rate Books show that Goostrey and Simkin continued to occupy the property until November 1824, in fact there is another announcement in the same Newspaper for March 2nd 1816 stating: 'Partnership dissolved between Daniel Goostrey and Hugh Simkin, manufacturers of chinaware, Lane Delph from 11 November 1815 (Martinmas)'.

The underglaze relief portrait of Daniel Goostry (*sic*) that we show here was one reason for trying to find out something about the Goostreys. It is such an unusual name and in the rate records is spelt in several different ways: Goostry, Goosetrey, and Goosetree. It may have derived from the village of that name near Jodrell Bank in Cheshire. There seem to have been three Daniel Goostreys resident in the Potteries. The Daniel Goostrey of Goostrey and Simkin may have been the one described in 1826 in the Probate of his Will as 'A Yeoman living at Pear Trees in Fenton Vivian', or he may have been Daniel, son of Obadiah Goostrey who would have been twenty-six in 1815, which would of course make the plaque of a much later date than we have suggested for it.

Hugh Simkin (or Simpkin) Goostrey's partner was living at Lane End from 1816. Simeon Shaw describes Simkin's manufactory in Market Place, Lane End, where 'he made a superior kind of porcelain'. Shaw continues in a eulogistic vein' . . . he is well known for his public and private virtues and his house, near Steel's Nook, is a beautiful tho' small edifice, with gardens of delightful arrangement for Flowers and Fruit'.[11]

The *Staffordshire Advertiser* of February 15th 1817 makes another mention of the Pratt family in announcing that Mr. Waller, a respectable manufacturer of Lane Delph had married Miss Pratt, daughter of the late Mr. Pratt of Lane Delph, at Stoke Church on February 12th. This was Mary Heath Pratt, William Pratt's youngest child. The respectable Mr. Waller was William Waller, Hugh Simkin's partner from 1817 to 1819 at what later became known as the Gladstone Works at Lane End. Waller continued working the pottery until 1821.

Felix Pratt, in partnership with his youngest brother Richard traded from the Fenton potteries from 1818 as Felix Pratt & Company.

In 1828 William Pratt, shopkeeper and maltster of Lane Delph died at the age of fifty leaving his brother Felix and his brother-in-law Henry Brassington of Penkhull (at one time innkeeper of the Cross Keys at Lane Delph) as executors. His wife must have predeceased him and apparently he had no children for he left his not inconsiderable estate to his brothers and sisters and their children.

By 1829 according to Simeon Shaw, John Pratt was living and working the pottery in Arks Lane near the Calvinist Chapel. It looks, from the Rate Books, as though John Bourne, a wealthy landowner, had bought up the property and leased it back to the Pratts. It is not at all clear how many properties the Pratts were working. They must have owned or been tenants of at least three.

From 1827 Felix Pratt, trading as Felix Pratt & Company, was still working the pottery owned by John Smith as well as another pottery owned by P. B. Broad, with two partners Thomas Hassall and Thomas Gerrard. Gerrard died, aged sixty-two, in 1833. In 1834 Felix Pratt is listed in a local

---

11.   Simeon Shaw, *History of the Staffordshire Potteries*, Hanley, 1829.

gazetteer[12] as an earthenware manufacturer at Lane Delph and also in partnership with his brother Richard at Fenton. So clearly the two firms were closely connected.

Felix Pratt died in 1859. His will (five great vellum sheets) made in 1853, presumably after the death of his wife, gives some indication of how successful the Pratts had become. His personal estate was worth about £10,000.[13]

F. & R. Pratt and Company continued to trade until 1916. From 1920 to 1926 their works became known as the Rialto Pottery, which was run by the British Art Pottery Company (Fenton) Limited. The potworks were demolished in 1933 to make way for the Workshops for the Blind.

The Lane Delph pottery was run by John Pratt and his son William from 1835 and by John Pratt and Company from 1850 to 1870, when it became Pratt and Simpson. In 1884 the firm became Wallis Gimson & Co. and maybe the Pratts still had an interest in it. In the early 1900s it had passed entirely out of their hands, when it became known as the Rubian Art Pottery Limited which continued in business until the 1930s. The site which had long been derelict, was cleared some time after the last war and old people's bungalows were erected, encircled by a lane bordered with cherry trees and called Delph Walk.

In 1977 we visited Mr Philip Varcoe and his brother Mr Beaumont Varcoe at Par in Cornwall, direct descendants of William Pratt and interestingly enough, still connected with the raw material of the pottery trade. Their knowledge of the family did not go back before Felix Edwards Pratt (William Pratt's grandson), but Mr Philip Varcoe had in his possession some little late eighteenth century agate ware boxes that had been handed down to him and were said to have been made by the Lane Delph firm. Mr Beaumont Varcoe had a number of relief decorated underglaze coloured jugs, several of which are illustrated in this book. Unfortunately not one of them was marked.

---

12. William White, *History, Gazetteer and Directory of Staffordshire,* 1834.
13. Stafford Record Office D3272/5/20/4/19. See Appendix III.

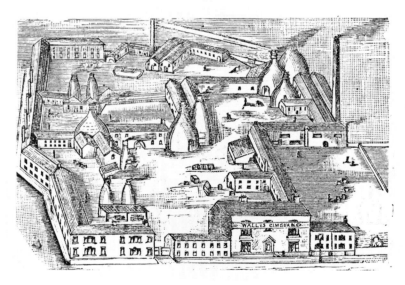

William Pratt's Pottery in Lane Delph
An engraving of William Pratt's pottery in Arks Lane as it had become by 1885. It was probably much the same in general appearance only smaller in the early years of the century.
From an advertisement in *The Pottery Gazette.*

2. The ware itself and its different types. Its place in the history of British Pottery. How it was made and the nature of the colouring

Underglaze coloured and relief decorated ware of the Pratt type occupied a transitional period after the coloured glazed pottery of Whieldon and Ralph Wood and before it was superseded by the over-glaze enamel coloured ware introduced at the end of the eighteenth century by potters such as Enoch Wood. This underglaze coloured ware consisted of either a cream-coloured earthenware, or more usually a pearlware body (which varied greatly in quality) with a transparent or blue tinted glaze, decorated with designs in relief, pressed from intaglio moulds. It was painted with a limited range of high temperature colours under the glaze, all of which are derived from metallic oxides. These colours were yellow, orange, green, blue, brown, black and occasionally a mulberry puce colour. It is the limitations of this palette that characterise the ware and make it so attractive. This underglaze colour technique is about the most durable way of retaining the brilliance of the colours, as they are protected by the coating of transparent glaze.

The ware was made from the early 1780s in Staffordshire, Shropshire, Liverpool, Yorkshire, Sunderland, Newcastle upon Tyne, Bovey Tracey in Devonshire and in Scotland, but does not appear to have been made in Bristol or in any of the Welsh potteries. Its quality gradually deteriorated and by the late 1830s, when the more versatile enamel colouring had come into general use, the production of this kind of ware practically ceased.

Though jugs are the most common pieces to be found, a variety of other both useful and decorative objects were made including teapots and tea-caddies, mugs, vases, flasks, cornucopias, money-boxes, candlesticks, plaques, busts, figures, cow creamers and other animals.

The last decade of the eighteenth century and the first decades of the nineteenth were periods of great disquiet and uncertainty. Relations with the United States of America, to where a considerable amount of pottery was exported, had long been precarious and came to an end in 1811 when they declared that all intercourse between the two countries should cease. The following year they declared war on England which lasted until 1814, after which trade was slowly resumed. On the Continent the French Revolution had taken place and in England there was the recurring fear of an invasion from the armies of Napoleon. It was a time of patriotism and hero worship which led to the production of many commemorative pieces of pottery. Though the industrial revolution in England was gathering pace, a large part of the population still lived and worked in the countryside; it is not surprising that, apart from commemorative pieces, the most common subjects decorating so-called Pratt jugs, mugs etc., were rural and rustic scenes of hunting, shooting, coursing, roistering and toping.

If the Pratts were the first to make this relief decorated underglaze coloured ware, it is clear that they must have been influenced by the work of other potters. Raised decoration on ware certainly dates back to classical times. The

'Colchester vase' (c.200A.D.) shows a lively combat between two gladiators in full relief. Mediaeval jugs were decorated with relief designs, stoneware bellarmines from the seventeenth century were embellished with relief masks and sprigged decoration appears on the red wares of the Astbury type and on early white saltglazed stoneware and of course on the jasper ware of Josiah Wedgwood and John Turner.

Many of the actual designs on Pratt ware have been copied or adapted from those used on jasper and other stonewares by Wedgwood, Turner and Adams, and border motifs were copied from some of William Hackwood's drawings.

John Turner, one of the most influential figures in the potteries in the middle of the eighteenth century, began potting at Stoke on the site of what was later to become the Copeland-Spode factory. Turner and his modellers James Lucock, George Ray and William Massey produced many designs in relief for use on stoneware, based on rural scenes of everyday life that were sometimes beautiful and often amusing. In the Spode Museum at Stoke-on-Trent, there are some hundreds of small master moulds of such scenes, many of them impressed TURNER or incised 'Turner' in a cursive hand. These master moulds are in relief, it is from these that pitcher moulds were pressed and fired.

At least a dozen of these subjects appear on Pratt jugs, mugs and plaques. Numerous border motifs of stiff straight leaves, curious lily-like plants and many versions of the acanthus leaf which are so typical of the decoration on Pratt jugs, also appear on these moulds. On such evidence, Turner plays a significant part in the Pratt ware story.

By the mid-1760s Wedgwood was producing a refined pale coloured creamware, which was composed of ball clay from Dorset and Devonshire mixed with a certain proportion of ground calcined flint. With the introduction in the late 1760s of china clay and china stone from Cornwall, Wedgwood perfected his product. The ware was finished with a transparent lead glaze of a slightly yellowish colour.

Pearlware or what Josiah Wedgwood referred to as 'Pearl white' ware[1] was first made by him in 1779. He considered this development from creamware as 'a change rather than an improvement'. The white earthenware body had rather more white clay and flint in it than the cream coloured ware.[2] A very small quantity of cobalt was added to the glaze and the faint blue coloration gave an impression of whiteness.

The same designs that are to be found on Pratt ware can also be seen on fine white smear-glazed stoneware and black basaltes. It is only in the fine white stoneware that one finds Pratt jugs in exactly the same form and from the same moulds as their more colourful cream or pearlware counterparts.

The Pratts or who ever invented this particular form of ware inspired a number of copyists. It was a simple but lively formula, far less sophisticated than Wedgwood's relief decorated jasper ware, yet retaining an artistic unity by the limited range of colours imposed on the potters by the high temperature firing. Once over-glaze enamel colouring came into fashion, this limited but effective colour scheme was soon abandoned.

---

1. Mentioned in a letter to Thomas Bentley 6 August 1779, Keele University Archives (E.18914-26).
2. For recipes for pearl white bodies see Taylor's *Complete Practical Potter*, Shelton, 1847. See also Appendix IV p. 292.

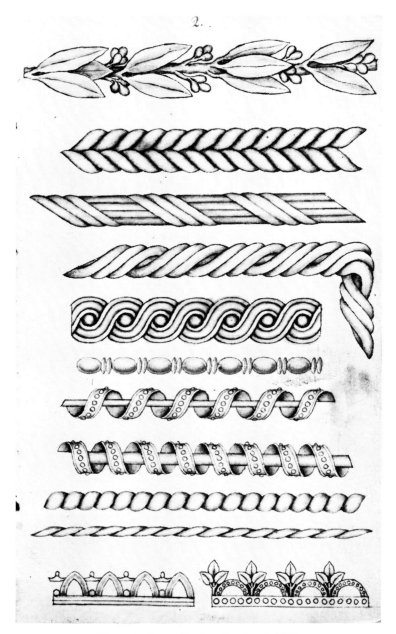

2.

Pages from William Hackwood's drawing book 1799
Some of Hackwood's meticulously drawn border designs, many of them
the inspiration behind the relief moulded borders used on underglaze
coloured ware. The laurel border at the top of the page was also used on
Wedgwood's jasper ware.

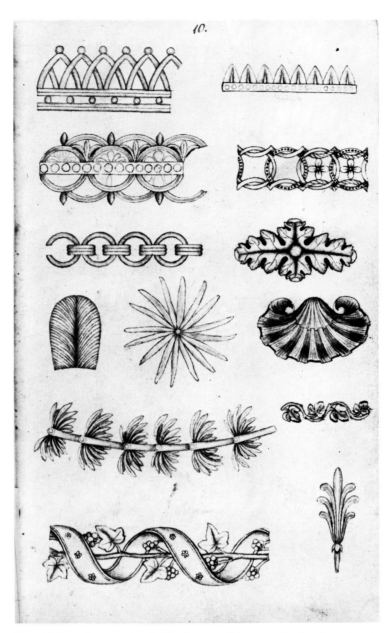

Page 10 from the same book. The bottom ribbon and ivy border is clearly the inspiration for the border used on the Duke of York and Royal Sufferers jug on page 129. No doubt many of these designs antedate the sketchbook by some years. Original size 168mm high. *Courtesy of the Trustees of the Wedgwood Museum, Barlaston, Stoke-on-Trent.*

Modern jasper ware border design *opposite*
This laurel border decoration was originally designed by William Hackwood for use on jasper ware made by Wedgwood in the late eighteenth century and was the inspiration for one of the border designs used on relief moulded underglaze coloured pieces. This design is still used today on contemporary Wedgwood jasper ware. *Courtesy Josiah Wedgwood and Sons Limited, Barlaston, Stoke-on-Trent.*

The moulds

The moulds from which relief decorated ware was produced were usually well made, the intaglio decoration being sharply defined. The best ware has a crisp quality, but as the moulds were often used until they were very worn (the average life of a mould was only about twenty-five pressings) examples pressed from them later in the run tended to be blurred and smeary.

Mould making was a specialised craft involving many skills. First the 'block cutter' or modeller made a model or block in clay, plaster or even wood, of the object or jug and from this a plaster cast or case was taken. (By the time Pratt jugs were being made, plaster of Paris had come into general use for this purpose). The original model was never used for making the working moulds. The sequence for making the working moulds was as follows:

1. The original model or block was made
2. Plaster cast or case taken from it
3. Second block made of clay and subsequently fired
4. Second plaster case from the second block
5. Final jug or object

For a simple shape like a jug, a two-or three-piece mould was used, the two side pieces and the base fitting together exactly, positioned by interlocking 'natches'. Even so, it is possible to see in the finished jugs a line where the two sides of the mould had met, when the piece had not been properly fettled (or even when it had been), that is, tidied up with a fettling knife and then by sponging over the seams left by the joins of the mould. The rims and bases also had to be fettled and sponged.

It is quite likely that the original blocks for these jugs were made without any relief decoration.[3] They may have been thrown and turned. Plain plaster of Paris cases would be made from these blank 'originals'. From these plain moulds further blocks would be made and then on to these the relief decorations would be sprigged.

Applied relief or sprigged decorations were made by taking a pressing from a small intaglio mould. The plastic clay was pressed into the mould, surplus clay scraped off, thereby flattening the back of the impression. It was then carefully lifted out of the mould and placed on the dampened surface of the unfired block and by the careful pressure of a finger or a wooden tool, was fixed in place.

From these sprig decorated blocks, further plaster of Paris moulds would be made and would become the moulds from which the relief decorated jugs would be pressed. The walls of these plaster moulds were quite thick, to enable them to absorb the moisture from the damp clay as quickly as possible.

In the process of press moulding, a layer of clay some 5mm thick was pressed into each side of a completely dry mould and on to the base. After pressing into position, it was smoothed off. Some of the old potters used a dampened cow's lip – the soft smooth lower lip, which in life was always moist. When the two sides of the mould and the base were joined up and firmly tied together, a thin roll of clay was worked into the seams and smoothed off in the same manner, a process known as luting. At the time when these jugs were made, small boys were employed as 'mould runners' to carry the moulds away from the presser

---

3. One of a number of helpful suggestions by Harold Blakey.

Turner mould c.1790
The Archery Lesson, a master pitcher mould, impressed mark
TURNER. This design appeared on many stoneware jugs and tankards
as well as on Pratt jugs. *Courtesy Spode Museum, Stoke-on-Trent.*

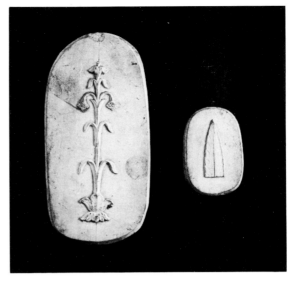

Turner moulds c.1790
Master pitcher moulds for decorative motifs for repeat
borders on various kinds of ware. Impressed mark
TURNER. *Courtesy Spode Museum, Stoke-on-Trent.*

to a warm drying place, often in another building, and to return with the
empty moulds.[4]

When sufficiently dry, the jug was removed from the mould, it was then
fettled and sponged and the handle was added. The handles were either press
moulded, for the more complicated shapes, or extruded in the form of a strip of
clay and formed into a loop. They were joined to the vessel with slip. Press
moulds were also used for the production of figures.

For casting, slip (liquid clay) of about the consistency of cream was poured
into the mould. The dry plaster of Paris absorbed the water from the slip,
leaving a thin layer of dehydrating clay adhering to the sides of the mould.
When the slip had been left long enough in the mould to form an adequate
thickness, the excess liquid was poured off.

Casting would seem to have many advantages over press moulding, but the
potters of the late eighteenth and early nineteenth centuries had problems.
Plastic clay suitable for pressing was not suitable for casting. It was difficult, if
not impossible to create a liquid clay with a minimum of water content that
would flow easily. Acid salts in the clay apparently caused the clay particles to
coagulate or flocculate. This resulted in a thin and impervious skin of clay
forming against the sides of the mould, preventing enough clay from building
up an adequate thickness for the walls of a vessel. So a deflocculating agent was
needed, such as sodium silicate and soda ash, of which potters at that time had
no knowledge.[5]

---

4. There are accounts of these children in Victorian times, who were employed by the workmen, and who
   were often as young as seven years old. They started work at 6 a.m. and finished their day's work at any
   time between 6 and 8 p.m. all for a shilling (5p) a week. At the end of the week they usually had to wait
   outside a public house, until their employer emerged with their pitiful wage. E.J.D. Warrilow, *A
   Sociological History of Stoke-on-Trent*, Etruscan Publications, 1960. The conditions were probably much
   the same at the end of the eighteenth and beginning of the nineteenth centuries.
5. Taylor's *Complete Practical Potter*, Shelton, 1847. This book gives a number of recipes for bodies suitable
   for pressing and casting. See also Appendix IV, p. 292.

Mould for the Loyal Volunteers jug c.1799
The side of the worn plaster of Paris mould showing the three Volunteers standing in firing position, now in the Abbey House Museum, Kirkstall, Leeds. It came from J.& G.Senior of Hunslet, who illustrated a jug made from this mould in W.W.Slee's Catalogue (see page 67). *Leeds City Council, Abbey House Museum.*

28

Loyal Volunteers jug c.1800
This creamware jug must have been pressed from a mould like that shown opposite. Some versions of this jug actually have LEEDS POTTERY impressed on the base. This specimen is unmarked. 155mm high. *Private Collection.*

These problems did not arise with the mixture used in making porcellanous stoneware, because of its high content of non-plastic ingredients. Hence examples of stoneware jugs of Pratt type do exist that are slip cast.

It is possible to tell a slip cast jug from a press moulded one by scrutinising the internal contour. Slip cast ware, unless very thickly cast will show a concave contour corresponding exactly to the external relief moulded form. Pressed wares merely show an ill-defined depression behind the external moulded relief. They are also thicker in section.

Press moulding caused much less wear on the plaster of Paris moulds because the water in the slip eroded the plaster surface more quickly. Even though press moulding was a slower process, the entire operation was quicker because the damp clay dried out much faster than the liquid slip.

After the first relatively high temperature firing (c.1150ºC) to biscuit, the colours were applied. The painting of the moulded decoration varied very much in quality from quite intricately painted specimens to pieces where the colours had been applied in a very simple, even slapdash manner, quite possibly by child labour.

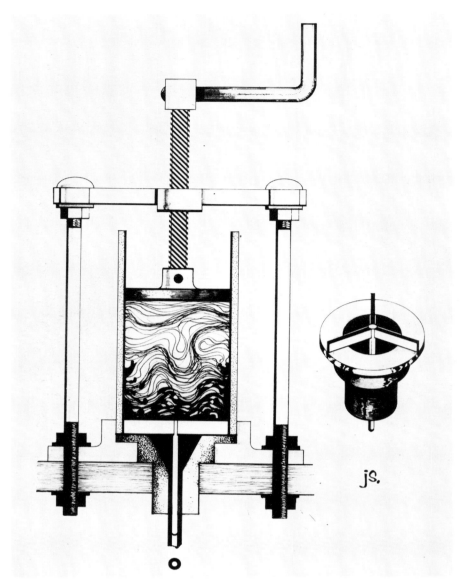

Diagram of a wad box
Wad box for extruding pipe stems, consisting of a cylinder, filled with clay, with a screwing down plate for forcing the clay through the aperture at the bottom. The drawing to the right shows the little inset bottom plate with the rod that forms the hollow stem. *Drawing by John Smith, Stourbridge.*

The making of pipes

The most indiosyncratic of all Pratt ware objects are the underglaze coloured pipes that often have stems of great length, twisted and bent and coiled into extraordinary shapes. These pipes were made from a white clay mixed with a high proportion of plastic ball clay, which was even softer than that used for throwing. It did not contain flint, normally used for qualities of whiteness and hardness of clay bodies.

The hollow pipe stem was formed in a small version of a 'wad box'. At the bottom of the cylinder was a metal core that made the hollow stem. The desired length of stem was extruded, by screwing down the pressure plate and forcing the soft clay through the hole in the base of the box. If very long lengths of pipe were wanted, extra clay could be added to the cylinder.

The extruded length was then coiled, folded or twisted into what ever shape was fancied. Acute bends had to be avoided, as they would have collapsed the hollow stem. This operation required much skill and delicate handling.

The bowl of the pipe was formed separately, pressed out from a small mould and then fitted to the end of the stem, the potter making sure that the pipe stem was not blocked. A brass crimping tool was used to finish off the mouthpiece. The complete pipe was then allowed to dry before firing; when fired and in biscuit state, the underglaze colours were applied, it was then dipped in glaze and fired again in a glost kiln.

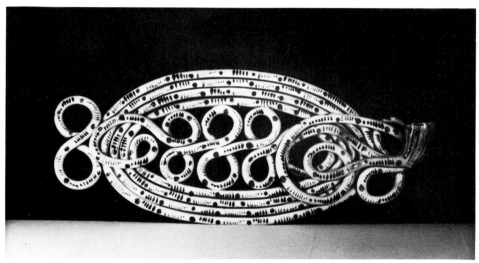

Coiled tobacco pipe c.1800
A tobacco pipe with a stem many feet long, intricately coiled and decorated with blue, ochre and green dashes under the glaze. 344mm long. *The Royal Pavilion Art Gallery and Museums, Brighton. HW 1500.*

The making of extruded handles

A 'wad box' was used for extruding handles. A small plate was fitted at the bottom of the box in which an aperture was cut out to the desired shape of the handle section.

Clay was then forced through this aperture by screwing downwards a pressure plate within the wad box, pushing out a continuous strip of plastic clay of uniform section. The operator then deftly removed the strip with a careful movement, so that the strip was not stretched or damaged in any way, and laid it down horizontally on a ware board. The operation was then repeated, until the board was filled with one layer of handle strips. The 'handlefolder' then measured off given lengths, using dividers; with a fettling knife, he then smoothly cut across the extruded lengths according to the measured marks. Taking up each separate piece, with a graceful and almost balletic movement of his hands the handlefolder bent the piece into whatever loop was needed. He repeated the operation until he had used up all the pieces from the extruded lengths. Each 'folded' loop being laid on its side with others added until small identical piles of handles covered the board. These would be left until they had dried a little, retaining their form and in a condition for applying to the jugs.[6]

---

6. Fortunately for posterity, John Smith of Stourbridge has placed this skilled technique on film, consequently recording a little-known method of handle-making.

Underglaze colours

The most striking feature of Pratt ware is the colouring. This relatively simple range of colours (a painter would describe them as earth colours) was achieved by the use of metallic oxides, as used in Italian maiolica. These oxides were painted on to the biscuit body which was then lead-glazed and fired to between 1000°C and 1100°C. Organic colours, such as vermilion would not have stood up to these temperatures.

The oxides used were lead, tin and antimony for yellow; for deeper yellow and orange the addition of iron oxide; cobalt was used for blue[7]; lead and copper for greens, browns were obtained by iron oxide with the addition of manganese. Manganese by itself made a purplish brown. Black was made by mixing iron oxide and cobalt.

The cost of producing cobalt led to a search for a substitute. In 1772, a process of manufacture of a cobalt substitute called 'Prussian Blue' was discovered in Germany. This process made use of bullock's blood. This was mixed with potash and calcined, forming a prussiate of potash, which when dissolved in water produced Prussian Blue.[8]

This process was taken up by a firm of manufacturing chemists in Newcastle upon Tyne called Davidson and Davenport. The Northumbrian potter and tilemaker Antony Hilcote, under licence from Davidson and Davenport, established a 'Blood-works' on the west bank of the Figgate on the Firth of Forth, where he manufactured Prussian Blue, much to his neighbour's annoyance.[9]

In 1777 Josiah Wedgwood was writing to his partner Bentley,[10] complaining about the price of the 'Prussian' cobalt, which had reached three guineas a pound. Nine years later, Wedgwood in another letter said '. . . the best prepared cobalt separated from nickel and all heterogeneous matter by reducing it to a regulus and then calcining it etc.[11] is worth from 27s. to 30s. a pound. It has been near three times that price through a scarcity of the material and want of skill in preparing it. But that scarcity and consequent high price has brought plenty to the market. . .'[12]

Because of the cost of imported cobalt various efforts were made to find it in these islands.[13] Cobalt is one of the most effective of the underglaze colours and was also used to tint the lead glaze to counteract any yellow coloration. The other typical Pratt colour is a strong burnt orange which was made from lead and iron oxides.

The cobalt blue is often almost transparent and can be seen at its best on the range of Toby jugs made by the pottery that used the large impressed crown mark (see page 85). It was mixed with a soft flux of lead oxide, or after 1828 of borax, when plentiful supplies of this were available from Tuscany, or with a mixture of common salt and ground flint. It had a tendency to trickle when laid on too thickly.[14] Even after the discovery of borax, cobalt frits based on the use

---

7. For details on the preparation of cobalt see M.J.A. Chaptal, *Chemistry Applied to the Arts and Manufactures*, (Vol. III), London, 1807. See also Appendix V, p. 292.
8. ibid. See also Appendix VI.
9. Patrick McVeigh, *Scottish East Coast Pottery 1750-1840*, Edinburgh, 1979.
10. E.18746-25. Keele University Library.
11. The 'regulus' is the term for the separated stain, removed from other materials and left in isolation. Calcining was a means of reducing ores and oxides to a powder by heat.
12. Letter to R.L. Edgeworth, 24 December 1786, quoted in *The Wedgwood Letters* Finer & Savage, Cory Adams & Mackay, London, 1965.
13. See Appendix X.
14. J. Arnold Fleming, *Scottish Pottery*, Glasgow, 1923.

Comparisons
The jug on the left is pressed from a well worn mould with arbitrary colouring, the other is from a crisp new mould and is carefully painted.

of lead oxide were still widely used. The cobalt ore when processed was in two forms – zaffre and smalt. Zaffre resulted from fritting calcined cobalt ore with sand; smalt was prepared by fusing zaffre with potash. Zaffre was used for deeper colours.[15]

The rich mulberry shade of brownish puce that sometimes appears on Pratt ware was produced by mixing oxide of iron with black oxide of manganese. J. Arnold Fleming described how at Portobello the manganese was supplied by the local chemical works that made bleaching powder from chloride of lime. Some of the chlorine remained in the manganese under the 'recovery' process and in the reaction formed chloride of manganese, a purple coloured salt. The addition of this 'recovered' manganese to underglaze brown colours was a fairly common practice.[16] This colour varied considerably in tone and sometimes gave the appearance of almost breaking through the glaze, producing quite a rough surface.

The painting was done by means of brushes – liners, squares, edgers and ones with long soft hairs called 'pencils'. Another method of applying colour was by the use of a small piece of sponge. This was dipped into oxide colour mixed with a suitable medium and dappled on to the ware, leaving an impression of the sponge's texture. It was a quick and economical way of colouring and can be seen on the bodies of Pratt ware horses and cow creamers or on the bases of some figure groups and money-boxes.

The particles of the oxide colours were probably held in suspension with gum arabic, which would burn away in the firing. If the colours had been mixed with oil or turpentine it would have been necessary to subject the painted wares to a 'hardening on' firing to fix the colours and to burn away the oily medium. This firing which would have taken place before the application of the glaze would have involved yet another stage in the process.

Samuel Parkes in his *Chemical Essays* written between 1806 and 1815 states that: 'In employing these various colours, the ground oxide is first mixed with a prepared flux, which is also reduced to an impalpable powder, and then this mixture is well incorporated with gum water, (or) the acid of tar, (or) oil of turpentine, or some other essential oil, as may be most suitable, in point of

---

15. Robert Hunt, F.R.S., *Dr Ure's Dictionary of Arts, Manufactures and Mines*, 7th Edn., 1875, London.
16. *Scottish Pottery.*

expense or otherwise, for the goods on which it is to be employed. The fluids are used merely to lay on the colour; for it is necessary that, whatever oil is employed, it should have the property of evaporating entirely.'

In other words, if you could afford an extra firing to fix the colours, you would use oil, probably boiled linseed oil. In the case of inexpensive ware, such as Pratt jugs, figures etc., Parkes goes on to say:

'It is here necessary to remark, that in painting on the biscuit no oil is used; the metallic oxides are mixed with water only; and it is owing to this circumstance that such ware may be glazed at once without being put into an oven.'[17]

Here at last is positive evidence of how these underglaze colours were applied. No doubt most potters had receipt books for the make-up of clay bodies and colours. A notebook of underglaze colour recipes and specifications for various bodies for ware and for underglaze painting was left by the potter Thomas Lakin. This was posthumously published by his widow.[18]. Lakin had been a partner in the firm of Lakin and Poole in Burslem and for a short while operated a little potworks at Bourne's Bank, also in Burslem. From there until 1799 he went to work at Davenports. He moved again to the Leeds Pottery and ultimately became manager there. He died in Leeds in 1824. The colours for Pratt ware must have been made from comparable recipes.

A similar set of recipes is in a notebook lodged in the Merseyside County Museum, Liverpool. These were compiled by a potter called Joseph Tomkinson (1784-1836) who had worked at the Herculaneum Pottery where Pratt jugs were made. He emigrated to America in 1826, taking his notebook with him.[19] Tomkinson's recipes largely agree with those of Thomas Lakin, except in the precise quantities of the ingredients. Yet another set of underglaze colour recipes was left in a notebook (c.1824) belonging to J. & R. Riley.[20]

Firing and glazing

When the painting was completed and dry, the vessel or figure was dipped in lead glaze and then fired again. The firing was in an oxidising atmosphere in the kiln, the best that could be achieved.

The quality of the lead glaze varied; sometimes it was quite transparent and at other times it was slightly tinted with zaffre, which gave a faintly bluish colour. No doubt the use of zaffre was to counteract the natural creamy colour of the lead glaze. The bluish tint can most easily be seen in the indented parts of the design where the glaze has settled a little more thickly. On some pieces the glaze has crackled.

It is not unusual to find examples of Pratt ware that are dark in colour. These are somewhat less appealing; the dark discoloration may be due to the clay or to some accident in firing. The use of the ware for holding hot liquids or even foods could stain the body, the liquids or juices penetrating the crackled glaze. Pots placed on a kitchen mantelpiece could absorb smoke and fumes from cooking, which would also tend to darken the ware. Occasionally pieces can be found that have suffered from 'sparkling', that is a black gritty effect which spoils the glaze with its texture and colour.[21]

---

17. Samuel Parkes, F.L.S., *Chemical Essays,* Vol. II, London, 1815.
18. *The Valuable Receipts of the Late Mr. Thomas Lakin,* Leeds, 1824. See also Appendix IX, p. 295.
19. These recipes are reprinted in *The Illustrated Guide to Liverpool Herculaneum Pottery 1796-1840,* Alan Smith, London, 1970.
20. Lodged in the City Art Gallery and Museum, Stoke-on-Trent, Staffordshire. See Appendix VIII.
21. See Hugh Owen, *Two Centuries of Ceramic Art in Bristol,* 1873.

3. Pratt jugs and other ware known to have been made by other potters in Staffordshire and Shropshire

Because of the number of potteries making creamware and pearlware in Staffordshire at the end of the eighteenth century, it would seem most likely that Pratt ware first appeared there, even if not from William Pratt's Lane Delph factory. The same designs appeared on ware with different potters' names as well as on many more unmarked pieces.

There was much plagiarism in the pottery industry which caused some concern to established firms like Wedgwoods: Josiah Wedgwood, writing to his nephew Thomas Byerley in December 1790,[1] tells him to be on his guard for a man who was going round taking casts of cameos etc., and copying their designs. No doubt there were many other complaints.

On the other hand, moulds were often acquired when potteries were sold up (a frequent occurrence in the late eighteenth and early nineteenth centuries). Mould makers also moved from pottery to pottery and district to district. Evidence of this is clear enough with identical Pratt type jugs and other pieces marked with potters' names in Staffordshire, Shropshire, Yorkshire, Newcastle, Liverpool and Scotland.

Subjects which one finds on relief decorated underglaze coloured cream and pearlware can also be found on stoneware pieces marked with the names of ADAMS and TURNER. It is more than likely that as mould making was a specialised trade, that moulds could be purchased direct from the mould makers in several sizes by any pottery who wanted them.

At least a dozen potteries in Staffordshire and Shropshire can be said to have made Pratt ware, either by the evidence of marked pieces or sherds dug up on the site of the pottery. It is more than likely that evidence of others may be discovered. We have not attempted to give detailed histories of all these potteries, which have been written up elsewhere, we have merely confined ourselves to the period when they were making relief decorated, underglaze coloured cream and pearlware.

These potteries include R.M. Astbury at Lane Delph, Richard Barker at Lane End, Edward Bourne at Burslem, Walter Daniel at Burslem, Thomas Harley at Lane End, Jacob Marsh at Burslem and later at Lane Delph and still later at Lane End, Jacob Tittensor at Stoke and Charles Tittensor at Shelton, Peter and Francis Warburton at Cobridge, Ralph Wedgwood at Burslem (and later at Ferrybridge in Yorkshire) and one of the Wood factories.

As for Shropshire, the only pottery for which there is evidence of the manufacture of relief decorated, underglaze coloured ware is that of Bradley & Co. at Coalport.

---

1. Josiah C. Wedgwood, *A History of the Wedgwood Family*, London, 1908.

Teapot c.1790

A fine pearlware teapot, straight-sided with serpentine panels decorated with a swagged blue curtain edged with yellow and with yellow and blue tassels. The two narrow panels on either side are enriched with pendants of blue bells tied at the top with blue and yellow ribbons. Round the base of the teapot is a deep border of stiff green leaves with wavy edges, topped by a raised line coloured blue. Round the opening at the top is an uncoloured narrow moulding below which is a finely modelled ring of acanthus leaves edged with green and with blue dots terminating the midrib of each leaf. The handle, which has an acanthus motif outlined in green at the top is ear-shaped;

unfortunately the lid is missing. The spout is stepped and rimmed with a blue line. Impressed mark ASTBURY on the base. 105mm high. *Private Collection.*

This teapot is almost identical in shape and decoration to a more thickly painted version in the Bulwer Collection in the Castle Museum, Norwich, which is marked HAWLEY (page 76).

A very similar teapot in a black basaltes body marked BRADLEY & CO COALPORT can be seen in the Victoria and Albert Museum *C.3392.1901.*

A drawing of a similar design can be found in one of the Leeds Pottery Drawing Books, in the Leeds Central Library.

Richard Meir Astbury

The Astbury family had been potting in Staffordshire at least since the seventeenth century. Traditionally John Astbury (b.1688) is said to have decorated his red earthenware with applied reliefs made of white pipe clay, but no marked pieces are known. John Astbury died in 1743 and his son Joshua in 1780. Richard Meir Astbury, Joshua's son (1765-1834) succeeded his father at the Foley Works at Lane Delph. Here useful wares of good quality were made, sometimes marked ASTBURY in capital letters on the bases. Among the underglaze coloured relief decorated pieces that are marked ASTBURY are a handsome pearlware teapot and versions of the 'Fair Hebe' jug.

The impressed ASTBURY mark.

36

Teapot c.1790
A teapot obviously from the same pottery as the teapot over the page, very similar in general shape and colouring but with many subtle differences. Although the handles are the same, the spouts are quite different and the lid with its flower knob and the gallery round the lid, the patterns at the foot and on the painted panel are dissimilar, though the landscape has obviously been executed by the same hand. The narrow panels flanking the painted landscape have also been given different treatment. Attributed to the Staffordshire Barkers. Impressed mark *BARKER*. 152mm high. *Collection Mr and Mrs Robert Allbrook.*

The Barkers of Lane End

The Barkers were well known as a potting family in Staffordshire. John Barker (who had worked for Thomas Whieldon) and his brothers William and Richard are listed in *Bailey's Western Directory* as making cream coloured earthenware at Lane End in 1784. Richard Barker appears again in *Holden's Triennial Directory 1805*. The Barkers continued potting at least until 1817.[1]

There is a Pratt ware teapot in the Victoria and Albert Museum *C.41.1948* with the impressed mark BARKER, attributed to the Staffordshire Barkers, but a very similar teapot in the Yorkshire Museum is attributed to the Mexborough Barkers. Another in the Doncaster Museum is also impressed BARKER and is also attributed to the Mexborough Old Pottery. In the Bulwer Collection, Castle Museum, Norwich, there is yet another teapot marked BARKER of similar design and attributed to the Staffordshire Barkers. At the present state of knowledge it is impossible to give a firm attribution. See also the entry for the Yorkshire Barkers under Low Pottery, Rawmarsh, page 75.

---

1. W. Mankowitz and R. Haggar, *The Concise Encyclopedia of English Pottery and Porcelain*, London, 1957.

4 & 5. Fair Hebe jug 1788

This example of the Voyez designed and modelled Fair Hebe jug is in underglaze colours of burnt orange, green, blue, yellow and manganese brown. This is almost a transitional example when the use of underglaze colours was replacing the earlier coloured glazes and is quite as attractive as any earlier model. This piece has a wealth of marks, including the initials RMA, the name VOYEZ and the date 1788 and underneath the base the impressed mark ASTBURY, and also on the scroll behind the standing figure is impressed 'A BUMPER A BUMPER'. 273mm high. *Collection Peter Manheim Ltd., London.*

Another version of the Fair Hebe jug in the Elias Clark Collection has 'A bumper, A bumper' replaced by LONG LIVE THE KING, and on the other side 'Fair Hebe' is replaced by

G.R.III
RESTORD (sic)

which probably dates it at 1789 when the king made the first of the recoveries from his mental illness: his return to health was greeted with popular enthusiasm.

6. Teapot c.1790

A teapot with moulded relief decoration painted in blue, green, brown, yellow and ochre with a small landscape painted in the same colours on the central panel on each side, between a border of leaves. There is a relief pattern of stiff leaves round the bottom of the teapot and a border of splayed out leaves and star-like flowers round the top of the pot, a pattern repeated on the lid above which is a dolphin knob. The crenellated gallery round the lid is decorated with a pattern of fan-like leaves in relief. Round the base of the spout and on the upswept handle there is an outlined acanthus leaf. Impressed mark on the base: *BARKER* in italic capitals. Made in either Staffordshire or Yorkshire, for there were members of the Barker family potting in both counties. The painted landscapes on this teapot have been executed in the rather free style of the decorations on many Dutch delft tiles. 165mm high. *Private Collection.*

A very similar teapot with the same mark is in the Merseyside County Museum. *26.12.84.5L.* Another, identical but unmarked is in the City Museum and Art Gallery, Stoke-on-Trent. *552.*

Teapot c.1790
A teapot with serpentine side panels decorated with painted
sprays of flowers in green blue and ochre and applied
'snowflake' decorations in the upper corners. There are
acanthus leaf borders round the top of the pot, round the lid,
which has a swan knob, and round the bottom part of the teapot.
There is a beaded border round the base of the gallery with a line
of upstanding small leaves above it. The lines are painted blue
and there is an outline acanthus decoration at the base of the
spout and on the top of the upswept handle. Impressed mark
*BARKER. Crown Copyright, Victoria and Albert Museum. C.41 & A.
1948.*

Impressed mark *BARKER* from the base of the teapot.

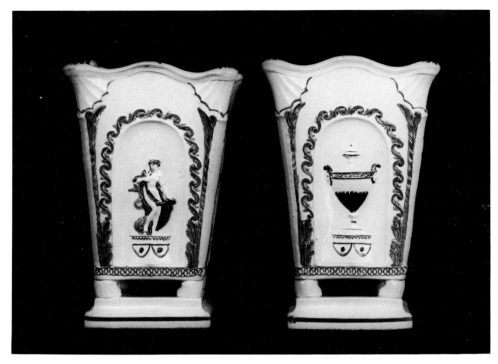

Fern Pots 1790-1810
Fern pots made by E.Bourne, in Burslem or Longport decorated in relief with Venus and her dolphin and classical urns set in niches on each face of the pot, surrounded by a scroll decoration in green and ochre.

They are mounted on block feet set on a square stepped base which is banded in brown. Impressed mark E.BOURNE under the base. 152mm high. *Peter Manheim Ltd, London.*
An exactly similar specimen, but unmarked is in the Victoria and Albert Museum *Circ. 414.1811.*

Edward Bourne

There were numerous potters of the name of Bourne working in Staffordshire at the beginning of the nineteenth century. These included Bourne, Baker and Bourne, potting at Fenton in 1801 and Edward Bourne who was working in Burslem in 1802 in quite a small way. His house and effects and his set of potworks and utensils were insured for only £200.[1]

There was an Edward Bourne working in Longport in 1787. Which of these Edward Bournes used the impressed mark which appears on a pair of relief decorated underglaze coloured fern pots, is in no way clear. There was also another Edward Bourne who had a potworks in Belper in Derbyshire in 1807.[2]

In the Keele University Archives there are a number of accounts from both 'the late' Thomas Wedgwood and from Josiah Wedgwood II to Edward Bourne at Burslem for supplies of frit for glazing. These were dated November 3rd 1772 to August 11th 1809. In this last one is written 'Six score of blue frit to be ground very fine. Please let the tub stand full of water till the glaze is ready'. On January 13th 1813 Edward Bourne is writing to Josiah Wedgwood II apologising for delay in settling his account. There is another account from Edward Bourne at Longport dated July 27th 1787 listing 'Shell Top tureens, Round Royal dishes and Royal plates'. Presumably these had been subcontracted. It would seem that it was the same Edward Bourne.

1. Guildhall Ms. 11,937. Sun Fire Insurance Policy 726658.
2. Guildhall Ms. 11,937. Sun Fire Insurance Policy 805759.

Quintal flower vase c.1815-25
A pearlware flower vase decorated with what might be termed peasant style sprays of painted flowers in dark blue, orange, yellow, brown and green, on the main body of the piece. The 'fingers' are decorated with counterchange green and yellow leaves, moulded in relief, and where they join the main vase there is a looped blue line with a moulded feather edge. The base is encircled with a single brown line. The impressed mark on the base is DAVENPORT in capital letters with an anchor. 235mm high. *Private Collection.*

John Davenport, Longport

John Davenport took over John Brindley's factory near the canal at Longport in 1793, when Brindley died (he was the brother of James Brindley the famous engineer and canal builder). The firm made good quality earthenwares and according to Reginald Haggar made wares 'painted with designs in a peasant style' in the 1815-35 period. When John Davenport retired in about 1830, his two sons Henry and William carried on the business.

The flower quintal shown here would seem to fit in to the 'peasant style' of painted decoration. The flowers are charmingly pencilled in underglaze blue, orange, yellow, green and brown. The actual leaves at the tops of the flower holders are moulded in relief. It is not strictly what one thinks of as Pratt ware, but the piece appears to be unique. It is coloured under the glaze and part is certainly relief moulded. The impressed mark DAVENPORT with an anchor appears on the base, in upper case lettering.

Davenport mark from quintal flower vase.

41

W. Daniel

Daniel was the name of an old potting family in Staffordshire. Many members are recorded as working in or around Stoke-on-Trent in the latter half of the eighteenth century and early nineteenth century. *Bailey's Northern Directory* of 1781 records that Walter Daniel was then making cream-coloured earthenware in Burslem. In *Tunnicliff's Directory* of 1786 he was recorded as a maker of creamware and red earthenware. He was working at the Waterloo Pottery at Burslem from 1784 to 1795. About 1793 he took his sons into the business, which then traded as Walter Daniel & Sons until 1801 when the father retired leaving his son Walter to carry on the business, which remained in production until 1804. They used the impressed mark W. DANIEL.

Walter Daniel must have been a man of some substance; an insurance policy issued by the Sun Fire Insurance Co. on February 11th 1797[1] shows that Walter Daniel of New Port near Burslem owned five potteries. Of these, one was let to Leigh and Wedgwood, one to Benson and Rhodes, one to Nathan Heath and Son, one to Thomas Lakin and the fifth he worked himself.

In 1809, according to another Sun Fire Insurance Policy[2] dated December 21st, Walter Daniel was living at Hassell Hall in the County of Chester. His son Walter was working the pottery at New Port in partnership with John Davenport. This extensive pottery with its numerous buildings was insured for £2,250.

---

1. Guildhall Ms. 11,937/17. Sun Fire Insurance Policy 664461. See Harold Blakey's article in *Northern Ceramic Society's Journal,* Vol. 3, pp. 110-1.
2. No. 838698.

Teapot c.1805
Diamond-shaped teapot in a stand, moulded with a border of stiff leaves with blue borders, enclosing sparsely painted floral decorations painted blue with a little gilding added. The lid is surmounted with a swan knob. Impressed HARLEY. 207mm high. *Courtesy Sotheby's.*

In other versions the same shape occurs but with widely differing decoration, some with underglaze blue transfer pseudo-Chinese scenes put on without regard to the relief moulded decoration. Teapots of a similar shape are illustrated in the 1808 Don Pottery Catalogue (see page 71).

Thomas Harley of Lane End 1778-1832

Thomas Harley was first in partnership with a family of potters called Weston in Lane End. This association came to an end in 1801, when he started work on his own. He must have been fairly successful and he obviously took an interest in current affairs, for his name occurs in various accounts of meetings about the abolition of the slave trade and so on. He married Myra, William Pratt's elder daughter and was liked and trusted by Ellen, William Pratt's widow, for she made him joint executor with her youngest son Richard in her will of 1814. He is listed in various local directories as an earthenware manufacturer from 1801-18, when he was in partnership with a man called Seckerson. At some stage he moved to St. Helens, where he owned a shop and other property, and where he died in 1832.

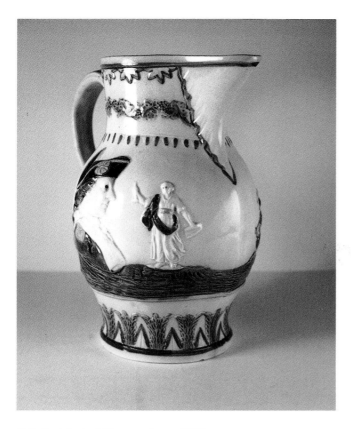

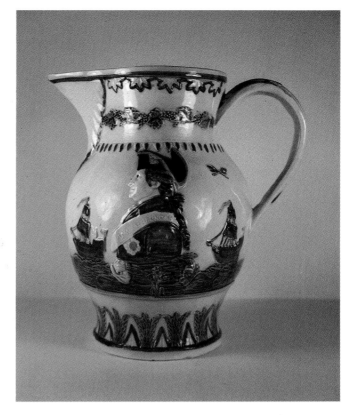

7 & 8. Admiral Duncan jug c.1797

A creamware jug with a bluish glaze decorated on one side with the head and shoulders of Admiral Duncan, with his name appearing in raised lettering on the sash he is wearing across his chest. His uniform jacket is dark orange, his brown hair is worn *en queue* and his black hat is trimmed with yellow. Below him in the mossy green sea are the faces of two dolphins and a flowering plant. He is flanked by two naval vessels, aboard which out of proportion men are sitting on the poops. On the reverse side is a portrait of Captain Trolop (sic) similarly dressed and flanked by

a naval vessel on one side and the draped female figure of Clio, the Muse of History on the other, she is clutching a scroll and a trumpet. This figure has been copied from a jasper medallion modelled by John Flaxman c.1776/7 and impressed Wedgwood & Bentley. The plain loop handle has a brown acanthus leaf outlined at top and bottom. Impressed mark on the base W.DANIEL. 195mm high. *Private Collection.*

For further versions of this jug see pages 112 and 147.

W.DANIEL mark impressed in capital letters 1.8mm high on base.

Wedgwood jasper ware bas relief of Clio

The Muse of History holds a trumpet in one hand and a scroll in the other. Modelled by John Flaxman c.1776-7. *Courtesy Josiah Wedgwood and Sons Limited, Barlaston, Stoke-on-Trent.*

Thomas Harley made good quality creamware and pearlware including some curious diamond shaped teapots moulded with borders of stiff upright leaves and painted underglaze decoration. The painting on these teapots varies from pseudo-Chinese landscapes to simple and rather sparse blue flowers and blue lines. (It is rather stretching a point to include these under 'Pratt' ware). Examples of his teapots can be seen in the Bulwer Collection at the Castle Museum Norwich, which are marked HARLEY in impressed capital letters on the base.

Jacob Marsh

Simeon Shaw in his book published in 1829[1] describes Jacob Marsh as 'Being long esteemed for his numerous private virtues... and for his integrity as a tradesman and master... descended from a family long engaged in the manufacture of different kinds of pottery, and of the first flint and salt-glazed ware, he alone remains to perpetuate the name...'

Marsh's pottery was situated in Burslem and is shown on a map dated 1800. On July 2nd 1803, a Sun Fire Insurance Policy shows that Jacob Marsh of Burslem was insuring his potworks for £300 and the stock and utensils for another £200[2] which means that he was in a fair way of business. In 1806 he moved to the Lane Delph pottery, which according to the Rate Books[3] he rented from a Thomas Griffin. In 1816 John Carey seems to have taken over

Jacob Marsh's mark pencilled under the base of the fishergirl in a cursive hand in blue.

Fishergirls c.1790-1800
The figure on the left, seated on a rocky mound and holding a basket of blue fish is after a Ralph Wood model. Her dress is spotted in brown and edged with ochre. The square base is marbled with blue lines and marked underneath 'Jacob Marsh'. 135mm high. *Private Collection.* The unmarked figure on the right has been attributed to Ralph Wood. Her dress is coloured blue and ochre. 127mm high. *Courtesy Sotheby's.*

from Thomas Griffin as his landlord. The factory made pretty little toys and figures in the Wood manner in underglaze colouring. They were marked occasionally with his name pencilled in blue under the base in a cursive hand. Whether he made useful ware as well, we do not know.

Though *Parson and Bradshaw's Directory* of 1818 lists Marsh among the Lane End potters, he was not listed as a ratepayer there until the following year. In 1819 Marsh sub-let his Lane Delph pottery to Carey jun. The Rate Books show him as owner-occupier of premises in Longton or Lane End from 1820 until 1832, when he handed over to a John Riley Marsh, which fact seems to disagree with Simeon Shaw. Shaw describes Jacob Marsh's factory as 'his very compact and well-arranged Manufactory is at the entrance to Lane End.' He is listed in *The History and Gazetteer and Directory of Staffordshire* in 1834, as 'Jacob Marsh of Golden Hill House, (Foley) gent.'

1. Simeon Shaw, *History of the Staffordshire Potteries,* Hanley, 1829.
2. Guildhall Ms. 11,937. Policy 749520.
3. Transcript of 1807/8 Rate Books. Alfred Meigh. Keele University Archive Library. Res. Local Coll NK 4087.57.A2. M3.

Tittensor

There were numerous potters of this name in Staffordshire at the end of the eighteenth century and at the beginning of the nineteenth. There is a Jacob Tittensor listed in the Stoke Parish Register for 1780 and 1791 and there is an underglaze coloured plaque signed by this potter and dated 1789. There was a William Tittensor working at Hanley in 1793[1] and another (or perhaps the same one) working at Fenton from 1802 to 1813, and then until 1823 at Shelton.

Charles Tittensor, who was born in 1764, was working at Hanley from 1803 in partnership with his brother John. In 1807 he entered into partnership with a man called Simpson, which lasted until 1813. From 1818 to 1823 he was working on his own account at Shelton. He made little figures, often set in front of a bocage, and marked his wares, which were sometimes decorated with underglaze colours with the impressed mark TITTENSOR in capital letters. The marked figure of the boy reading illustrated here is almost certainly by Charles Tittensor.

In the Ernest Allman Collection there was a vase with looped handles flanked by the figures of a boy and a girl (a copy of a Ralph Wood design)[2] in underglaze colouring of brown, green, burnt orange and blue with the impressed mark TITTENSOR.[3] We have also seen a figure of a spaniel lying on a green glazed oval mound with flowered sprays round the borders in a cream coloured body with blobs of manganese decorating it and with brown ears and tail, with the same mark, and also a comparable model of a sheep.

1. Guildhall Ms. 11,937. Sun Fire Insurance Co. Policy 622497. December 2nd 1793.
2. *Apollo,* May 1943. 'An unrecorded family of potters', an article by H. Boswell Lancaster, based on researches by Ernest Allman, who made a collection of marked pieces. (After a sale at Sotheby's on 12th January 1965, I bought a marked Astbury teapot that had been in the Allman Collection from Mr. Peter Manheim, who told me that he had known the old collector. 'Allman was a great character,' Mr. Manheim said, 'he was a fish and chip merchant in a Bootle back street. He kept his entire collection in a room behind the shop. He had an obsession for marked pieces. He apparently did not need much sleep, for he always kept me up until at least 2 a.m.!' G.M.L.).
3. The Ralph Wood original is illustrated in Frank Falkner's, *The Wood Family of Burslem,* London, 1912.

9. Figure of a boy reading c.1810-20 *top left*

A figure of a boy seated on a grassy mound. Impressed mark TITTENSOR in capitals on the back of the green washed base. 180mm high. *Collection Peter Manheim Ltd., London.*

The fact that the figure is wearing trousers, which did not come into general fashion until after 1807 is a help in dating this piece.

10. Boy, girl and oaktree group c.1790

This version of these figures is more carefully finished than the one opposite. Though unmarked it is highly probable that it was made by Charles Tittensor. It is clearly based on the Wood flower vase group and is similar to a marked Tittensor piece. The outsize acorns on the bocage are an amusing feature. The group is quite thinly pressed and in the unglazed part of the interior, the potter's finger prints are clearly obvious. 187mm high. *Private Collection.*

11. A drunken man holding a foaming jug of ale plaque. 1789

An oval plaque in a white frame with a blue bow at the top and a chain of blue swagged laurel leaves above the figure's head. Incised on the back of the plaque are the words 'Jacob Tittensor made this 8 October in the year of Our Lord 1789.' 195mm high. *Collection Peter Manheim Ltd., London.*

Boy, girl and toper group c.1790
The derivations of this rather crudely painted underglaze coloured group, decorated in blue, brown and burnt orange, can clearly be traced. The figures of the children have been copied from the Ralph Wood vase group and the little man on the barrel derives from a much earlier figure of the Whieldon type. 172mm high. *Courtesy Sotheby's.*

The flanking figures also appear on the Dixon Austin watch stand (see page 104). Another version of this vase was once in the Ernest Allman Collection. It had the impressed mark TITTENSOR on the base. In *The Wood Family of Burslem* Falkner illustrates a similar piece and quotes a letter from Ralph Wood to Mr Thomas Wedgwood written in 1784 and asking for payment for flower pots of this type.

Impressed mark TITTENSOR from the back of the figure of the seated boy opposite.

Urn-shaped vase with figures c.1780
A vase designed by Ralph Wood and decorated in relief with blue and yellow leaf borders in relief. The relief on the front is of a young woman in a blue dress with a child. The girl is dressed in a garment of Naples yellow and the boy has similar yellow drapery round his waist. 197mm high. *Courtesy Sotheby's.*

Toper 1760-70
A Whieldon-type figure of a small, fat man sitting astride a barrel, blotched in green and manganese coloured glazes. 82mm high. *Private Collection.*

This figure is the forerunner of the man on the pedestal. Versions of this toper can also be found in underglaze colouring.

Teapot with classical decoration c.1790 *opposite*

A creamware teapot decorated over the glaze with blue and jade green with blue outlined niches enclosing classical figures and ornaments in relief against an orange-peel textured background. The gallery is painted green with a blue rim and there is green feathering above the niches and on the spout. Marked WOOD impressed and filled in with blue on the base. Presumably from Enoch Wood's factory at Burslem. The knob is in the form of an inverted flower with reflexed petals. 159mm high. *Private Collection.*

An identical shaped teapot, (apart from having a 'widow' knob) is impressed SPODE on the base and is illustrated in Arthur Hayden's *Spode and his Successors.* The reason for showing this enamel decorated Wood teapot here is that similar pieces are to be found with underglaze colouring.

Boy with grapes 1795-1802

The figure of a boy is standing on a green mound. He is strongly coloured, wearing a black hat, ochre coat and brown breeches. He holds a bunch of grapes in his hand. 178mm high. *City Museum and Art Gallery, Stoke-on-Trent 402p.49.*

An identical uncoloured creamware figure in the same Museum is marked P.F.WARBURTON. A similar figure also appears on a cruet stand holding three bottles lettered in red in German. This is illustrated in Donald Towner's *Creamware.*

Peter and Francis Warburton

The Warburtons were a family of potters working at Cobridge and Fenton Low from early in the eighteenth century until well into the nineteenth century. They were one of the three largest exporters of earthenware in their day and they also did much of Josiah Wedgwood's enamelling.

Peter Warburton (1773-1813) was originally in partnership at Bleak Hill, Cobridge with his younger brother Francis. As well as cream tableware they made figures in the manner of Ralph Wood. Their mark was P. & F. WARBURTON impressed. In 1802 the partnership was dissolved and Peter Warburton continued on his own at Bleak Hill. He also became a partner on the resignation of Jacob Warburton in the New Hall Pottery. He married Mary Emery (daughter of Francis Emery) who outlived him by many years. In 1802 Francis Warburton left Staffordshire for France and became established at a pottery at La Charité-sur-Loire, where he produced cream coloured earthenware.[1]

---

1. See Reginald G. Haggar, 'The Warburton Family of Cobridge', *Apollo,* 1955.

Impressed mark WOOD, the letters filled in with blue, on the base of the teapot.

Wood

The mark WOOD was apparently sometimes used by Enoch Wood, who started potting on his own account at Burslem in 1784. The same mark appears on figures made between 1820 and 1830, possibly by Ephraim Wood who was potting from 1805 till 1830 in Burslem. It seems most likely that the teapot marked WOOD that is illustrated here comes from the Enoch Wood factory, where cream coloured earthenware was known to have been made in considerable quantity.

Wedgwood

The impressed mark WEDGWOOD in capital letters was the mark used by Josiah Wedgwood on his cream-coloured earthenware from about 1760 onwards. This mark appears on some pearlware Pratt jugs, but in a slightly different typeface from that used on many Etruria products. The Wedgwood Museum at Barlaston has no record of this kind of ware ever having been made at Etruria. However, when demand outstripped manufacturing capacity the firm of Wedgwood commissioned other potters to make ware for them, even instructing them to mark the goods with the Wedgwood mark. Josiah Wedgwood is said to have referred to such subcontractors as his 'pot-banks', inferring that he could draw on them when necessary.[1]

There were other Wedgwoods in Staffordshire in the late eighteenth century who would have been entitled to use the name on their productions, Thomas Wedgwood's son Ralph, for one and Joseph Wedgwood for another, (he who supplied the Castleford Pottery with 'infamous stuff, scandalously packed...' for shipment to America).[2] As these marked WEDGWOOD relief decorated underglaze coloured pearlware pieces are all of a very good quality, they were not likely to have been made by Joseph.

Ralph Wedgwood's Hill Pottery might have made relief decorated underglaze ware of this nature, there are certainly pencil drawings in his Ferrybridge scrap-book of ware with acanthus decoration, or it is possible it might have been made at Ferrybridge during his association with Tomlinson and Foster (see page 77).

---

1. Letter to John Wedgwood March 13th 1765. Eliza Meteyard, *The Life of Josiah Wedgwood*, London, 1865.
2. Diana Edwards Roussel, *The Castleford Pottery 1790-1821*, Wakefield, 1982.

Ralph Wedgwood

Ralph Wedgwood (1766-1827) was the son of Thomas Wedgwood (1734-88). Thomas had worked with his cousin Josiah from 1759, firstly as a journeyman and then from 1766 until 1788 as a partner in the side of the business connected with the production of useful cream coloured earthenware, which was first made at Burslem and later at Etruria. Very near the end of his life Thomas Wedgwood decided to set up in business on his own.

He was married to Elizabeth, the daughter of John Taylor, master potter of the Hill Top Brick-house at Burslem. In 1788 Thomas Wedgwood fitted up the Hill works for the manufacture of cream coloured earthenware. He persuaded Peter Swift, Josiah's accountant, to go into partnership with him. On a previous occasion, Swift had tried unsuccessfully to run two separate businesses, in addition to his work for Josiah Wedgwood. Josiah thought highly of him, describing him as 'My Cashier, Paymaster General and Accountant General and without him we would all be in confusion at once.'[1] Swift had originally been hired by Wedgwood in 1766. He was described as being tall, thin and formal and dressed in a brown suit and a bobbed wig. He was elaborately precise, painstaking and highly conscientious (and incidentally a very bad speller).[2] Thomas Wedgwood died before he could put his scheme into operation.

Ralph Wedgwood, as Thomas's eldest son, took upon himself the task of looking after his brothers and sisters, no doubt with help from Josiah Wedgwood and his son, who between March 15th 1788 and September 5th 1789 paid him various sums of money amounting in all to £888. 16s. 0d. These drafts were all signed by Josiah Wedgwood II.[3] The first thing Ralph did was to finance his brother Samuel, so that in partnership with Peter Swift he could start work at the Hill Pottery.[4] Unfortunately Samuel died in 1790, so Ralph took over the business himself; he has been described as the most original of all the remarkable men that the Wedgwood family produced. 'At sixteen he began a series of experiments which persued him like Frankenstein throughout his life, encouraged in this by his older cousin Josiah Wedgwood with the words: "Remember Wedgwoodykin, everything gives way to experiment".'[5]

It was on December 12th 1790 that Josiah Wedgwood was writing to Tom Byerley in much less complimentary terms about his young cousin. He said: 'And you know that one of our people who was in our warehouse some time ago furnished a man of this sort in Oxford road or Holborn with casts from our own bas relief...We have had several potters, particularly Rph Wedgwood, send to our works for pieces, apparently intended to take moulds from to supply our customers...'[6]

In the same year, as well as setting himself up as a potter, Ralph Wedgwood married a lady from Worcester called Mary Yeoman, who had been his sister's school mistress. She had 'the somewhat doubtful distinction of being included in the Rev. Samuel Burder's *Memoirs of Eminently Pious Women'*.[7]

Ralph Wedgwood, while at the Hill Pottery, Burslem, lived in a house

1. Josiah C. Wedgwood, *A History of the Wedgwood Family,* London, 1808.
2. Eliza Meteyard, *The Life of Josiah Wedgwood,* London, 1856.
3. Keele University Archives. The Mosley Collection W/M 1729 dated 1775, 1785-1813.
4. Usually referred to as the Hill Top Pottery, but in the sale notices of May 1798 it is called 'Hill Pottery'. The *Staffordshire Advertiser* also calls it 'Hill Pottery'.
5. Josiah C. Wedgwood, *A History of the Wedgwood Family,* London, 1908.
6. Ed. Ann Finer & George Savage, *The Selected letters of Josiah Wedgwood,* London, 1965.
7. Josiah C. Wedgwood, *A History of the Wedgwood Family,* London, 1908.

12. Smokers and drinkers jug c.1795

An alfresco drinking scene decorates the other side of this fine quality pearlware jug. Two men, their right hands clasped, are seated at a table upon which rests a jug of ale, two churchwarden pipes and a plate of food. The man on the left is wearing a blue coat, knee breeches and a fancy brown hat adorned with feathers. He toasts his companion, a sailor, who is sitting nervously opposite, his free hand clutching the back of his chair. He is dressed in an orange coat, white trousers and a brown hat. On the side of the jug shown here is a scene of a soldier and a civilian sitting on green rocks at an up-ended brown barrel, upon which rests a jug of ale. The soldier, in plumed shako and blue coat holds his sword in one hand and an ale glass in the other, from which he is drinking. The civilian opposite in an orange coat, brown beaver hat and white trousers is smoking a long churchwarden pipe. He conceals a dagger in his other hand and his face wears a cunning expression.

The jug is brown banded at top and bottom and has an additional blue band at the base of the neck below which is a band of pendant stiff green leaves. Round the lower part of the jug is a border of large stiff leaves picked out in green and brown. Below the line round the top of the jug is a scalloped border of demi-florets painted in blue and bordered with an orange line. These same florets also occur on Castleford teapots.

The jug has an attractive upswept double-scrolled handle with a knobbed thumb-rest. Impressed WEDGWOOD on the base. 157mm high. *Private Collection.*

It is by no means certain that this marked jug and the very similar stoneware jug shown on page 61 were made by the Etruria firm. However entries in their Oven Book for June 1800[1] list white stoneware jugs 'with a group of Dutch figures on the front', with a marginal sketch showing a jug with an upswept handle of similar shape. If the Smokers and Drinkers jugs were not made at Etruria, the likelihood is that they were made by Ralph Wedgwood, either at the Hill Pottery, Burslem or at Ferrybridge.

1. E53-30018 Vol. II. *Wedgwood Museum, Barlaston.*

Wedgwood mark impressed in capital letters 2mm high on the base.

13. Smokers and drinkers jug c.1795

An almost identical unmarked jug showing the scene on the other side of the jug above, but with slight colour differences and a plain loop handle. 157mm high. *Private Collection.*

A smaller version (122mm high) can be seen in the Yorkshire Museum and an almost identical one is in the Victoria and Albert Museum. Both are impressed WEDGWOOD.

Admiral Duncan jug c.1797

On one side is a bust of the Admiral in ochre uniform with a white sash with his name in relief on it. He is flanked by two dolphins and a couple of naval vessels. The jug is ochre banded at top and bottom. The upswept handle is slightly rococo in shape with a knobbed thumb-rest. The spout is feather-edged in blue where it joins the body.

On the reverse side are two classical female figures, one holding a basket of fruit or flowers on her head (taken from a Flaxman design 'Offering to Ceres' for a jasper ware plaque) see page 203. Marked impressed WEDGWOOD on the base. 134mm high. *Crown Copyright, Victoria and Albert Museum. C.72.1952.*

A similar model, also impressed WEDGWOOD with slightly different colouring but with the same shaped handle can be seen at the Butan Museum of Wedgwood, Merion, Pennsylvania. For further versions of the Admiral Duncan jug see pages 43 and 147.

adjoining the works. He used the mark WEDGWOOD & CO, sometimes in capital letters and sometimes in upper and lower case. In the Doncaster Museum and Art Gallery there is a fine big underglaze coloured jug with relief decoration marked WEDGWOOD & CO. Whether he actually used the word WEDGWOOD by itself while at Burslem, is not clear; certainly when he arrived at Ferrybridge a handbill published in July 1798, which refers to the new partnership, stated that the pottery mark should be the one word WEDGWOOD followed by a small crown.[8]

Ralph Wedgwood made cream coloured earthenware, black basaltes, jasper ware and stoneware at the Hill Pottery. In the papers lodged at the Keele University Library, there are references to Ralph Wedgwood also making lustreware and figures for Josiah Wedgwood II. He certainly made sprig moulds for cherubs etc. It has been suggested that he may have manufactured moulds for the trade.[9] This mention of sprig moulds is the nearest reference to relief decorated ware.

In 1793 Ralph Wedgwood had a London warehouse at 35 St. Paul's Churchyard.[10] His stock was insured for £900 which indicates that as a manufacturer, even if he could not match the production of the Etruria firm, he was certainly a potter of some importance.

Meanwhile at Burslem he was devoting much of his time to experiments, to the detriment of his business and he was frequently in financial difficulties, gradually selling off the various properties he owned. Without doubt he was an inventive genius, but he was no kind of businessman. In spite of Swift's

8. By permission of Josiah Wedgwood & Sons Ltd., Barlaston, Stoke-on-Trent and Keele University Library where the manuscript (31414-56) is deposited.
9. Harold Blakey: 'Ralph Wedgwood' a talk given to Morley College Ceramic Circle Seminar, November, 1982 and article in the NCS Journal 1978-9.
10. This is shown in an insurance policy of 1793, now lodged in the Salop Fire Office.

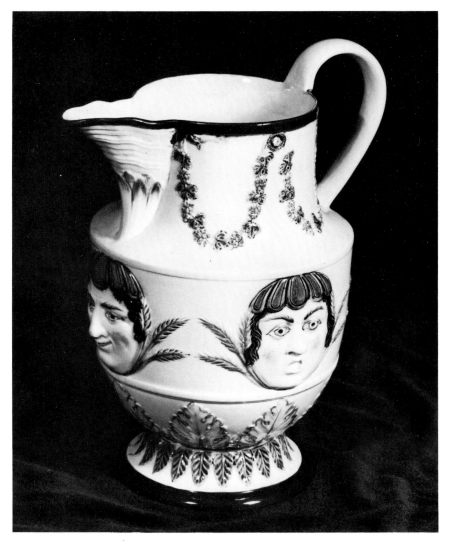

Impressed mark WEDGWOOD & CO on the base of the jug.

Four faces jug c.1790-1800

This well-modelled jug is decorated with four faces in relief, each with a different expression. One sick with disgust (literally), one open-mouthed, registering horror, one with a cross expression with the corners of the mouth turned down, and one smiling. Their petal-like caps are either blue and green or orange and green and the faces, picked out in black and ochre are flanked by ears of corn, alternatively green and orange. On the neck of the jug are swags of grapes, orange with green leaves and tied with blue ribbons at the top. There is a thick brown stripe round the top and the foot of the jug. The acanthus leaves round the foot are outlined in grey-green. It is impressed on the bottom WEDGWOOD & CO. Made by Ralph Wedgwood's pottery when he was still in Staffordshire, or at the Knottingley Pottery near Ferrybridge in Yorkshire during the years when they used this mark. Height 254mm. *Museum and Art Gallery, Doncaster.*

A similar but enamel coloured jug in the Northampton Museum is described in *Jugs in the Northampton Museum* by Jo Draper as representing the different stages of drunkenness. It differs from the Doncaster jug in having a merman for a handle.

accountancy skills, the company failed, finally being sold up in May 1798. Seeing no future at Burslem, in the following July Ralph Wedgwood entered into a formal agreement with Messrs. Tomlinson and Foster of the Knottingley Pottery, near Ferrybridge in Yorkshire. In spite of what looked to be a profitable relationship, the Knottingley Pottery partners were a hard-headed lot and there was a rider in their agreement[11] with Ralph Wedgwood to say that they could call in an independent arbiter if they were not satisfied with his work.

11. By permission of Josiah Wedgwood & Sons Ltd., Barlaston, Stoke-on-Trent and Keele University Library where the manuscript (31411-56 June 26th 1798) is deposited.

The terms of the agreement conclude with the proviso that a majority of the partners can dissolve the co-partnership at any time but that the agreement with Ralph Wedgwood shall hold for ten years should Tomlinson, Foster & Co. wish to resume trading.

The partnership only lasted until 1800, for the partners became exasperated by Ralph Wedgwood's endless and often fruitless experiments and the high proportion of breakages that occurred in the firing. Tomlinson and Foster finally paid him the not inconsiderable sum of £1,025 to relinquish any rights he had in the concern and to be off the premises on or before January 1st 1801.[12]

So ended Ralph Wedgwood's career as a potter, yet, one of his experiments had resulted in his taking out a patent in 1796 for the use of the newly discovered borax in the manufacture of glaze. Borax was then in short supply and was very costly. It was not until 1828 when the Tuscany borax fields were tapped, that this now universal flux for glazes came into general use.

In 1805, Ralph Wedgwood, having by then got through the £1,025 from Tomlinson and Foster, wrote to his daughter Mary from London telling her of his privations there. 'For lack of money even nakedness when I send my sole shirt to the wash!' He continues in the letter '...I have had three bitter reproachful letters from my namesakes, or rather by their direction (probably Josiah Wedgwood II and Tom Byerley), for the use of the WEDGWOOD & CO. imprint on the Ferrybridge ware. It seems that they have not a right understanding of my circumstances. On explanation, perhaps I may stand in a more favourable light...'[13]

In 1805 Josiah Wedgwood II had written to the Ferrybridge directors complaining about their use of the Wedgwood mark on their wares. Some pieces were marked with the single word WEDGWOOD, followed by a numeral, thus WEDGWOOD 12. This must have been the last straw, as far as the Etruria firm was concerned. As a result of that correspondence the WEDGWOOD marks were dropped by the Knottingley firm and FERRYBRIDGE was used instead.

In spite of being exasperated by Ralph's continual begging letters, always dignified, sometimes amusing and often desperate, Josiah Wedgwood II went on sending his unfortunate kinsman small sums, just enough to keep him from the debtor's prison. Ralph and his family moved from one sordid London lodging to another. At one time they had but three doors to serve as beds and a few tea chests for furniture. It is sad that a man of his brilliance and culture should have been reduced to such straits. In 1790 his library had been insured for £300 — as much as his house was worth.

By 1834 Ralph was suffering badly from bronchitis and rheumatism, but he was cheerfully making a model of Stonehenge. His son, Ralph junior wrote to Josiah Wedgwood II in the following terms:

'He is so completely absorbed in several schemes he has in hand that he foregoes the common duties of the husband and the father and instead of providing for his and their wants he applies nearly all his funds to carry into effect every chimera that obtrudes itself into the mind, some of which have proved him to be sadly devoid of *common* sense...'[14]

---

12. By permission of Josiah Wedgwood & Sons Ltd., Barlaston, Stoke-on-Trent and Keele University Library where the manuscript (31415-56) is deposited.
13. Josiah C. Wedgwood, *A History of the Wedgwood Family*, London, 1908.
14. Keele University Archives 19531-27. Letter from Ralph Wedgwood Jun. dated December 23rd 1834 to Josiah Wedgwood II.

Bradley & Co. of Coalport 1796-1800

An advertisement appeared in *The Shrewsbury Chronicle* in May 1797[1] stating that Walter Bradley & Co. had opened a warehouse at the Canal Wharf, Castle Foregate in Shrewsbury where 'Dealers and others may be supplied with EARTHENWARE (for ready money) on the lowest terms.'

The pottery that made this ware was situated on land belonging to William Reynolds on the opposite bank of the canal at Coalport to John Rose's porcelain factory. Bradley & Co.'s Coalport Pottery was only in business for a matter of four or five years. Recent researches suggest that the pottery was founded by Walter Bradley with the assistance of William Reynolds, who owned the land. Reynolds, a Quaker like Bradley, helped to promote various industries on this land, including a chain works, a rope works, a large building yard, Bradley's Pottery and John Rose's China Works.

In 1796 a Joshua Gilpin recorded in his diary how he had been through Mr. Reynolds' pottery lately established and had seen 'yellow ware'[2] being made. This probably refers to cream coloured earthenware.

This pottery was also referred to by Joseph Plymley, writing in 1799 describing it as 'a manufacture of earthenware in imitation of that at Etruria' and in the same year Thomas Telford described the pottery as being of a considerable size.

After 1800 it seems likely that the pottery was taken over or absorbed by Reynolds, Horton and Rose (Thomas Rose, John Rose's brother), and on the death of William Reynolds, his share was taken up by his cousin Robert Anstice and the firm became Anstice, Horton and Rose, and they manufactured porcelain.

An excavation trench was begun in the autumn of 1975[3] on the site of one of Bradley's old buildings and this revealed many earthenware sherds in the lower levels of the trench, many of them were plain biscuit but some decorated pieces were also found, some with border patterns in the manner of Wedgwood Queensware borders, some blue transfer fragments were found as well as sherds of mocha and banded wares, but the most interesting of all in level 8 of the trench were fragments of some 'Gretna Green Marriage' jugs. Some of these were biscuit, some coloured and some glazed and fired. They indicated that there were at least three sizes of the design with differing relief acanthus borders at top and foot.

It would seem from the site of the dig that the sherds and wasters were Bradley productions. The porcelain fragments in the upper layers of the trench indicated that John Rose's hands wheeled their wasters across the little bridge over the canal and dumped them on Bradley's site at a later date.

As several marked Bradley pieces exist, including a teapot, a candlestick and a jardinière in the form of two swans decorated in relief and in high temperature underglaze colouring, it seems more than likely that the Gretna Green Marriage jugs were made at the Bradley Pottery.

1. R.S. Edmundson, 'Bradley & Co. Coalport Pottery 1796-1800', *Northern Ceramic Society's Journal*, Vol. 4, 1980-1.
2. ibid. See also *Diary of Joshua Gilpin*, Pennsylvania State Archives.
3. Denis and Gaye Blake Roberts, 'The result of recent excavations in Coalport, Shropshire', *English Ceramic Circle Transactions*, Vol. II, Part 1, 1980.

Gretna Green elopement and marriage jug 1796-1800

This relief moulded unmarked pearlware jug, showing on one side an elopement by closed carriage drawn by two galloping horses, and on the other side a marriage ceremony at the blacksmith's forge at Gretna Green, is decorated in the usual underglaze colours. The neck of the jug is painted with a meandering design of leaves and flowers, and the lower part is plain except for a single brown band. 159mm high. *Private Collection.*

The body and the glaze on this jug are identical to the sherds from Coalport.

Sherds from Coalport 1796-1800

These sherds from very comparable Gretna Green jugs were recovered from Level VIII in Trench I at a dig on the site of Bradley & Co's factory at Coalport in the autumn of 1975. They consisted of fragments of biscuit, some with the coloured oxides painted on them, and some glazed and fired pieces, all showing parts of the Gretna Green marriage and elopement scenes. The relative sizes of the figures on these sherds indicate that there were at least three different sizes of jug. Two of the jugs had different moulded acanthus borders, whereas the third one just had a painted decoration round the neck as on the complete jug illustrated here. *Courtesy Ironbridge Gorge Museum.*

Teapot c.1797-1800 *opposite*

A moulded pearlware teapot, decorated with stiff leaves and oak leaves. On one side in a central oval pointed medallion is a relief decoration of Venus with Cupid at her side and the dolphin. A winged putto decorates the medallion on the other side. The teapot is sparsely coloured in blue, orange and dark green. Impressed mark BRADLEY & CO COALPORT in a small rectangular panel 3mm x 14mm on the base. 122mm high. *Courtesy Roger Edmundson.*

A teapot from the same mould in a black basaltes body and also marked BRADLEY & CO COALPORT is in the Victoria and Albert Museum *C.204.1926.*

4. Marked pieces and others known to have been made in the Yorkshire Potteries

The potteries include factories at Castleford, Leeds and Ferrybridge and in South Yorkshire at Swinton, Rawmarsh, Mexborough and Kilnhurst. Many of these potteries were interlocked through family connections on their boards of management, such as members of the Green family who were part owners of the Don Pottery at Swinton, or Peter Barker who moved from Rawmarsh to take over the Mexborough Old Pottery. Skilled workers also moved from one pottery to another, so it is hardly surprising that the wares from the different Yorkshire potteries are in many cases so similar. If it is not marked, it is almost impossible to say that a certain piece was made by a particular factory, unless there is other and conclusive evidence.

There is one unsolved problem of identity that we think may belong to Yorkshire. There are some Toby jugs, richly coloured in cobalt and burnt orange, that are marked with a large impressed crown on the base. We suggest tentative attributions, but once this crown has been identified it will establish the provenance of a whole range of Toby jugs, animal and figure groups, which are among the most colourful of all the underglaze coloured pieces.

A cow group from this pottery has recently come to light with the name WESLEY impressed on the base. If this name can be identified with any pottery in Yorkshire or elsewhere our problem of identification will be solved.

Castleford-type fine white stoneware

Since several of the designs that appear on relief decorated underglaze coloured pearl or creamware jugs also appear on this type of fine stoneware body, it is perhaps worth mentioning a little of what is known of the Castleford Pottery, where much of this ware is believed to have originated.[1]

The pottery was established at Castleford, just south of Leeds by David Dunderdale (1740-99) a successful linen draper in Leeds and John Plowes (who put money into the business), about 1790. The pottery made cream-coloured earthenware in the Leeds or Wedgwood manner as well as black basaltes, blue and brown printed ware and also this fine white stoneware.

The marks used by the pottery were

D D & CO CASTLEFORD	D D & CO CASTLEFORD POTTERY	CASTLEFORD POTTERY

though marked pieces are very rare.

One imagines Dunderdale to have been something of an entrepreneur who had already established an export market for his textiles in Spain and France and who saw an opportunity of adding to his trade by going into the pottery business and exporting to America as well. There exist some acrimonious letters from David Dunderdale written in 1792 to Joseph Wedgwood of the Churchyard Works at Burslem in Staffordshire, complaining about the

---

1. It is impossible to write about the various Yorkshire potteries without referring extensively to Heather Lawrence's book, *Yorkshire Pots and Potteries*. Her help we gratefully acknowledge.

White stoneware teapot c.1800
This fine white stoneware teapot has relief decorations of a seated female in the central panels bordered by demi-florets, which also appear on the gallery round the lid. The bottom border consists of a line of ferns, again repeated round the lid. Below the gallery is a border of broad, stiff leaves. The spout is elaborately moulded with leaves and flowers and the scroll handle is finished with an acanthus moulding and a double simulated strap. The decoration is enhanced with blue lines. Underneath the base is the mark D D & CO . 120mm high. *Crown Copyright,* CASTLEFORD
Victoria and Albert Museum. 3581-1901.

'wretchedly bad' crates of earthenware he had received for the American market. Joseph was one of Josiah Wedgwood's nephews.

When Dunderdale died in 1799 he left his share of the pottery business to his son of the same name (1772-1824). Though times were very difficult at the beginning of the nineteenth century, one is tempted to wonder whether the younger David Dunderdale had inherited his father's flair, for though the pottery continued in business until 1821, it went through a series of difficulties with mortgages and bankruptcies until its final liquidation. Oxley Grabham, one time Keeper of the Yorkshire Museum, nearly seventy years ago stated that Pratt jugs were made at Castleford, but what evidence he had for saying that, we do not know.[2] Whether the white stoneware jugs of the same design as the underglazed coloured cream and pearlware jugs were actually made at the Castleford Pottery or at any of the other Yorkshire potteries, at the moment it is impossible to say.

A fine white smear-glazed felspathic stoneware similar to that for which Castleford has come to be known (especially when decorated with blue enamelled lines) was used by many other potteries, including Wedgwood,

---

2. Oxley Grabham, *Yorkshire Potteries, Pots and Potters,* York, 1916.

American eagle teapot c.1800
This fine white stoneware teapot has a sliding lid bordered with acanthus leaves. It is decorated in relief on one side by the American eagle with shield and stars and a ribbon in its beak impressed 'E PLURIBUS UNUM'. On the other side is the head of Liberty in a Phrygian cap. The teapot is decorated with blue lines and borders of acanthus leaves interspersed with attenuated bell-like forms and ferns. The scroll handle is also decorated with an acanthus leaf, as is the lid which is surmounted by an oval knob in the form of a flower with reflexed petals. Impressed 36 on the base. 160mm high. *Private Collection.*

White stoneware teapot with painted landscapes c.1800
This teapot has a sliding lid. It is decorated in relief with an acanthus border round the bottom and another border of acanthus leaves interspersed with bluebell-like forms round the top of the body. The gallery round the lid is made up of a pattern of interlocked circles enclosing daisies and the knob is in the form of a reflexed flower. On the centre panel on each side are painted small naturally coloured landscapes. The teapot is also decorated with blue lines. 140mm high. *Private Collection.*

There is an identically shaped teapot, except that the centre panels have a relief moulded design of a child with a lion in place of the landscape in the Bulwer Collection at the Norwich Castle Museum. Under the base of this is impressed S & Co and also 22. It was probably made by Sowter & Co at Mexborough.

Herculaneum, Adams and Turner. Turner's body can usually be identified by the marked orangy glow when held up to a strong light, showing that there was a certain amount of iron contamination in the clay body.

Straight-sided teapots with crisp acanthus decoration and moulded panels picked out with fine blue lines enclosing classical figures or little hand-painted landscapes were also made in this stoneware body by Clulow of Fenton, Heath and Son of Burslem, Benjamin Plant of Longton and Sowter & Co. of Mexborough; the latter made teapots with sliding lids. All these potteries were functioning within the 1780-1820 period.[3]

The following are some of the white stoneware jugs of the Castleford type that are to be found also in a pearl or creamware body and decorated with high temperature underglaze colours.

Admiral Jervis   The Sailor's Return and Farewell
Peace and Plenty   Sportive Innocence and Mischievous Sport
Peacocks   Smokers and Drinkers

3. For further information about the Castleford Pottery see Diana Edwards Roussel, *The Castleford Pottery 1790-1821,* Wakefield, 1982.

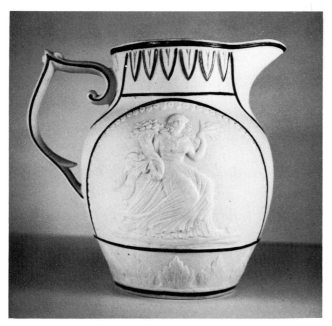

Four Castleford type stoneware jugs c.1795-1800
Above: Peace and Plenty, identical in shape to the pearlware jug of the same size and subject. It is banded in blue with touches of green, brown and puce on the leaves round the neck. 185mm high.

Above: the Smokers and Drinkers jug, identical to the pearlware jug marked WEDGWOOD. The floret design under the rim is similar to that on a marked example of a Castleford teapot (see page 59). The jug is banded in blue with the additional colours of green, yellow and puce. 157mm high.

Below: Mischievous Sport and Sportive Innocence, identical in size and shape to a pearlware jug. It is banded in blue and enamelled with the additional colours of yellow, orange, green, brown and turquoise. 117mm high. All the jugs on this page have been cast and not press moulded.

Below: the Peacock jug, identical in shape and size to the middle size of a set of three pearlware jugs (see page 194). The handle is of a type used by the Herculaneum Pottery at Liverpool. 153mm high. *Private Collection.*

The Leeds Pottery

The Leeds Pottery was founded in about 1770 by Joshua Green and his nephew John, and Richard Humble, who had bought the land on which the pottery was built. It was situated in the parish of Hunslet, on the wagon route from Leeds to the Middleton Collieries. It was, in 1812, on this three and a half mile long tram-line, that John Blenkinsop, who was the manager of the collieries, first tried and brought into regular use his rack-rail and cog-wheel driven steam locomotive, which was a complete commercial success. The Middleton Collieries paid the Leeds Pottery £7 per annum for allowing this line to cross their land and they also allowed them a discount on the price of coal supplied to the pottery.

By 1774 Joshua Green's cousin Savile Green had joined the firm which was then known as Humble, Green & Co. A couple of years later William Hartley put money into the firm which became known as Humble, Hartley, Greens & Co. Humble retired in 1781 and from then on the three Greens and Hartley ran the business between them. By 1800 John Green had already sold his shares in the Leeds Pottery and he was declared bankrupt. He left Leeds and moved to Newhill, near Swinton where he established the Don Pottery with the financial help of John and William Brameld of the Swinton Pottery and Richard Clark of Leeds.

William Hartley proved to be a good business man, endowed with much energy and the Leeds Pottery prospered greatly under his direction. After his death in 1813, things began to go wrong and in 1820 the firm became bankrupt. The pottery struggled on, passing through various hands until about 1880. It is sad to think that about that time a whole warehouse full of old Leeds creamware was discovered and that it was broken up and disposed of as refuse.[1]

But the time we are concerned with was the Hartley, Greens & Co. period 1781-1820, when the firm was competing with Wedgwoods, particularly with their fine quality cream-coloured earthenware and black basaltes or Egyptian Black as they called it. Many of the moulds used by the pottery for making the raised decorations on this black ware show acanthus and other leaf forms.

From looking at the old pattern books it is possible to see many pieces such as candlesticks and vases with acanthus and stiff leaf moulded decoration so often found on Pratt ware, and from one of the drawing books (the *No. 1 Teapot Drawing Book* in the Victoria and Albert Museum,) it can be seen that underglaze colours were used.

Though none of the pattern books list them, there are at least two Pratt ware commemorative pieces to be found with the impressed mark LEEDS POTTERY on the base. One is a 'Nelson and Berry' jug, rather creamy in body and the other is the 'LL Volunteers' jug. The former is in the City Museum, Stoke-on-Trent. The latter was a smaller jug (133mm high) than the one illustrated on page 169). Moulds of both these jugs are lodged at the Abbey House Museum, Kirkstall, Leeds.

Figures were also made at the Leeds Pottery. J.R. & F. Kidson, writing towards the end of the last century had some interesting observations to make which are worth quoting in full.[2]

'It is not generally known that the Leeds Pottery made figures and busts, but

---

1. J.R. & F. Kidson, *Historical Notes of the Old Leeds Pottery,* Leeds, 1892.
2. ibid.

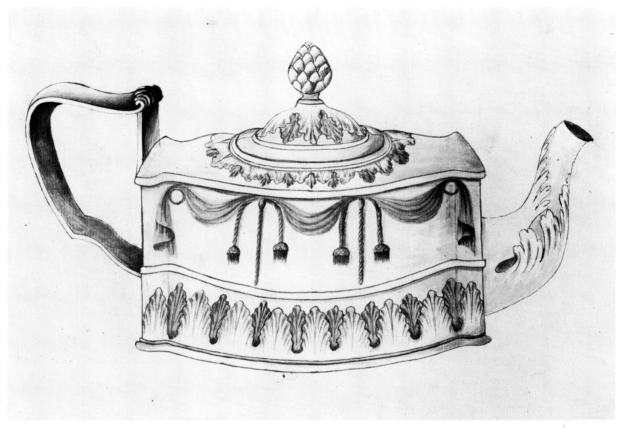

Leeds Drawing Book design c.1800
In one of the Leeds Teapot Drawing Books there is a drawing of a creamware straight-side teapot decorated with acanthus borders and tasselled swags that might well have served as an inspiration to the designer of the teapot marked HAWLEY. *Leeds Central Library. SF. 738. 30942 (L517).*

It is also remarkably like the teapot marked ASTBURY (see page 36).

this is certainly the case though marked specimens are rarely met with. The figures made by all potteries about the end of the last and the beginning of the present century are so much alike as to render positive identification of unmarked pieces exceedingly difficult.

There is every likelihood that in the very early days of the Pottery's existence, figures of a rude type decorated with slip colour would be extensively made, but like all ware made by the Brothers Green in those days, we have no means of any certain recognition. We can but conjecture that such are of Leeds make of this period by their being found in cottages in the immediate vicinity of the Pottery. Of this class are small figures of sheep of a peculiarly wooden character, coarsely coloured, evidently a staple product, as they were in much request for the adornment of the parlour mantel shelf. Cows, too appropriately turned into milk jugs, the tail twisted up to form a handle, and the milk finding an exit by the cow's open mouth. Watchstands again were manufactured in the shape of an old-fashioned longcase clock, with a boy and a girl standing on either side. All these, besides many others, are in a thin white body with a bluish glaze, and are splashed rather than painted with slip colours, principally orange, green and blue.' He might well have been describing the products of the factory whose mark was a large impressed crown.

Three-part flower vase c.1790
A fine quality pearlware flower vase, very light in weight and with a bluish glaze. The decoration is confined to blue feather-edging, a little ochre on the dolphin's head and tail and green for the main part of the dolphin's body. Impressed mark on the base LEEDS POTTERY. 191mm high. *E.2436. From the collection of the Laing Art Gallery, reproduced by permission of Tyne and Wear County Council Museums.*

Almost identical vases are to be found marked WOOD.

Quintal flower vase c.1800
A pearlware flower vase with blue feathered shell edges at top and foot. The splayed foot is mounted on a plain base with ogee shaped sides. On the front of the vase, an orange cartouche encloses a spray of orange and green leaves and flowers. The cartouche is enclosed with green acanthus leaves at the sides. The base is impressed LEEDS — POTTERY 18. 175mm high. *Leeds Art Galleries, Temple Newsam House. 16.127/47.*

Leeds Pottery mark in impressed capitals from the base of the quintal flower vase.

Venus and Neptune c.1805
A pair of figures, heavily coloured, very much in the Hawley manner, in dark blue, ochre and dark green on square bases. The green dolphins have ochre tails. This pair is unmarked, but there are also in the collection at Temple Newsam House an uncoloured pearlware pair from identical moulds (*16.304/47 & 16.306/47*) marked LEEDS POTTERY, and a Venus from the same mould finished in delicate enamel colouring (*(16.207/47*). The pair illustrated here is attributed to Leeds or the Don Pottery. 190mm high. *Leeds Art Galleries, Temple Newsam House. 16.201/47 & 16.209/47.*

This pair could well have been made by the Hawleys at either Rawmarsh or Kilnhurst, as the colouring has the intensity of so many of the marked Hawley pieces.

Model of a horse c.1810
A large pearlware figure of a horse, sponged in underglaze colours with a black mane, tail and hooves, standing on a stepped rectangular base with chamfered corners, colour washed green on top. Made by the Leeds Pottery. 406mm high. *Courtesy Sotheby's.*

These big Leeds horses are technically remarkable, for they are free-standing on quite thin legs. They are mostly from the same basic mould but treated with different types of colouring, underglaze and later enamel colours.

Joseph Kidson writing about the Leeds Pottery in 1892 said that he did not think that these large models of horses, originally produced for saddlers' and druggists' window display, were made by any of the Staffordshire potteries or any of the other Yorkshire potteries either. He said: 'We have been fortunate enough to obtain from cottages in the neighbourhood of the Pottery several fine examples of these earthenware horses, all having the history that they were made at the Leeds Pottery, generally by the father or grandfather of those who then held them.'

Leeds Drawing Book design 1800
In the drawing book for Black Ware dated 1800, this teapot (No. 15 in the book and titled Swinton No. 2) is decorated with leaf borders of various sorts reminiscent of many of the borders found on Pratt ware teapots made by the Barkers, Astburys, etc., and on other unmarked underglaze coloured specimens of the period. *Leeds Central Library. SF 738. 30942 (L.517).*

Swinton Old Pottery

The Swinton Old Pottery, which in 1826 became the Rockingham China Works, was situated some four miles north of Rotherham and at the time with which we are concerned (1785-1806) was linked to the Leeds Pottery through the Greens and Hartleys. The ware produced there was of much the same type as that made at Leeds. At one time Joseph Barker, who (according to Oxley Grabham[1]) came from Staffordshire, was employed at this pottery. It was his son Peter who took over the Mexborough Old Pottery in 1812 and worked it until 1822.

At the time when Swinton was affiliated to the Leeds Pottery, it is said that Leeds concentrated on creamware and a more decorated class of goods was manufactured at Swinton, so it is possible that Pratt ware was made here. From 1785 to 1806 the Swinton Pottery traded as Greens, Bingley & Co. Things did not go too well with the Leeds partners and in 1806 John and William Brameld became sole proprietors and all connections with Leeds were severed. In spite of establishing a trade with Russia and all parts of the United Kingdom, the Bramelds, like many other English potters, had a difficult time during the Napoleonic Wars. They were twice declared bankrupt and in 1843 the pottery was sold up. There are no known marked Pratt ware pieces from this pottery.

---

1. Oxley Grabham, *Yorkshire Potteries, Pots and Potters,* York, 1916.

Page from W.W.Slee's catalogue c.1913-18
Page 24 from an undated catalogue of reproductions of Leeds
Pottery made by the Seniors for W.W.Slee at a pottery at
Hunslet, shows reproductions of 'Pratt' ware jugs described and
priced.

602 Jug, Coloured Hunting	6″	4/6
581 Teacaddy Beau and Belle	3¼″	2/6
601 Jug, coloured Peace and Plenty	6″	4/6
574 Jug, coloured Volunteers	6″	3/6

551 Jug, coloured, Nelson	7″	4/6
603 Jug, coloured, Shooting	6″	7/6

These with the possible exception of No. 603 are copies of
very well known 'Pratt' ware models made between
1790-1830, presumably by the Leeds Pottery (see pages 68
and 28 for the Nelson and Volunteers jugs). *Leeds Central
Library.*

Reproductions

Pratt ware jugs and tea caddies have not been extensively copied with the
exception of the reproductions of J.W. Senior (who had worked at the Old
Leeds Pottery in 1865) and his sons George and James who were working from
about 1888 in a pottery in Hunslet, Leeds. W.W. Slee, who was a well-known
antique dealer in Leeds, marketed their wares and in 1913 issued a catalogue.
In the Leeds Central Library there is a photostat of this crown octavo
catalogue; bound up with it is another catalogue of landscape shape (140 x
192mm). On the title page is W.W. Slee's address at 30 Duncan Street, Leeds
and his telephone number, 3810 Central. If in 1913 Slee had had a telephone,
no doubt he would have put the number on his catalogue. In 1918 the Leeds
telephone exchange altered all the numbers to five digits so the likelihood is
that this second catalogue was produced during the 1914-18 war.

According to an historical note in Slee's catalogue 'The manufacture of
Leeds Pottery (was) revived in 1888 by W.W. Slee and using many of the
original moulds and patterns obtained from the old works'. Many of these old
moulds were destroyed by George Senior, but some were given to the Abbey
House Museum, Kirkstall, Leeds, where they are still. There is no way of

Mould for the Admiral Nelson and Captain Berry jug c.1798
One side of the worn plaster of Paris three-piece mould showing the bust of Admiral Nelson flanked by two men-of-war. It came from J.& G.Senior of Hunslet, who had acquired some of the original moulds from the Old Leeds Pottery in the 1880s. Later versions of the jug made by the Seniors from the same mould are impressed LEEDS*POTTERY on the base. *Leeds City Council, Abbey House Museum.*

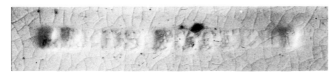

Admiral Nelson and Captain Berry jug 1888-1918
This pearlware jug is marked LEEDS*POTTERY. It may well have been made by J.W.Senior or his sons George or James at Hunslet. See No. 551 from the Slee Catalogue on page 67. 178mm high. *City Museum and Art Gallery, Stoke-on-Trent.*

An enamel coloured version of this jug, using a virulent green, is in the National Maritime Museum. Captain Hardy's name is substituted for Berry's. It may have been made by the Seniors at the centenary of Nelson's death.

The Senior's mark from the base of the jug above.

telling which of these moulds were from the old factory and which were copies by the Seniors.

In the Slee catalogue numerous examples of Pratt ware subjects cast from the Leeds Pottery moulds were listed, including a hunting jug, a Peace and Plenty jug, an Admiral Nelson jug, a Ll Volunteers jug, an uncoloured figure of a shepherd carrying a sheep and another uncoloured figure of Venus with a dolphin (listed as 'Charity'), an uncoloured bust of a man blowing out his cheeks, called 'Air', and another uncoloured bust of Shakespeare. There was also a Macaroni tea-caddy; the prices ranged from half a crown for the tea-caddy to ten and sixpence for the Shakespeare bust.

The few uncoloured subjects listed above are often to be seen decorated with underglaze colours. Among other subjects made by the Seniors were a relief decorated tobacco jar with the arms of the City of Leeds and a cream jug in the form of a woman's head, enamel coloured. In the National Maritime Museum in London there is a Nelson and Berry jug and also a Nelson and Hardy jug, both coloured over the glaze, that were most probably made by the Seniors, though neither of them is marked.

According to Heather Lawrence, who quotes an interview with G.W. Senior, he said that various versions of the large Leeds horses were made at Hunslet by

Shooting and Gardeners jug c.1800-10
This fine quality pearlware jug is coloured in brown, orange, yellow and green only, shows a shooting scene of a man with a gun and three brown spotted dogs in a wooded landscape against an orangepeel textured background. On the other side are a man with a spade and a girl with a watering can. It is fluted and scalloped at the bottom and scalloped at the top with a feathered edge. The neck is decorated with a painted orange line and a serpentine trail of leaves, below which is a line of swagged orange bunting. The handle is fastened to the body at the top with a simulated strap and the lower part of the handle has a leaf shaped terminal. 155mm high. *Private Collection.*

A larger version, 186mm high with the handle terminating in a dolphin's head, is in the Victoria and Albert Museum *C.70.1952.* Though the jug shown here is unmarked, it seems more than possible that it was made at Leeds, because of the later copy which was made by the Seniors and impressed LEEDS POTTERY.

Shooting and Gardeners jug c.1888-1920
This rather crude pale creamware jug, cast from a worn mould, is decorated in relief with a similar shooting scene and pair of gardeners. It is painted over the glaze with a pale pea green, a bluish green, black and Indian red. The scalloped design at the top and bottom of the jug is feathered in Indian red. It is marked LEEDS POTTERY in small capital letters on the base and was made by J.W. or J. and G.Senior at their pottery in Hunslet. This jug is illustrated in a catalogue issued by W.W.Slee some time before 1918. It is number 602 on page 24, and it was priced at 4/6d, a perfectly reasonable price at that time for a reproduction. It could not possibly be mistaken for one of the earlier Leeds pieces. 170mm high. *Leeds Art Galleries, Temple Newsam House. 27/6/3179.*

This jug is obviously based on the earlier model, shown above left, but with one or two significant differences. The figures of the gardener in this later version are widely separated with a tree and dogs between them. On the other side the tree has been moved to behind one of the dogs and the orange peel background so noticeable in the earlier version is missing.

them.[1] We have not been able to discover if these horses were decorated in underglaze colours. In fact, as far as we have seen, most of the Seniors' coloured reproductions were enamelled over the glaze. Many of the copies they made were marked LEEDS POTTERY, sometimes with an asterisk between the words.

George Senior continued in business until 1957, his reproductions were made in a pale creamware, many of them from worn moulds. As for examples of Pratt ware, there is no record of it being made after 1918, though it may well have been. An overglaze decorated Ll Volunteers jug that we saw a few years ago marked LEEDS POTTERY was easily identifiable as a late reproduction from the Seniors' pottery.

---

1. Heather Lawrence, *Yorkshire Pots and Potteries,* Newton Abbot, 1974.

The Seniors, no doubt, were merely intending to carry on the tradition of the Old Leeds Pottery in making modern reproductions, for their prices were very modest. According to the illustrated catalogues, quite apart from the Pratt ware examples, most of their output was confined to typical Leeds pierced creamware.

Another firm that made reproductions was William Kent Ltd of Burslem. They were established in 1878 and made copies of some Pratt subjects (but not with underglaze colouring) which included cottages, pastille burners etc (see page 255). The Kents remained in production until December 1962.

The Don Pottery

This pottery was founded at the beginning of the nineteenth century on the north-west bank of the canalised river Don at Swinton, by John Green (who had left the Leeds Pottery in 1800) in partnership with John and William Brameld from the Swinton Pottery and Richard Clark, a rope manufacturer from Leeds. At the end of 1803, John Green's two sons, John and William had joined the firm; John as a partner and William as a clerk. Two years later John Green senior died and the two sons took over the running of the pottery, trading first as Greens Clark and Co.; it was not until 1822 that John and William Green became sole proprietors, trading under their own names. Beset by money troubles they went bankrupt in 1834, like their father who had had to leave the Leeds Pottery for the same reason. After various vicissitudes, in 1839 the pottery was sold to Samuel Barker of the Mexborough Old Pottery.

In 1808 the Greens issued a pattern book that was very similar to the Leeds Pattern Book. In it are illustrated some teapots with relief decoration and a vase with an acanthus leaf border.[1]

In its heyday the Don Pottery produced more goods than any of the other Yorkshire potteries, with the exception of the Leeds Pottery. The great similarity of the Don creamware to that produced at Leeds must be due to the fact that John Green had been one of the partners there. It is highly likely that the Don Pottery made underglaze coloured relief decorated cream or pearlware, but apart from the pattern book, to date there is no absolute evidence to confirm that they did.

There is a group of Toby jugs, sheep with shepherds and shepherdesses, cows with cowherds, clock money-boxes flanked by figures, horses and cow creamers, all with similar underglaze colouring and with sponged or speckled bases which we have identified as all being made at a pottery that used a large impressed crown as its mark. These are often attributed to the Don Pottery. We have been quite unable either to substantiate or deny this claim.

---

1. 'Engraved Patterns of the Don Pottery' 1808, Victoria and Albert Museum Library 11.RC.M3.

Engraved vase design 1808
No. 222 from the Don Pottery Catalogue issued in 1808 showing a typical creamware vase design with relief decoration and feather edging. Similar vases were made at Leeds. *Crown Copyright, Victoria and Albert Museum. 11.RC.M3.*

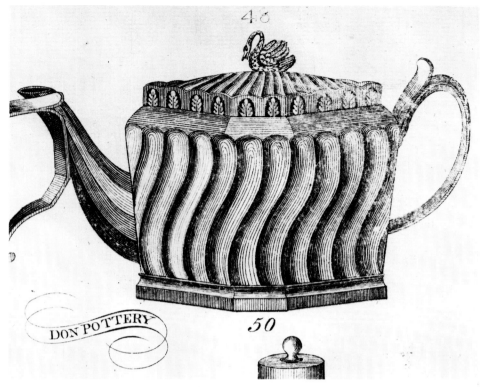

Engraved teapot design 1808
No. 48 from the Don Pottery Catalogue issued in 1808, showing acanthus leaf moulding on the gallery around the lid and a swan knob, so often seen on underglaze coloured relief decorated teapots. The basic diamond shape is one much used by T. Harley (see page 42). *Crown Copyright, Victoria and Albert Museum. 11. RC. M3.*

Engraved teapot design 1808
No. 46 from the Don Pottery Catalogue issued in 1808 showing the complicated kind of design made in black basaltes as well as in underglaze coloured cream and pearlware. The pointed oval medallion and vertical fluting can also be seen on teapots made by the Bradley Pottery at Coalport (see page 56). *Crown Copyright, Victoria and Albert Museum. 11. RC. M3.*

Kilnhurst Old Pottery

White's Directory of 1837 describes this pottery, which is on the west bank of the Dearne and Dove canal, as being founded in 1746; William Malpass was thought to have been one of its founders. Thomas Hawley, brother of William Hawley of Rawmarsh was working at the Kilnhurst Old Pottery in 1783. He continued working there until his death in 1808; his son Philip succeeded him and remained at Kilnhurst until his death in 1830.

Whether the Kilnhurst Old Pottery used the impressed mark HAWLEY is not clear. As there are two versions of this mark, one in a straight line of capital letters and the other in a crescent shape of capital letters, it is possible that the Kilnhurst Pottery used one design and the Top Pottery at Rawmarsh used the other. There are also some underglaze coloured pieces impressed THO HAWLEY, including some busts of John Wesley which must have been made by Thomas Hawley at the Kilnhurst Old Pottery between 1783 and 1808.

Top Pottery, Rawmarsh

William Hawley established the Top Pottery at Rawmarsh in 1790. Hawley came from a family of potters working both in Yorkshire and Staffordshire. There are references to a Hawley working in Staffordshire in the early nineteenth century and a John Hawley was working at the Foley Pottery from 1842 to 1887, (too late for our purposes).

William Hawley had formerly been a partner in the Rotherham Old Pottery a couple of miles up the river Don. Thomas Hawley (probably William's brother) was working the nearby Kilnhurst Old Pottery. There is an unresolved debate as to which pottery made the examples of underglaze coloured relief decorated ware and figures impressed HAWLEY.

These Hawley figures, jugs and teapots are in a pearlware body with a markedly bluish glaze and are most richly coloured. The opaque oxide colours are applied very thickly, which produces a relatively deep toned appearance, particularly in the blues and greens. The eyes and other features are also heavily outlined in black. There are several marked examples of these Hawley pots in the Yorkshire Museum, including a fine small jug with the design of the heads of the French royal family and the Duke of York; a shepherd (after the Ralph Wood 'Lost Sheep' figure), the Bacchus jug and a teapot similar to one marked Astbury (see page 36).

A traditional type of Toby jug, impressed HAWLEY on the rim of the base passed through the London Sale rooms in 1972. At the Castle Museum, Norwich, there is another teapot, richly coloured and marked HAWLEY. In this piece there was a discoloured piece of paper with a handwritten note in faded ink saying that Hawley once worked at the Foley Works in Staffordshire, where the similar Astbury teapot originated. Maybe it is a coincidence that a William Astbury worked for the Hawleys for over sixty-three years as a model maker and mould cutter.

William Hawley continued to trade as Hawley and Co. until his death in 1818, when the business was carried on by his redoubtable widow and her sons.

14. The Royal Sufferers and Duke of York jug c.1795

The vertical fluting on the neck and lower part of the jug is picked out with blue and ochre lines. The figures are strongly painted with black hair and their features heavily outlined in black. Louis XVI is wearing a blue uniform with a yellow sash and Marie Antoinette is wearing a blue dress trimmed with yellow. The group is enclosed in a medallion edged with green leaves and ochre fruits. On each side of the spout is an unusual yellow panel, triangular in shape and pricked to simulate orange peel, it is flanked by a green leaf. Down the centre of the spout runs an orange band. At the back of the jug under the rather heavy scrolled handle is a similar large leaf design with blue veins, edged with green and orange. This well-potted jug impressed HAWLEY on the base, was made at Kilnhurst or the Rawmarsh Top Pottery. 127mm high. *Yorkshire Museum. Ht 5087.*

There is another marked specimen in the Nelson-Atkins Museum of Art (Burnap Collection) *B.625 (BI 912)* Kansas City, Missouri; and also one is on loan to the Rotherham Museum.

15. The Lost Sheep c.1795-1810

The figure of a shepherd, after a Ralph Wood model, wearing a very dark green coat, dark ochre breeches, a yellow waistcoat and blue speckled stockings, stands on a mount mottled in ochre, green and black. The sheep is uncoloured and is supported on his shoulders with its feet tied to a white stick. Impressed mark HAWLEY on the base. The glaze is markedly blue and all the colours have an opacity and thickness that seems typical of the Hawley productions. From the Kilnhurst Old Pottery (Thomas Hawley) or the Top Pottery at Rawmarsh (William Hawley). 222mm high. *Yorkshire Museum. Ht 4472.*

See page 263 for another version of this figure.

The HAWLEY mark in impressed capital letters on the base.

Teapot c.1795-1815

A teapot with a pearlware body, richly decorated in green, ochre, blue and yellow, featuring a Chinaman on both sides, one holding an umbrella and the other playing some musical instrument. The impressed mark HAWLEY on the base is semi-circular. From the Kilnhurst or Rawmarsh Top Pottery. 145mm high. *Private Collection.*

The HAWLEY mark in impressed capital letters on the base of one of the candlesticks opposite.

Bacchus jug c.1800-15

This extraordinary jug originated from the Wood factory and is said to have been designed by John Voyez. This particularly richly coloured underglaze version has the rather heavy outlining of the eyes that characterises so many of the Hawley pieces. The spout should be in the form of a dolphin's head, but has been damaged and repaired. Made either at Kilnhurst or at Rawmarsh Top Pottery. Impressed HAWLEY on the base. 304mm high. *Yorkshire Museum.*

For a similar but unmarked version see page 216.

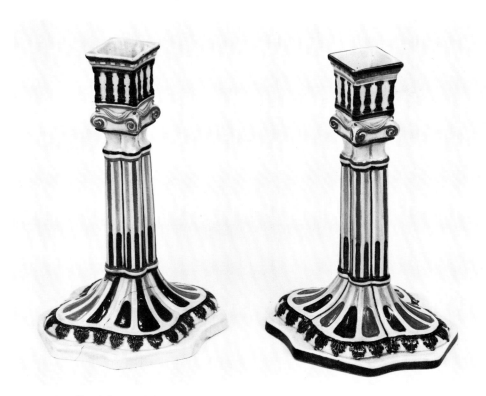

Pair of Candlesticks c.1805
Two pearlware candlesticks with square topped sconces on elaborately moulded pillars and bases with a border of dark green acanthus leaves round the foot. Coloured richly and opaquely with orange, brown, dark green and blue. The glaze has a strong bluish tinge. One of them is impressed HAWLEY on the base. Made at Kilnhurst or the Rawmarsh Top Pottery. 229mm high. *Doncaster Museum and Art Gallery. 356.82 a & b.*

Low Pottery, Rawmarsh

Situated about a quarter of a mile from the Top Pottery, the Low Pottery was leased in the early 1790s by John Wainwright and Peter Barker, from the widow of Robert Hall, where they traded under the name of Barker & Co. Peter Barker only remained with this pottery until 1812, when he moved to Mexborough.

Whether or not the relief decorated underglaze coloured pieces, such as the dolphin knobbed teapot, which has the impressed mark BARKER on the base was made here or at Mexborough, or at Lane End in Staffordshire is not clear.

Mexborough Old Pottery

This pottery was established on the branch canal at Mexborough, at the end of the eighteenth century by Sowter & Bromley. In 1804 they were trading as Robert Sowter & Co. It is said that they made fine white stoneware teapots, certainly some of these are marked 'S & Co', and it is reasonable to suggest that Sowter & Bromley may have made them.

In 1809, the pottery was let to Jesse Barker. Two years later, with the help of his brother Peter, Jesse Barker bought the pottery and was joined by his brother in 1812. In due course, Jesse's son Samuel succeeded the two brothers in the management of this pottery. Relief decorated underglaze coloured teapots marked BARKER (in both Doncaster and Yorkshire Museums) are attributed to the Mexborough Old Pottery.

16. Teapot c.1795-1815
A richly coloured straight-sided teapot decorated in ochre, dark green and blue, with a lid with a rounded knob. The side panels are decorated with tasselled and swagged drapery and stiff leaves in relief. Impressed HAWLEY on the base. From Kilnhurst or Rawmarsh Top Pottery. 155mm high. *Bulwer Collection, Norwich Castle Museum.*

There is a similar teapot in the Royal Scottish Museum *1973.129* differing in that it has a 'widow' knob coloured in ochre. Impressed HAWLEY. Another example, also with the same impressed mark, but lidless and with a broken handle is in the Yorkshire Museum. Yet another teapot of the same design but in a fine pearlware body is impressed ASTBURY (see page 36). There is a black basaltes teapot of the same design marked Bradley & Co Coalport, in the Victoria and Albert Museum *3392.1901.*

17. Huntsmen at a meet jug c.1805
This full-bodied squat shaped jug with a pronounced spout is coloured blue, brown, yellow, burnt orange and dark green with uncoloured acanthus moulding at the base and a vine border at the top. On the other side of the jug is a scene with Toby Fillpot sitting outside an inn with a hanging sign. Impressed FERRYBRIDGE on the bottom. 117mm high. *Private Collection.*

Ferrybridge Pottery

The Ferrybridge Pottery was first called the Knottingley Pottery and was situated on the south bank of the river Aire, about a mile downstream from the bridge at Ferrybridge, and some twenty miles from Leeds. The Knottingley Pottery was founded by William Tomlinson in 1793, partnered by Seaton, a banker from Pontefract, Foster a ship owner from Selby, Thompson a gentleman of leisure, and a coal proprietor called Timothy Smith.

The title of the firm was Tomlinson, Foster & Co. until Ralph Wedgwood joined the firm in 1798, when the name was changed to Tomlinson, Foster, Wedgwood & Co. As the lithographed circular, issued in July 1798[1] shows, they started out with high hopes of what their new partner could do for them which were not to be fulfilled, for the partnership was dissolved in 1800. The style William Tomlinson & Co. was assumed and so continued until 1804. In 1804 the name of the actual pottery was changed from Knottingley Pottery to Ferrybridge Pottery and traded as Tomlinson, Plowes and Co. The new partner John Plowes was the son of a former partner of David Dunderdale at Castleford. From 1805, the firm used the one word FERRYBRIDGE for their mark, impressed in small capital letters which are often barely decipherable.[2] By 1828 William Tomlinson had bought out all his partners and had become the sole proprietor of the Ferrybridge Pottery. He was then 82 years of age.[3] The impressed word FERRYBRIDGE sometimes had the 'D' reversed.

The production of the pottery was mainly cream coloured earthenware, caneware, black basaltes, printed ware and pearlware; there are various Pratt type pearlware jugs marked FERRYBRIDGE. The ones we have seen are all of a squat shape with large spouts decorated with bucolic or classical subjects. The body of the ware is of a good quality, the modelling crisp, and the painting careful and intense in colour.

The Ferrybridge Pottery not only had an extensive local and coastal trade, but a large export business, including in their early years with Russia, until Napoleon put an end to their trade with the entire Continent.

In the Wedgwood Museum at Barlaston, there is a large scrap-book cum ledger (368 x 248mm) called *Wedgwood & Co. Ferrybridge Shape and Pattern Book*, that once belonged to Ralph Wedgwood.

The entries cover a very wide range of wares and include lists of exports to New York and Leghorn, with prices. The illustrations show dozens of hand painted decorative borders as well as engraved patterns. There are also many pencil sketches, some of relief moulded jugs decorated with acanthus leaves, flutes and figures and there is a carefully drawn relief moulded teapot which is headed 'March 30th/99 The Newest Pattern in the Pottery'. In this book are several references to underglaze decoration. There is one tantalising reference to 'Jug, coloured, Franklin and Washington'. It would be nice to be able to assume that this was a relief decorated underglaze coloured jug, but as there are several engraved portraits of these two men in the book, probably the jug referred to was decorated with a hand-coloured engraving.

---

1. Keele University Archives, 31414-56.
2. A Sun Fire Insurance Policy 788873 issued on 7 April 1806 to Messrs. Tomlinson, Plowes & Co. gave them cover for house, pottery and contents for £5,600 and a further £400 for the water flint mill at Brotherton, which shows it was a substantial business. Guildhall Ms. 11,937.
3. Heather Lawrence, 'Wedgwood & Co.', *The Connoisseur*, 1974.

unnecessary. — *The various shapes, models, & designs of goods made by Mr Wedgwood & Co are adopted in this Concern, & Mr Wedgwood, having obtained his Majestys letters patent for various improvements in the manufacturing of his Wares, it is agreed to mark our goods WEDGWOOD 👑 ——— Referring you to our respective signatures.*

We have the honor to subscribe ourselves,

Your obedient, humble Servants,

The Signature of Messrs Tomlinson, Foster, &c. ~~Tomlinson, Foster, Wedgwood & Co~~

The Signature of Mr Ra. Wedgwood. ~~Tomlinson Foster, Wedgwood & Co~~

Knottingley-Pottery. July, 1798.

Lithographed circular issued by Tomlinson, Foster, Wedgwood & Co

The last few lines of the agreement signed by Tomlinson, Foster, Wedgwood & Co. of the Knottingley Pottery, dated July 1798. This shows the crown mark that the pottery was intending to use. *Courtesy Josiah Wedgwood & Sons Limited, Barlaston, Stoke-on-Trent, and Keele University Library 31414-56, where the manuscripts are deposited.*

Toby Fillpot jug c.1805

This is the reverse side of 'The Meet' jug illustrated in colour on page 76. *Private Collection.*

Old Mother Slipper-Slopper jug c.1805

This full-bodied squat jug (a shape unique to the Ferrybridge Pottery) is decorated with a border of dark green vine leaves and blue grapes round the neck. The continuous frieze pictures the orange fox carrying off the goose with the farmer in his blue smock stumbling in pursuit and John, in blue coat, black hat and orange breeches looks on while the farmer's wife, also dressed in blue, unleashes the brown spotted hounds outside their orange and yellow kennel. The acanthus border at the base of the jug is uncoloured. Very faintly impressed mark FERRYBRIDGE. 116mm high.
Wakefield Art Gallery and Museums. 164.

Venus jug c.1805

This full-bodied, squat shaped jug with the large spout and wavy top peculiar to Ferrybridge has a relief design of Venus, draped in a blue garment and standing in a yellow scallop shell drawn by a pair of dolphins, with Cupid swimming along behind through the green sea. The vine border at the top and the acanthus leaves at the foot are similar to the other jugs of the same shape. Impressed FERRYBRIDGE on the base. The handles on these marked Ferrybridge jugs are all similar with their upswept line and thumb-rest. 116mm high. *Wakefield Art Gallery and Museums. 169.*

The other side of the Venus jug shows a putto mounted on an eagle, flying over the waves, beside a man-of-war sailing away with pennants flying. The eagle and putto motif had been used earlier by Turner on his jasper ware and also appeared on that made by Adams. It can be seen in underglaze colouring on an 'apprentice plaque' (see page 149).

The Sailor's Return jug c.1805

This squat shaped jug is bordered at the top with a trailing vine coloured with green, blue and manganese. On one side the cheerful homecoming sailor in blue jacket, white trousers and yellow waistcoat waves his black hat as he runs towards the yellow and orange public house. On the other side his girl-friend, standing in a landscape with trees, wearing a yellow skirt and blue bodice, awaits him with open arms. Impressed mark FERRYBRIDGE (rather faint) on the base. 116mm high. *Wakefield Art Gallery and Museums.*

Modern jasper ware border design

This vine design was originally probably drawn by William Hackwood and must have been the inspiration for many of the vine borders used in relief on underglaze coloured ware. It is still used on contemporary Wedgwood jasper ware. *Courtesy Josiah Wedgwood and Sons Limited, Barlaston, Stoke-on-Trent.*

Clock group Money-box 1838
A money-box in white earthenware in the form of a longcase clock, flanked by the figures of a man and a woman; the man is wearing a black hat, blue coat and white trousers; the woman, who has black hair is wearing a black bonnet, a yellow blouse trimmed with puce and a white skirt. In front of the clock are two black and white spotted dogs with yellow collars. There are blue line decorations around the clock face and its base. The whole group is mounted on a rectangular base, green washed on top, the sloping sides sponged in puce, green and blue. The clock is almost identical to the one bearing J.Emery's signature. 229mm high. *Courtesy Sotheby's.*

Emery's Pottery, Mexborough

This little pottery lay about a quarter of a mile to the west of Mexborough Old Pottery, some six miles north of Rotherham. Very crude Pratt type of ware was made there by James Emery towards the end of the 1830s. A grandfather clock money-box is incised in a rather shaky cursive hand on the back 'J. Emery Mexbro' 1838'. The pottery continued in business until the 1880s, though James Emery died in 1874 at the age of 81.

Clock group Money-box 1838

A very similar group from which the female figure and one of the spotted dogs are missing. It is surmounted on an oval base, the sides crudely splashed with dark green, blue and puce. The modelling of the clock is identical with the other two. The additional colours used are black and yellow. It is incised on the back '*J. Emery Mexbro' 1838*' in a cursive hand. 229mm high. *Museum and Art Gallery, Doncaster. 199.83.*

Clock Money-box 1838

This white earthenware money-box has been removed from its base. It is most probable that it was once the central piece of a similar group to the two other money-box groups illustrated here. Inscribed on the back in a cursive hand is '*J. Emery Mexbro' 1838*'. The piece is crudely decorated in very dark blue, ochre and black. 200mm high. *Private Collection.*

These money-box groups must be almost the last underglaze coloured pieces of Pratt ware to be made.

J.Emery mark incised on the back of the clock money-box.

The pottery that used a large impressed crown mark

The most colourful and intriguing of Pratt ware pieces are found in a particular range of Toby jugs, sheep, horse and cow groups, figures and tall clock money-boxes and watch stands. Their colouring is remarkable for a very intense burnt orange and a strong cobalt blue. What makes them intriguing, tantalisingly so, is a large and unidentified impressed crown mark that appears on the bases of various Toby jugs. The sheep, horse and cow groups are united to the Toby jugs by certain characteristics including their colouring, and bases stippled or sponged in ochre, cobalt and black and also eyebrows that are indicated by a row of black dots. In addition, identical figures appear in different groups.

The large Toby marked with the impressed crown is typical in feature of the most common of the Ralph Wood Tobys. It is in the form of a seated man wearing a white tricorne hat with the rim scalloped in black, a strongly coloured blue coat and orange breeches. In his right hand he holds a mug and in his left a small jug, in some cases a miniature Toby jug. As far as we know none of the Ralph Wood Tobys holds a comparable miniature Toby, nor do the Wood jugs have such elaborate handles. The handle on this particular jug has a caryatid forming the top part. Placed between the feet of one of these Toby jugs is a small spaniel from the same mould as that of the dog at the foot of one of the tall clock money-boxes. None of the Ralph Wood Tobys is accompanied by a similar animal.

The most idiosyncratic of the animal groups consists of very large sheep or rams standing a clear head higher than the attendant figures alongside them. These gigantic sheep or rams are entirely white except for dark brown or black marks on their horns or ears and the eyebrows are dotted in black. A pair of lambs lie beneath the large animal. Accompanying one ram, facing to the right is a gardener with a spade. A sheep, also facing to the right is attended by a lady gardener with a watering can. An identical pair of figures flank a clock case money-box group, the only difference being in the colouring of their clothes.

Other figures appear with these large sheep and on money-box clock cases. A different clock is flanked by a man in a top hat, blue coat and ochre coloured trousers (not breeches); the girl in this group wears an exaggeratedly wide-shouldered, high-waisted dress, splodged in a dusty green. Her black hair is uncovered and she wears a blue kerchief round her neck. A similar girl is to be found with an orange blotched cow. The costumes of these figures, the top hat and trousers of the man and the high-waisted, puff-sleeved dress of the woman would indicate that these figures could not have been made before about 1807, when trousers for men replaced breeches for informal wear.

All these groups stand on similar green-topped bases, the sides of which are sponged in ochre, cobalt and black. These figures, animals and Tobys are made of a good quality white body with a slight bluish cast to the glaze. They must all be from the same factory, which is sometimes referred to in auctioneers' catalogues as the Don Pottery (with, as we have already stated, no apparent justification.) The only hint to their origin is the very large impressed crown mark on the base of some Toby jugs and, on the base of one cow group, the word WESLEY in large capital letters. We have been unable to trace any potter of this name, so it may just have been a *jeu d'esprit* of a potter, bored, or out of sympathy, with making busts of the famous preacher. These busts were made by numerous potteries, including, so it would seem, the pottery that marked some of their wares with a large impressed crown.

Cow with farmer's wife c.1820

The cow is facing to the right, with an elaborately attired female attendant wearing her black hair piled up and a low cut dress with a blue frill round her shoulders. The dress is dotted with blue spots encircled with puce, and has a flounce at the hem with a pattern of flowers in ochre and green with blue bands. She wears blue shoes and has a string of black beads round her neck. The woman is a little like the Josephine figure in the watch stand group on page 91.

The cow is blotched with aubergine blotches on its back and face and she has the usual dotted eyebrows. The recumbent calf by her hind foot is speckled with green and lies on the green-washed top of the base, the sides of which are speckled with ochre, blue and black.

Under the base, in impressed capital letters 5mm high, is the name WESLEY. These letters have been stamped in from single printers' sorts and the 'S' is upside down. We can trace no potter of this name, which is not a common one in the potteries. We can only think that a potter who may have been working on busts of John Wesley suddenly for a joke took it upon himself to impress the cow group with the famous Methodist preacher's name. 153mm high. *Private Collection.*

Girl in a carriage drawn by a lion c.1810

The seated girl wears a blue hat and a white dress with a yellow collar and brown polka dots. The carriage is coloured orange and has brown wheels. The yellow lion wears a brown harness, its eyes are brown and white and it has an orange mane and forelegs. The base is partially brown banded. 79mm high. *Colonial Williamsburg Foundation. 1963-478.*

The figure of the girl is very similar to the farmer's wife with the cow marked WESLEY. This group was formerly in the C.B.Kidd Collection.

Bust of John Wesley c.1800

A very small bust of Wesley, who is dressed in black with white bands. He is mounted on a waisted socle, ochre banded at the top and speckled in ochre and black around the base. He has the same dotted eyebrows as the Toby jug, etc., from the pottery with the impressed crown mark. 121mm high. *The Royal Pavilion Art Gallery and Museums, Brighton. HW 829.*

The impressed mark on the base of the cow group above.

Toby jug c.1800-20
Rear view, showing the caryatid handle, of the Toby marked with an impressed large crown. This one differs from the one shown in colour, having no spaniel between his feet and having the addition of the mulberry puce colour to the sponged base, to the coat and the hat of the small Toby jug that he is holding, and to his lips and scarf. The treatment of the hair is also different, being heavily sponged with black. 250mm high. *Private Collection.*

Toby jug c.1800-20
A similar Toby, but holding a striped and spotted full-bodied jug. This piece is also marked with a large impressed crown. *Private Collection.*

All these large Tobys have a broad green-washed stripe down their backs, beneath the caryatid handle.
Another example of this marked Toby jug is in the Merseyside County Museum, Liverpool *5.10.26.7.*

It has been suggested that the crown might be a mark used by the Mexborough Pottery. Another possiblity is that they were produced at the Swillington Bridge Pottery, which was known to have used various crown marks. This pottery was situated at Woodlesford, some five miles south-east of Leeds and close to the river Aire. It was being worked by William Taylor in 1797 and was still being worked by him in 1805 when William and Thomas Wildblood took over. This pottery is known to have made very good quality creamware and black basaltes ware.[1] A round creamware plaque with a figure in relief but enamel coloured, has a scene of a bearded man with a short jerkin and an anorak-like hood, holding blacksmiths' tongs in his right hand. In the background is a classically draped woman holding a shield and standing on a pedestal. The back of the plaque is incised 'John Wildblood Swillington Bridge Pottery July 12th 1831.'[2] A stamp for marking a crown in relief was found near the site of this pottery. However, this is but a tentative suggestion and until further evidence is forthcoming, we suggest these figure groups and Toby jugs are referred to as the products of the pottery that used the large impressed crown mark. The ware certainly has the kind of robustness that one might associate with Yorkshire, but that is as far as we are prepared to take it.

---

1. A. Hurst, *A Catalogue of the Boynton Collection of Yorkshire Pottery,* 1922.
2. Illustrated in Oxley Grabham's *Yorkshire Potteries, Pots and Potters,* York, 1916.

18. Toby jugs c.1800-20

Three generations of Toby, obviously from the same pottery, though only the largest one is marked with a large impressed crown. A black and white spaniel rests between his feet. The middle-sized Toby has been designed so that the limbs are in relief on the body of the jug and are not fully modelled as in most Toby jugs. The base is green washed on the top and the handle is in the form of a caryatid. 195mm high. There is another version of this in the Royal Pavilion Art Gallery and Museum, Brighton *HW 1448*. The smallest Toby of the same design and colouring as the middle-sized one, holds a vestigial bottle and mug to his stomach. The handle is decorated with a trailing pattern of blue leaves. 102mm high. *Private Collection.*

There is an illustration of a group of three similar Toby jugs with sponged bases in Major Cyril Earle's book. He attributed them to 'a Yorkshire Pottery'.

Impressed crown mark from the base of the large Toby jug.

19. Cow, calf and milkmaid 1800-20

The cow, facing to the left is coloured with burnt orange patches, speckled with black; the ears are outlined with black and there is a black patch on the head between the horns, a black tail and hooves, and an orange udder speckled with black. The milkmaid has a high shouldered white dress spotted in blue, a puce kerchief round her neck and an orange apron. Her black hair is piled on top of her head. She is the same figure that flanks a tall money-box clock. The calf, lying at her feet is spotted in ochre, blue and black. The group is mounted on a base with a green-washed top with the sides sponged in ochre, blue and black. 153mm high. *Private Collection.*

This group must have come from the pottery with the large impressed crown mark. Similar groups to this are to be found made of a buff coloured body.

Ram and Gardener c.1800-20

A very large ram facing to the right with horns, eyes and feet picked out in black. The eyebrows are treated in the same manner as those on the large Toby from the pottery that used the impressed crown mark (see page 84). The gardener with the spade who stands at the ram's head is the same figure as on one of the tall clock money-boxes on page 89. He is dressed in a black hat, blue coat, yellow spotted waistcoat and ochre breeches. A shepherd's crook leans against the ram's foreleg, spotted in blue, black and yellow. Two lambs rest on the top of the green-washed base, which is sponged in blue, black and orange. 160mm high. *Private Collection.*

Ram and Shepherdess c.1800-20

A very large ram facing to the left has a small figure of a girl in attendance holding her hat to her head. She is wearing a dark blue apron and burnt orange splashed dress and carries a basket on her right arm. This figure also appears riding pillion on her horse (see page 279) and accompanies a cow (see below). The usual pair of lambs rest on the green washed base which has a slightly different moulding and sponging on the sides, with rather more solid patches of black and orange. 150mm high. *Private Collection.*

Opposite

A pair of cows with cowman and milkmaid c.1800-20

The cow faces to the right with the cowman, the doleful one with the milkmaid faces to the left. They are patterned with orange blotches spotted with black, the cowman wears a blue coat and yellow breeches, the milkmaid a hat like a crown, a white skirt spotted in ochre and black, an ochre blouse and a white apron spotted in yellow, ochre and black. A calf rests on the green-washed base of the cowman group and another spotted calf lies at the feet of the milkmaid. The edges of the bases are sponged in a similar manner to the sheep groups. 152mm high. *Courtesy Sotheby's.*

Cow with milkmaid c.1800-20

A large cow, facing to the left with a milkmaid holding her hat to her head (the same figure as on a sheep group above and also sitting pillion on horseback, see page 279). The milkmaid's dress is mottled with brown and spotted in black. A calf reclines on a grassy mound at her feet. The cow and calf are splashed in ochre, black and brown. The group is mounted on an oval base, the sides of which are speckled with blue, manganese brown, ochre and black. Clearly made by the pottery that used the large impressed crown mark. 140mm high. *Courtesy Sotheby's.*

Cow, calf and lady gardener c.1800-20
A cow, blotched in ochre and spotted in black, with the same dotted eyebrows and other details as on other pieces from the pottery that used the large impressed crown mark. The girl with the watering can standing by the cow's shoulder is the same figure, wearing a poke bonnet, that appears on the large sheep group, the watch stand and the clock money-box group. The green-topped base is speckled in ochre, blue and black, the calf is blotched with purple. 152mm high. *Wakefield Art Gallery and Museums. B1 390.*

Cow with cowherd c.1800-20
The putty coloured cow is decorated with black and grey sponged patches. The cowherd is made of white clay, as is the seated calf. The boy is dressed in a blue coat with an orange sash and he stands on a small green mound. On both cow and herd the eyebrows are dotted in black in the same manner as the subjects marked with the large crown. The figures are mounted on a putty coloured base, sponged with black and mauve. 140mm high. *Courtesy Leonard Russell.*

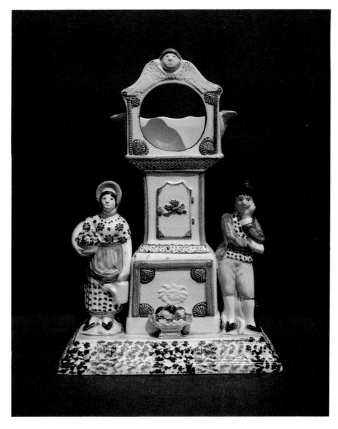

21. Watch stand c.1800-20

A delicately made and precisely painted watch stand. The top receptacle is shaped with small side brackets to fit a large turnip watch. The top of the longcase clock is in the form of an angel's head with outspread wings and there are moulded scallop shells in the four corners, a detail repeated on the base of the clock. The very carefully painted diaper pattern above and below the door is unusual.

The flanking figures of the pair of gardeners appear on cow, sheep and money-box groups, though it is rare to find the man wearing a puce coat. Puce usually appears on small areas in many of the figures in these groups, perhaps in the pattern of a dress or a kerchief.

On the floor in front of the clock there is a bowl of fruit. The stepped base is moulded with a repeat leaf pattern and sponged with ochre, blue and black. 218mm high. *Private Collection.*

20. Clock money-box c.1800-20 *top left*

A money-box in the form of a longcase clock, flanked by figures. The man wears a black top hat, blue coat, black waistcoat and orange trousers, his right hand is in his pocket; the woman is wearing an elaborate coiffure and a high waisted puff-sleeved dress, spotted in green, with a blue kerchief round her neck and an orange apron. A lion crouches at the foot of the clock. The base is green washed on top and sponged in blue, orange and black round the sides. 220mm high. *Private Collection.*

The same lady appears on a cow group (see page 85). Seated versions of this female figure can be seen on page 90.

22. Sheep and Lady Gardener c.1800-20

A very large sheep faces to the right with a lady gardener carrying a watering can beside it. The girl wears a white sun-bonnet and a short sleeved dress, patterned with blue and mulberry. Her crook is spotted with mulberry and black. She is an identical figure to that on the watch stand above. Two lambs rest on the green-washed base. 150mm high. *Private Collection.*

Clock money-box 1800-20
A money-box in the form of longcase clock flanked by unusually small figures only 69mm high. The man wears a puce coat and the lady a puce bonnet and a blue coat. The clock is of putty coloured clay and is edged with black decorations lightened by touches of puce. The oval base is sponged with black, blue and ochre and at the foot of the clock is the same spaniel that rests between the feet of the large Toby jug. 220mm high. *Courtesy Leonard Russell.*

Clock money-box 1800-20 *top right*
A money-box in the form of a longcase clock, flanked by small figures of a man dressed in black hat and shoes, blue coat, puce spotted waistcoat, burnt orange breeches and white stockings, resting his face on his hand and leaning on a spade; and a girl in a sun-bonnet trimmed with orange, a blue speckled dress and an orange apron holding a basket of flowers and a watering can. A black spotted spaniel rests at the foot of the clock. These are the same figures that appear with very large sheep and cows. The dog is the same as the one between the feet of the large Toby, which must have come from the same factory. The mounds that the figures stand on are washed in green, the sides of the base are sponged in black, blue and orange. 220mm high. *Private Collection.*

Cow with cow girl c.1800-20
A putty coloured cow decorated with mulberry purple patches edged with black. The girl is wearing an ochre apron over a white skirt patterned with blue, a blue blouse and a large ochre and white sun-bonnet. The oval base is speckled with black. 146mm high. *Courtesy Elias Clark.*

Clock money-box 1800-20

A money-box in the form of a longcase clock, flanked on the right by the figure of a woman wearing a dress with puffed sleeves, as the one on page 88 and on the left by a different figure of a man in a top hat. A typical sponged base with a green top, obviously from the pottery that used the large impressed crown mark. 220mm high. *Museum and Art Gallery, Doncaster. 308.78.*

Cow group c.1800-20

The cow is of a putty coloured body decorated with mulberry purple patches heavily outlined in black. The pearlware milkmaid wears a mantilla-like head-dress, a blue spotted bodice and a striped and spotted skirt. Her apron is ochre coloured and she stands on a small mound impressed with little circles. The top of the base is green washed and the sides are sponged in black. A putty coloured reclining calf is spotted with mulberry purple. From the pottery that used the large impressed crown mark. 152mm high. *Museum and Art Gallery, Doncaster. 87.80.*

Seated women c.1800-20

A pair of figures, seated on green chairs, very similar to the standing women in the cow and money-box groups on pages 88 and 85. They have the same elaborate coiffures and high-waisted puff-sleeved white dresses, one spotted in green and ochre and the other in dark blue and ochre, both with blue kerchiefs round their necks. Probably made by the pottery that used the impressed large crown mark. 100mm high. *Crown Copyright, Victoria and Albert Museum. C.44 & A 1938.*

Clock money-box c.1800-20
A similar money-box to the one on page 89, but in this case the female figure is wearing a very dark green blouse and blobbed skirt. She has been given a very much larger sun-bonnet. Her partner is wearing a top hat, a dark brown jacket and yellow trousers (which date him nearer 1810 than 1800). The edges of the clock are decorated in blue. 220mm high. *City Museum and Art Gallery, Stoke-on-Trent. 58P 1958.*

Clock money-box c.1800-20 *top right*
Very similar to some of the others from the same pottery, but the male figure is unusual with his little round ochre hat and cummerbund and blue jacket. 220mm high. *Courtesy Jonathan Horne.*

Watch stand c.1800-20
A watch stand in the form of a longcase clock decorated in relief with the head of an angel with outspread wings at the top, almost identical to the one illustrated in colour on page 88. The clock, picked out in ochre and blue, is flanked by the standing figures of Napoleon, and the Empress Josephine who is wearing a plumed hat and a short dress with a relief decorated hem. A lion, identical in form to that on the money-box with the woman with puffed sleeves, is crouching at the foot of the clock. *Courtesy Sotheby's.*

These watch stands were sold complete with a small pottery model of a watch that could be suspended in the open clock face. There is a complete example in the City Museum and Art Gallery, Stoke-on-Trent. One imagines that perhaps as so few have survived intact, that they might have been given to children as playthings. One recently turned up in excavations on the site of one of the Hawley potteries at Rawmarsh in Yorkshire.

Mounted soldier c.1800-20

A soldier seated stiffly on a skewbald horse, wearing a black Napoleonic hat, blue jacket and white breeches with black boots. The horse has an arched neck, black mane and a docked tail, it is blotched irregularly with burnt orange patches edged with black. The ochre saddle is on a blue saddle-cloth. The rectangular base has a green washed top and the sides are speckled with orange, blue and black. 223mm high. *Northampton Central Museum. 1920/d/182.*

Mounted horseman c.1800-20

In a similar group the horse is decorated with large patches of ochre, edged with black and the rider is wearing a green coat. The horse has the same dotted eyebrows. The ochre saddle rests on a puce saddle-cloth edged with yellow and black. It is clearly from the same pottery as the others shown here. There is no trace of cream in the body of the ware, which is light in weight and of very good quality. 235mm high. *City of Manchester Art Galleries. 1923.939.*

Mounted horseman c.1800-20

A horseman wearing a black top hat and seated on a horse with a docked tail sponged in black and orange. It is mounted on a rectangular base with rounded corners, the top washed in green and the sides sponged in blue, black and orange. The treatment of the horse's eyes is similar to those on the sheep. 235mm high. *Courtesy Sotheby's.*

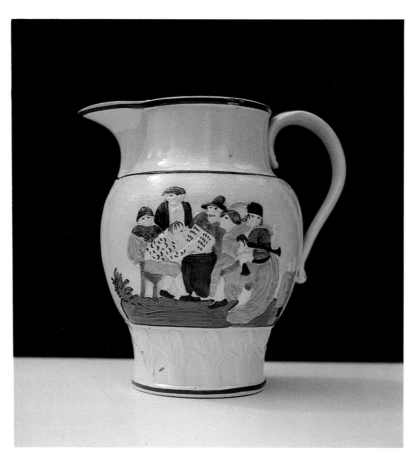

23 & 24. Peasants drinking and village musicians jug c.1796-1810

This relief decorated pearlware jug, with the faintest tinge of green to the glaze, shows a group of peasants. On one side a man is haranguing or toasting three seated figures who are drinking and smoking, on the other side is a group of village musicians. The jug is thinly potted and light in weight. The colouring is limited to yellow, orange, green and blue with a brown band round the top of the neck and the bottom of the foot. Impressed on the foot-rim in very small capital letters is HERCULANEUM.[13]

165mm high. *Private Collection.*

The design of the drinking scene, from a Turner mould, is copied from a Sadler and Green tile, which in its turn was adapted from part of an engraving by Philip Mercier after a painting by David Teniers the Younger, who specialised in painting groups of intoxicated peasants. The original painting and engraving are interior scenes, the adaptations set the groups alfresco.

The scene with the musicians is also taken from a Turner mould, which was also probably after a Teniers painting. The marked Turner version can be found on stoneware jugs and the same design was also used by Adams. There is another relief decorated underglaze coloured example of this jug in the Mattatuck Museum, Waterbury, Connecticut.

Herculaneum mark, impressed capital letters 1.5mm high on the footrim of the Peasants drinking and village musicians jug.

5. Marked pieces from Liverpool

The Herculaneum Pottery 1796-1840

In 1796 a merchant called Samuel Worthington made the decision to start up a pottery in Liverpool for the manufacture of cream coloured earthenware. Since 1763 Wedgwood had been shipping his Queensware up to Liverpool from Staffordshire, to be decorated with transfer printed designs by the firm of Sadler and Green.

There are accounts of how Worthington recruited the bulk of his workforce in Staffordshire and had them transported to Toxteth, along with their wives and children. By 1805 at least a hundred and fifty people were working at the factory which he called the Herculaneum Pottery. By 1827 twice that number of people were employed there. In 1833 it was put up for sale and by 1840 its days were over.[1]

In addition to cream coloured earthenware the factory produced pearlware, fine white stoneware and from 1801, porcelain. Relief decorated, underglaze coloured jugs were certainly made there. One particular jug which shows on one side a group of men drinking at a table and on the other a party of musicians, is marked HERCULANEUM on the footrim of the base in very small capital letters (the mark used by the factory from 1796 to 1810).

Moulds of Peasants drinking and village musicians c.1770
Master moulds made by John Turner of the scenes of the drinking peasants and village musicians which were later reproduced on the Herculaneum jug. *Spode Museum. TMMS/35 and TMMS/36.*

Teniers pinxit   *P.M. del. et Sculp.*

Engraving of Peasants drinking 1730-40
An engraving by Philip Mercier (1689-1760) after a painting by David Teniers the Younger (1610-90) which was the inspiration for the Sadler and Green tile, the Turner mould and the later creamware relief decorated Herculaneum jug. *Trustees of the British Museum.*

David Teniers the Younger was an Antwerp painter of peasant genre scenes. Philip Mercier, a Huguenot born in Berlin, came to London about 1716. He was a friend of Watteau's and an interpreter of his paintings, but he also made engravings from four of Teniers' works, including this scene of peasants inside a tavern. When the design was adapted for use on the tile and the jug, the scene was transferred to the open air.

Engraved transfer decorated tile of peasants drinking c.1770
Engraved transfer printed tile by Sadler and Green, after Philip Mercier's engraving from the Teniers painting. The tile is printed in black. 127 x 130mm. *Merseyside County Museums. 28.12.74.4.*

A Pratt type teapot is also impressed with the Herculaneum mark. This piece appears to come from a similar but much larger mould of a teapot marked BARKER, (see page 38). The painting however is cruder, though the colours are very bright and clear.

In addition to the useful wares, the Herculaneum factory also made plaques and figures. There is a relief decorated plaque dated 1815 (see page 98). The figure of a soldier, said to be a Volunteer Officer called Colonel Tarleton who was a local Liverpool celebrity, is attributed to the Herculaneum factory, though it is unmarked. The same attribution is given to a set of Faith, Hope and Charity, based on the Wood models, but these figures were copied by numerous factories. These so-called Herculaneum ones stand on high square tapered bases decorated on their sides with stiff upright leaves in relief and they are more strongly coloured than the Staffordshire versions of the same figures. They are crudely splashed in orange and blue. H.B. Lancaster shows an illustration of such a group in his book.[2] He describes them as very crude models coloured in yellow, blue and brown. Lancaster baldly states that they were made at the Herculaneum Pottery. Alan Smith, in his more recent book on Liverpool pottery states that these figures were attributed to Liverpool by Peter Entwistle, a local authority, and a former Keeper of Ceramics at the Museum there.

---

1. Alan Smith, *The Illustrated Guide to Liverpool Herculaneum Pottery 1796-1840*, London, 1970.
2. H. Boswell Lancaster, *Liverpool and her Potters*, Liverpool, 1936.

Teapot 1796-1810
A large pearlware teapot with relief moulded decorations of putti on one main side panel and a classical female with a child on a lead accompanied by a putto on the other is rather crudely banded in brown and has a pattern of upright stiff leaves round the bottom. The upswept handle is modelled with a leaf decoration painted in green and brown and there is a blue outlined acanthus decoration at the base of the spout, with a crude tree-form in relief beside it. The whole decoration is strongly coloured in orange, green, blue and brown. Made in Liverpool at the Herculaneum factory. Impressed mark HERCULANEUM in small capital letters on the base. 191mm high. *Merseyside County Museums. 1968.417.*

Rustic scene plaque 1815
This pearlware plaque is moulded with a scene of four figures
and a dejected dog, mourning the death of a goose and decorated
in the usual underglaze colours. On the back is incised 'July
18th 1815 Eli Till, Liverpool'. It was presented tò the Liverpool
Museum by Joseph Mayer who had obtained it from Eli Till's
widow. Presumably Till was one of the hands working at
Herculaneum. His son and daughter-in-law also worked at the
pottery for many years. 234 x 285mm. *Merseyside County
Museums.*

6. Marked pieces from Tyneside and Sunderland

Tyneside Potteries

The Tyneside potteries at the beginning of the nineteenth century catered mainly for the cheaper end of the market. As far as we have been able to discover from marked pieces so far, only four of the potteries made underglaze coloured sponged animals. The potteries of Tyneside certainly made relief decorated ware, but only with pink lustre or enamel colouring.

At the City Museum and Art Gallery, Stoke-on-Trent there are about seven hundred cows and cow creamers of various sorts. By the nature of the Keiller Bequest, at least four hundred and fifty of them are on permanent exhibition: massed together in a vast herd, they make a remarkable impact.

There are many underglaze coloured ones among them, but in the whole collection there are only about six or seven marked specimens, which all come from the Tyneside area.

These cows were also made in other parts of the country, many no doubt in the Yorkshire and Staffordshire potteries, though so far we have not come across any marked specimens.

St. Anthony's Pottery, Newcastle upon Tyne

Cow creamers and dappled horses were produced by this pottery. Very occasional pieces are marked ST. ANTHONY in impressed capitals or pencilled in black on the bases. At the end of the eighteenth century the pottery was run by William Huntley. Messrs. Foster and Cutter bought the pottery from Huntley in 1800 and in 1804 sold it to Joseph Sewell who produced creamware similar to the Leeds creamware and also these underglaze coloured cow creamers and horses. Some of these are impressed SEWELL (or sometimes SEWEL). In 1819 Joseph Sewell retired and the name of the firm was changed to Sewell & Donkin, who made the best of the Tyneside lustred wares.[1]

St. Peter's Pottery, Newcastle upon Tyne

This firm was established at St. Peter's Quay by Thomas Fell and Co. in 1817. They traded until 1890. They manufactured all kinds of cream and whiteware, sponged, printed, underglaze coloured and enamelled. They used the impressed mark FELL from 1817-30.

Tyne Pottery, Newcastle upon Tyne

This pottery was run by Tyler and Company from 1821 to 1823 when they were succeeded by Taylor & Son, who later moved to the Newcastle Pottery, Skinnerburn. It seems probable that the mark TAYLOR & CO refers to this firm.

---

1. R.C. Bell, *Tyneside Pottery*, London, 1971.

Horse c.1810

A standing figure of a horse in white earthenware with manganese sponging and wearing a blue saddle-cloth with a brown girth-strap, mounted on a green rectangular base plate. Marked on the bottom of the base ST ANTHONY impressed.

Made at the St Anthony Pottery, Newcastle upon Tyne. 146mm high. *City Museum and Art Gallery, Stoke-on-Trent. 47P.1963.*

Impressed mark on the base of the standing horse from St Anthony's Pottery.

Goat c.1810

A standing figure of a goat in white earthenware with manganese sponging, mounted on a green-washed rectangular base plate, slightly waisted. On the bottom of the base is the impressed mark ST ANTHONY.

Made at the St Anthony Pottery, Newcastle upon Tyne. 135mm high. *City Museum and Art Gallery, Stoke-on-Trent. 46P.1963.*

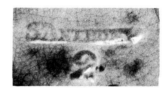

Impressed mark on the base of the goat from St Anthony's Pottery.

Cow creamer with calf c.1810

White earthenware cow with calf, sponged underglaze in grey and set on a green rectangular base plate. Marked SEWEL impressed on the bottom of the base. Made at St Anthony's Pottery, Newcastle upon Tyne. 130mm high. *City Museum and Art Gallery, Stoke-on-Trent. 294P.1963.*

There is another very similar animal in the same Museum also marked SEWEL. 134mm high. *293P.1963,* and another cow creamer marked ST ANTHONY. 111mm high. *50P.1963.*

Impressed mark SEWEL used by St Anthony's Pottery.

Cow creamer 1817-30

White cow with pale manganese markings, set on a green rectangular base. There are traces of cobalt in the glaze. On the bottom of the base is the mark FELL impressed. Made at St Peter's Pottery, Newcastle upon Tyne. 124mm high.. *City Museum and Art Gallery, Stoke-on-Trent. 47P 1967.*

There is also, in the same Museum another pair of cow creamers with patches of yellow sponging, mounted on rectangular green bases, both impressed FELL. 124mm high. *68P.1963 & 69P.1963.*

Impressed mark on the base of the cow creamer from St Peter's Pottery.

Recumbent Sheep 1817-30

This small figure of a sheep is spotted in ochre and rests on a hollow green mound base. Inside the base is the impressed mark FELL in capital letters. Made at St Peter's Pottery, Newcastle upon Tyne. 141mm long. *Crown Copyright, Victoria and Albert Museum. 3657.1901.*

Cow creamer 1820-25

White earthenware cow with a milkmaid in a patterned dress. The cow is decorated with orange and manganese sponging. The base plate is green-washed and shaped to accommodate the milkmaid. It is marked underneath in impressed capital letters TAYLOR. Made at the Tyne Pottery, Newcastle upon Tyne.
& CO
126mm high. *City Museum and Art Gallery, Stoke-on-Trent. 189P.1963.*

There is a pair to this cow creamer in the same Museum marked TAYLOR impressed. *188P 1963.*

Another cow and calf group from the same collection with black mottled decoration, mounted on moulded base with green and yellow sides is marked I. MOLE impressed. So far it has not been possible to identify this potter, though he was presumably from Tyneside. 130mm high. *47P 1963.* Not illustrated here.

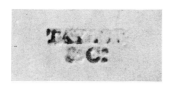

Impressed mark on the base of the Tyne Pottery cow creamer.

The Sunderland or 'Garrison' Pottery, Dixon, Austin & Co.

There had been potteries at the east end of Sunderland since the middle of the eighteenth century, but exactly when the Sunderland or 'Garrison' Pottery (as it came to be called because of its proximity to the army barracks) was founded is somewhat obscure. It was leased by Thornhill & Co. to John Phillips of the North Hylton Pottery in 1807.

Robert Dixon (1779-1844) and Thomas Austin (whose dates are uncertain, but who died about 1839) both worked at the North Hylton Pottery when they were young, so they were probably much of an age. By 1813 Phillips had become part owner of the Garrison Pottery and the firm used the marks PHILLIPS & CO. and DIXON & CO., which shows that Robert Dixon had become a partner by that date. From 1815 the North Hylton Pottery was under the same ownership as the Garrison Pottery. Similar ware was produced by both potteries. By 1820 Dixon and Austin had come together as partners and the firm used the mark DIXON, AUSTIN & CO. By 1826 Alexander Phillips had joined the firm (he was the nephew of the John Phillips who had leased the pottery in 1807), so the mark DIXON, AUSTIN & CO. only lasted for about six years.[1]

As well as an extensive home market, much of it by the coastal trade, the pottery had a large export market. They produced a variety of goods, among the most popular was probably the transfer printed and pink lustred ware, but among the most interesting of their productions were the underglaze coloured figures and relief decorated longcase clock watch stands flanked by figures. These were inspired by the 'Seasons' of Ralph Wood and also by some of the figures that accompany some of the Wood vases, and are of a naïve robustness of colouring that is particularly charming. They also made busts of Nelson and John Wesley, but we have yet to find a marked bust in underglaze colouring from this pottery.

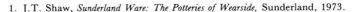

1. J.T. Shaw, *Sunderland Ware: The Potteries of Wearside,* Sunderland, 1973.

Coloured glaze figure of Flora or Spring c.1780
A figure of a young woman standing on a green mound holding a bunch of flowers to her bosom, with an upturned cornucopia of flowers by her side. She is wearing a pale green robe, her hair is coloured with manganese and the flowers are in green, yellow and blue glazes. The whole supported on a square socle with blue flowers painted on the front. It is one of the Ralph Wood models, but unmarked. 280mm high. *Courtesy Sotheby's.*

25 & 26. The Seasons 1820-26
Four classical figures mounted on flat square bases, after models by Ralph Wood. They are thickly painted and richly coloured, particularly with a strong yellow, also with a deep cobalt, burnt orange, mossy green, brown and black. The names of the seasons are pencilled in brown capital letters on the front of the bases. A brown band encircles the other three sides. Impressed on the bases DIXON, AUSTIN, & CO. Made at the Garrison Pottery Sunderland. Average height 217mm. *Private Collection.*

There is a set of these figures in the Sunderland Museum & Art Gallery, *TWCMS D.2044, D.2153, D.2159 and D.2152.*

Dixon, Austin & Co mark impressed in capital letters in a half circle on the bases of the figures.

Watch stand 1820-26
An underglaze coloured watch stand in the form of a longcase clock, decorated in relief with small groups of classical figures, coloured in orange, yellow, green and blue. The central figure is framed in a border of stiff leaves painted in green and orange. We have seen versions of this group with different relief designs on the clock including 'Charlotte weeping at the tomb of Werther'. The tall clock is flanked by the figures of two children wearing orange and blue drapery. These small figures are crude copies of the Ralph Wood figures which are sometimes seen supporting an elaborate two-handled flowerpot, mounted on a square stepped base (see page 47). The figures have manganese washed hair and are leaning against pedestals. The flat rectangular base plate has DIXON AUSTIN & CO impressed on the top at the foot of the clock case. 285mm high. *Private Collection.*

Two groups of women and boys c.1810-20

Two groups each of a woman and a small boy, possibly intended to represent the Seasons, for the children are carrying in one case a yellow sheaf of corn and the other a receptacle rather like a hat, full of fruit. The women are dressed in long dresses decorated in blue and ochre with patterns of flowers or circles. One of the women is wearing a blue apron edged with ochre and a yellow cloak edged with blue. Their poke bonnets are ochre, edged with blue and white. The boys are in blue coats and ochre trousers.

The high oval bases are decorated with a blue and ochre fern-like rococo decoration and there are tufts of green vegetation between the feet of the figures. 235mm high. *Courtesy Wynn A. Sayman, Richmond, Massachusetts.*

A similar group to the one on the left is illustrated in *Sunderland Ware the Potteries of Wearside,* where it is attributed to the Garrison Pottery.

7. The Indio Pottery, Bovey Tracey, Devonshire

This somewhat unlikely situation for the production of Pratt ware was brought to light by Norman Stretton in a paper published in the *English Ceramic Circle Transactions*.[1] He illustrated the underglaze coloured 'Parson and Sexton' jug shown here, which has 'Bovey 1800' inscribed on one side of the neck and the initials 'W.M.' on the verso. Mr Stretton suggested that these may have been the initials of William Mead who was the occupant of the Indio Pottery in 1800.

The Indio Pottery had been in production for some years when Josiah Wedgwood, accompanied by the potter John Turner of Lane End, visited it in 1775, on a journey into Devon and Cornwall in search of growan stone and clay. Wedgwood, writing in his Diary[2] dismissed the pottery with 'It is a poor trifling concern and conducted in a wretched slovenly manner. . .' and goes on to say: 'Notwithstanding all which advantages, besides labour being much cheaper with them than us, we can carry their clay and flints from Devonshire into Staffordshire, there manufacture them into ware, and send it back to their own doors, better and cheaper than they can make it. . .(they have) clay within 5 or 6 miles of them, from the same pits which furnish our potteries in Staffordshire and their flints from Exeter or Halldown Hill. The coals are only 2/6d per ton, at the pit, and so near the works, that only wheelbarrows are used for their conveyance to the works. . .'

The Indio Pottery was started by William Ellis and financed by him; George Tuffnell, the local squire and owner of Indio House, provided the site where the pot kilns, etc. were built. They first made salt-glazed ware, but by the time of Wedgwood's visit they were making cream-coloured earthenware. They also made pearlware. Norman Stretton showed in his article a pearlware plate with the impressed mark INDEO. It seems that both spellings were used. Indio House was on the site of a mediaeval monastery, hence the alternative spelling.

Ellis remained at Indio until 1787, when it was taken over by a Mr Foster, who, a year later was succeeded by John Crane. In 1800 William Mead was the occupant and he was succeeded in 1801 by Joseph Steer, who ran the pottery until 1831. It finally closed down in the 1840s.

Another pottery was established by William Mead and a Mr Lamble sometime between 1800 and 1810, known as the Folly Pottery, situated on the Heathfield, near to the coal pits and it is just possible that this example of Pratt ware illustrated here was made at this pottery and not at the Indio. The Folly Pottery was not finally closed down until 1956.

---

1. Norman Stretton, 'The Indio Pottery at Bovey Tracey', *English Ceramic Circle Transactions,* Vol. 8, Part 2, 1972.
2. Josiah Wedgwood's 'Diary of his journey into Cornwall' is published in full in *The proceedings of the Wedgwood Society,* Vols. 1 and 2.

Parson, Clerk and Sexton jug 1800
This familiar design is on a baluster-shaped jug. The colours used are blue, brown, tan and green. This piece is inscribed 'Bovey 1800' on one side and the initials 'W M' appear on the other side. It is likely that this piece, though unmarked, might have been made at the Indio Pottery, Bovey Tracey in Devonshire. The initials on the jug might have been those of William Mead who was running the pottery in the year 1800. 160mm high. *Private Collection.*

8. Marked pieces and others thought to have been made by the Scottish potteries

The East Coast potteries

There is a strong tradition that underglaze coloured relief decorated ware and figures were made by the Scottish East Coast Potteries. Attributions to such origins at both Huntly House and the Royal Scottish Museum in Edinburgh, where there are many examples of the ware, date back many years.

Arnold Fleming, himself a practical potter, writing in 1923[1] stated categorically that jugs with relief moulded scenes with underglaze colouring of Toby Fillpot, the Gretna Green Blacksmith's forge and the cavalryman leaping over a cannon were all made at Gordon's Pottery. He also identified Watson's Pottery with the manufacture of underglaze coloured figures during the period 1800-15. The Watsons employed over eighty potters, many of them from England. The pottery had been established about 1750 on the shores of the Firth of Forth at Prestonpans. It had three kilns and was locally referred to as the 'Pott works'.

A charming figure of 'Spring' inspired by one of the Wood Seasons may well have been made here, for she is clutching to her stomach a thistle, instead of the usual conventional bunch of flowers, and another thistle nestles among the roses that decorate the rocky mound on which she is standing.

It would seem that the potteries most likely to have made Pratt type jugs were the Gordon's Bankfoot Pottery at Prestonpans, Hilcote's Pottery at Portobello and William Reid's pottery at Musselburgh. The Bankfoot Pottery was taken over in 1795 by Robert Gordon and his son George, who had previously been potting at West Pans. The pottery seems to have prospered, and in 1812 the Gordons enlarged their activities by buying the old vitriol works at Cuttle and by taking over the lease of the Old Hyndeford (Hilcote) Pottery at Morison's Haven. In the same year Charles Belfield, who for the previous four years had been working at Bankfoot, took over their tenancy of that pottery, even though the Gordons continued to live there. The Gordon's enterprise came to an end with Robert Gordon's death and the dispersal of his estate in 1836. Charles Belfield moved into the old vitriol works and established a pottery business there that lasted for many years.[2]

Antony Hilcote had been potting at Morison's Haven in the parish of Prestonpans, but for various reasons in 1769 he moved to Figgate in what is now Portobello, a suburb of Edinburgh. The new pottery was on the site of a seam of clay which was already being used by a brick works. Hilcote certainly did not use this coarse material for his creamware, for which he must have imported his clay and flints; the Hilcote Pottery seems to have closed at the turn of the century.

Scottish subjects appear on several Pratt type jugs. One very handsome specimen has a thistle decoration under the spout and a border round the neck of fleurs-de-lis;[3] the Scots of course had close ties with France. A version of the

1. J. Arnold Fleming, *Scottish Pottery,* Glasgow, 1923.
2. Patrick McVeigh, *Scottish East Coast Potteries 1750-1840,* Edinburgh, 1979.
3. ibid.

Spring and Autumn c.1800
An unusual pair of figures (probably from a set of the Seasons), with yellow hair and dresses spotted in brown and yellow. Spring holds a thistle in one hand and supports a brown cornucopia from which tumble roses and a thistle, which suggests that they might be from one of the Scottish East Coast potteries. Spring stands on an uncoloured rocky mound, while Autumn, holding a yellow wheat sheaf and a brown sickle, stands on a green flowered mound. She wears a brown ribbon with a locket round her neck. 194 and 197mm high. *Royal Ontario Museum, Toronto, Canada. 964.221. 1 & 2.*

Admiral Duncan jug is thought to have been made at one of the East Coast potteries. Baron Duncan of Lundie was a Scot, and became a popular hero after his defeat of the Dutch Admiral de Winter off Camperdown in 1797.

At an exhibition of Scottish East Coast Pottery, sponsored by the Scottish Arts Council in Edinburgh in 1980, the overall impression was that the ware was of less good quality than that produced in Staffordshire or Yorkshire; there were many pieces that were well modelled and well painted, though the main body of the ware was on the whole darker and of a less refined appearance than similar pieces known to have been made south of the border.

In this exhibition there was however, a striking large relief-decorated

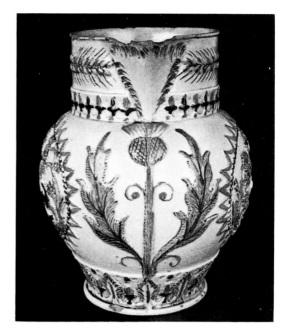

Thistle jug c.1790
A jug with a thistle decoration beneath the spout and a border of ears of barley round the neck. A bird with blue, yellow and orange colouring is hovering over her nestlings whose nest is enclosed by green foliage. The scene is set within a blue beaded oval frame. On the other side of the jug a similar medallion encloses some blue peacocks. The jug as a whole is coloured in yellow, brown, burnt orange, green and blue. It has a double scroll handle and is illustrated in *Scottish East Coast Potteries 1750-1840.* 165mm high. *Courtesy Patrick McVeigh.*

There are similar jugs in the Royal Scottish Museum with different flowers beneath the spout.

In most aspects this is unlike any English made Pratt jug. In addition to the yellow thistle on the front, the ears of barley on the neck and the fleurs-de-lis border also appear on other jugs attributed to Scotland. On the other hand the beaded oval frame appears on the octagonal Sailor's Farewell and Return jugs and the stiff leaf border surrounding the medallion is somewhat similar to the Peacock jugs, which is not surprising as peacocks appear on the reverse side of this jug. The scene of the bird coming in to feed her nestlings is as far as we know, quite unique. The border round the foot is similar to those on the other Scottish jugs shown on the opposite page.

underglaze coloured cornucopia wall vase, moulded with the figure of a boy holding a brazier, symbolising Winter, which was attributed to one of the Prestonpans potteries.

In both Huntly House and the Royal Scottish Museum there are further examples of Pratt ware attributed to the East Coast potteries. These include a rectangular dish with a relief portrait of George IV set within a border of crowns, floral ornaments and Prince of Wales feathers. The same royal portrait also appears on a circular plate with woven cane pattern borders. These must have been made at the time of the King's visit to Edinburgh in 1822. Versions of the Miser jug are also to be found in one or other of these museums, and also the jug with the Mischievous Sport and Sportive Innocence designs, where the figures are not set in the usual cartouche. All these examples are in a deep cream coloured body.

A figure of Charity rather crudely modelled, coloured in burnt orange and yellow on a square base is in the Huntly House Museum and is attributed there to either Prestonpans or Portobello. As we have no means of knowing what

Drunken Toper jug, c.1800

This jug has scenes of a drunken man leaning over a table, being comforted by a friend, and on the side shown here being grabbed by his irate wife. The scenes are set within medallions with an orange peel textured background with zig-zag borders. The colouring of the jug is limited to yellow and ochre and thin washes of blue and green. The neck of the jug is decorated with a border of ears of barley and below that a border of stiff vertical leaves. The bottom of the jug has a formalised pattern of large and small leaves, coloured alternately with ochre and green and outlined in brown. The jug has been attributed to Prestonpans. 191mm high. *Royal Scottish Museum, Edinburgh. 1907.166.*

Drunken Toper jug c.1800

This jug is decorated with the same themes except that in the scene with the irate wife the chair and table are replaced by a spotted dog jumping up at his master. The jug has a most unusual diamond pattern painted in blue round the neck, below which is a relief border with pointed decorations almost in the form of fleurs-de-lis. 191mm high. *Royal Scottish Museum, Edinburgh. 1923.772.*

contributory evidence was available when these attributions were made, it would seem that some consideration must be given to them. Unfortunately the pieces never seem to bear a mark and for us to attribute them to any particular Scottish pottery would be unwise.

As there was considerable intercourse between the Staffordshire potteries and Scotland, it is difficult to say with any degree of certainty where any of these pieces were made. Even if they were found on the site of a pottery, it is not necessarily proof that they were made there. It is likely that some of the ware was imported from Staffordshire.

However, having looked at literally hundreds of examples of Pratt ware over the years, there does seem to us to be something quite distinctive about these pieces that are attributed to the Scottish East Coast potteries, though it is very hard to put into words. The picture of the two jugs on this page in the Royal Scottish Museum shows something of this quality; on the front of these jugs different flowers are moulded, in one case a thistle — a likely enough decoration to come from a Scottish pottery.

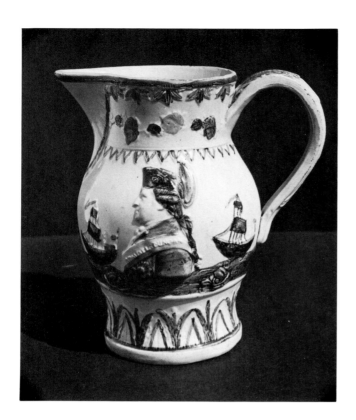

Admiral Duncan and Captain Trollope jug c.1798
This rather coarse and gritty small creamware jug has a very slightly blue-tinted glaze. On one side there is the bust of Admiral Duncan wearing an ochre uniform trimmed with yellow and a white sash with his name across it in raised capital letters. He is wearing a black hat trimmed with orange and his brown hair is *en queue*. He is flanked by two naval vessels and two dolphins can be seen in the green sea below him. Beneath a blue line at the top of the jug is a border of half vine leaves in blue and orange and below that a crudely painted band of grapes and vine leaves in brown yellow and green. Below that, a narrow band of triangular leaves outlined in orange and blue decorate the base of the neck of the jug. At the slightly splayed out foot is a decoration of sprays of green leaves alternating with stiff triangular leaves in orange and blue outline, a blue band encircles the foot. The loop handle is moulded quite carefully on the outside with an acanthus leaf at the top, and is serpentine in section. The spout is feather-edged and outlined in blue where it joins the body of the jug.

From the rough quality of this jug and the fact that Duncan was a Scottish hero, it might well be a production from one of the Scottish East Coast potteries. 139mm high. *Private Collection.*

After defeating the Dutch Admiral in 1797, Duncan, who was born at Lundie in Forfarshire was created Baron Duncan of Lundie and Viscount Duncan of Camperdown. The Scots were intensely proud of him.

George IV plate 1822
A plate with the relief portrait of George IV, made to commemorate his visit to Edinburgh in 1822, has the monarch's head facing to the left, crowned with green-brown laurel leaves. The rim is decorated with a basket-weave border and a thistle crossed with a rose with a crown in the middle. 'King George IIII' is in raised lettering on a scroll. This plate is attributed by the museum to George Gordon's pottery at Prestonpans. 203mm dia. *Huntly House Museum, Edinburgh. HH2353/11/62.*

George IV plate c.1822
A larger version, possibly a soup plate, again commemorating the King's visit to Edinburgh. This plate however is enamel coloured with green leaves, crown and Prince of Wales feathers decorating the rim. 242mm dia. *Huntly House Museum, Edinburgh.*

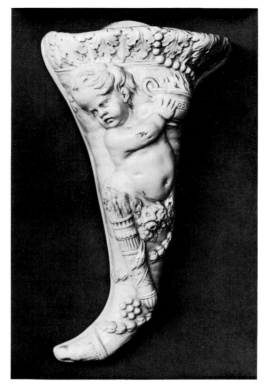

Cornucopia wall vase 1808

This creamware cornucopia is moulded in high relief with the figure of a child holding a flaming brazier, emblematic of 'Winter'. He is wearing round his waist a quiver full of arrows and his torso terminates in a bunch of flowers. It is coloured in the usual blue, burnt orange, brown yellow and green; yellow and orange predominating. On either side of the figure are the initials 'J' and 'C'. On the back is incised in a cursive hand 'James Cuthbertson Gardner July 16th 1801'. 280mm high. This piece was exhibited at the Scottish Arts Council Exhibition in Edinburgh in 1980 and is illustrated in Patrick McVeigh's *Scottish East Coast Potteries*.

The term 'Gardner' in Scotland signified a market gardener and not a jobbing one. This cornucopia is an imprecise and slightly smaller copy of one of a pair of uncoloured cream coloured earthenware cornucopias in the Victoria and Albert Museum *II 335*, (the other one represents 'Autumn'). There is another creamware version to be seen in the Manchester Museum and Art Gallery *775 (1923.843)*. There is also a pair of underglaze coloured cornucopias of the same design in the Nelson-Atkins Museum of Art (Burnap Collection) Kansas City, Missouri. *B639 (895)*.

Cornucopia wall vase c.1790

A similar creamware cornucopia showing a boy holding up a brazier of fire in high relief, emblematic of Winter. A quiver is at his side and his lower limbs are concealed by flowers. The top is bordered by acanthus leaves. Possibly made at the Leeds Pottery, but unmarked. 254mm high. *Crown Copyright, Victoria and Albert Museum. II 335.* This must have been the inspiration for the underglaze coloured version.

Miniature plates c.1810-20

Three very small plates, presumably from a child's dinner service, with a rouletted band around the rim, are decorated with a large central flower, in one case a thistle, and with Prince of Wales' feathers on the rim. Coloured in blue, yellow, green and black under the glaze on a dark cream rather gritty body. Attributed to one of the Scottish potteries. 82mm diam. *Art Gallery and Museum, Glasgow. 38.10.mx, my and mz.*

113

Peace and Plenty jug c.1800

A small and rather crudely modelled jug decorated with a classically draped figure of Plenty holding a cornucopia and flanked by lions and another seated figure of Peace holding an olive branch. The design is repeated on the other side of the jug, and is painted in the usual underglaze colours with the exception of blue. There are brown bands at the top and bottom of the neck below which are moulded acanthus leaves outlined in green with brown midribs. A similar border decorates the bottom of the jug. It is attributed to Prestonpans. 120mm high. *Royal Scottish Museum, Edinburgh. 1907.595.*

Mischievous Sport and Sportive Innocence jug c.1800

The creamware body is round and sparely coloured, the neck brown banded at the rim and encircled with blue and brown acanthus forms. The body of the jug has a well spread out border of acanthus leaves round the top coloured orange and blue. Below this the scenes are not enclosed in the usual way within medallions, but are separated by a classical female figure holding an olive branch, symbolising Peace. The base is also brown-handed. 149mm high. *Huntly House Museum, Edinburgh. HH 2353.667.62.*

Hunting jug 1800-05 *opposite*

The hunting scene on this jug, showing two horses standing beside each other and two men, one scrambling over a fence with a hound jumping over it is a very familiar design. It was used by Spode on fine stoneware in the 1760-80 period and by Wedgwood, Davenport and later by David Wilson in the early years of the nineteenth century. In this underglaze coloured version the order of the figures has been reversed, the horses being to the left of the design.

The floriated decoration around the neck of the jug in yellow, orange, blue and green is very similar to a relief decoration used by William Adams on his jasper ware c.1800, and also by the Wood factory on teapots.

The anthemion borders are outlined with green and the jug is banded in blue. The body is a rather rough darkish creamware, like that usually associated with the Scottish East Coast potteries. It is attributed by the museum to Prestonpans. 144mm high. *Royal Scottish Museum, Edinburgh. 1938.585.*

Opposite

A master mould of one of the elements in the design. This is incised 'Spode 5' on the back. 75mm high. *Spode Museum. SMMS/42.*

Bacchanalian cherub jug c.1800

A nicely modelled small pearlware jug decorated with a Bacchanalian scene of cherubs tumbling about among a fruiting vine. On the other side there is a seated figure of a tipsy female holding up a bunch of grapes. Under the spout there are crossed laurel branches in relief and some freely painted flowers. A wide band of brownish green encircles the foot and above there is an alternating pattern of acanthus leaves and fleurs-de-lis. The original design was by William Hackwood and can be seen on a black basaltes rum kettle of about 1775, and also on a

Wedgwood caneware teaset. This jug has been attributed to Prestonpans. 119mm high. *Royal Scottish Museum, Edinburgh. L.226.2 (1919).*

This innocent scene derives from the orgiastic festivals of Bacchus, at which the grossest debaucheries took place. The Roman Senate in 186 B.C. issued an edict prohibiting such entertainments. In spite of this, according to Livy, they continued in southern Italy for a very long time.

Reid's Pottery, Musselburgh

William Reid in 1800 was working a small pottery at Dam Brae at Musselburgh. Later in the same year he moved to 32 The Newbiggin, then a hamlet between Musselburgh and Fisherrow, where he worked for the rest of his life.

Newbiggin was a convenient site for a pottery, both because of the nearby coalfields and the harbours at Fisherrow and Morison's Haven. Through these harbours came a steady supply of Cornish clay from Fowey and flint stones from Ramsgate and Rochester in Kent. Reid's flint was probably ground for him at the flint mill at Mill Hill, a bare mile away towards Inveresk.

Reid's work can be identified by a presentation creamware jug in the Royal Scottish Museum. This jug, decorated with the arms of the Royal Burgh of Musselburgh, has on the base 'Wm. Reid May 14 1822'. The shape and satyr mask under the spout are very similar to the jug illustrated below.

By the 1820s Reid's Pottery was quite a large concern, and a map of Musselburgh of 1824 shows this sizeable works.[1] Reid himself was clearly a competent potter and his cream and pearlware was of excellent quality. The pottery continued after Reid's death in 1837, under the direction of Jonathan Foster who had worked at Watson's Pottery at Prestonpans, making both earthenware and porcelain. However by 1845 – Foster had died in 1840 – the pottery was in difficulties, finally closing down in the 1850s.[2]

Reid on occasions used a crown mark, either raised or impressed. This is not the same mark as that used by the pottery (possibly in Yorkshire) of uncertain origin.

---

1. Gerard Quail, 'Newbiggin Pottery, Musselburgh', *Archive News,* No. 4. 1979, Scottish Pottery Society, Edinburgh.
2. Patrick McVeigh, 'The Musselburgh Pottery' in *Scottish East Coast Potteries 1750-1840,* Edinburgh, 1979.

Reid's Pottery raised crown mark on the base of the jug illustrated in *Scottish East Coast Potteries 1750-1840.*

Queen Caroline jug c.1820
This jug is described in detail in the chapter on commemorative pieces (see page 137). It is by no means certain that it was made in Scotland but it is worth showing the satyr head spout here, which is identical to that on a jug with the impressed mark 'Wm Reid May 14 1822', illustrated in McVeigh's book. Otherwise these jugs are quite differently decorated. The thistle gives some substance to a Scottish origin. 151mm high. *Private Collection.*

Scottish fishergirl 1820-30

The figure of a well-built lass wearing a blue jacket, a yellow blouse and a yellow and black striped white skirt. Her tucked up apron is striped in mulberry-puce, the same colour as her head scarf. She is carrying on her back a brown creel of fish, supported by a black head band. She is holding a fish in one hand and three well modelled fish rest on the top of the basket, their heads and backs painted with a bluish green. The features of both fish and girl are picked out in black and her lips are indicated by a line of the mulberry colour. She stands on a round white base with a raised back and the flat surface is marked out to indicate stone paving. The edges of the base are sponged in black, yellow and a dusty green. 150mm high. *Private Collection.*

The figure certainly comes from one of the Scottish East Coast potteries. For illustrations of a comparable figure see Patrick McVeigh's book.

Girl harvester c.1810

A figure of a girl in a blue skirt and ochre blouse carrying a sheaf of yellow corn and standing on a green sponged mound. This rather sparely glazed little figure might well have been made at one of the East Coast Scottish potteries. 153mm high. *Courtesy Elias Clark.*

The Delftfield Pottery, Broomielaw

The Delftfield Pottery was one of the first potteries to become established in Scotland, and was also at one time, one of the most important. It was started in 1747 at Broomielaw on the north bank of the Clyde outside the Glasgow City boundary by Laurence Dinwoodie, a former Lord Provost of Glasgow, his brother Robert Dinwoodie (who later became Governor of Virginia), Robert Findlay a tanner, and Patrick Nisbet.

After one or two abortive attempts they succeeded in manufacturing a satisfactory tin-glazed ware. James Watt, the inventor, joined the firm in the early 1760s, becoming a partner in 1764. He helped them in various ways, with experiments in kiln-building and in the use of china clay, which led Delftfield to the manufacture of cream coloured earthenware. Watt's experiments were taking place at the same time that Wedgwood was perfecting his Queensware.

Watt first met Josiah Wedgwood in 1770 and they soon became close friends. It was about this time that his relationship with the Delftfield partners became a little uneasy, no doubt because of his many other interests, particularly in the development of his steam engines. He later supplied one of these (a 10hp Sun and Planet engine) to the Etruria Works.[1]

It was the habit at the Delftfield Pottery to dump broken kiln wasters on the nearby streets, which helped to give some kind of substance to their muddy surfaces. In August 1977, the pavement on the south west corner of James Watt Street (formerly Delftfield Lane) was dug up by the Electricity Board. Quantities of sherds were found. At the same time the G.P.O. was digging a trench in Carrick Street where further wasters were unearthed. Among these was a biscuit fragment of a jug, depicting in moulded relief an eighteenth-century gentleman holding a churchwarden pipe in his right hand. This must be a piece of the 'Parson, Clerk and Sexton' jug.[2] This is good enough grounds for us to assume that among their creamware, the Delftfield Pottery probably made relief decorated earthenware of the Pratt type.

In 1811, the pottery at Delftfield was closed down and the machinery and workers were transferred to the Caledonian Pottery on the north bank of the Monkland Canal at the head of Castle Street, St. Rolox, and on the other side of Garngad Hill. Here, using the same moulds, the same kind of ware (and so perhaps relief decorated underglaze coloured earthenware) was produced for some years.

1. Gerard Quail, 'James Watt at Delftfield', *Scottish Pottery Historical Review*, No.6, 1981.
2. Gerard Quail, 'Preliminary Report of Waster finds at Carrick Street and James Watt Street from the Delftfield Pottery, Glasgow', *Scottish Archive News*, No.3, Spring 1978.

Parson, Clerk and Sexton jug c.1790
A large well-modelled baluster-shaped jug with the Parson, Clerk and Sexton drinking and smoking. The stiff leaf borders are coloured green and the feather-edging at the top is blue. The initials 'J E' are pencilled on the front of the jug below the spout. 229mm high. *The Royal Pavilion Art Gallery and Museums, Brighton. HW 806.*

A sherd from what was clearly one of these jugs was found in excavations in Carrick Street Glasgow in 1977. There are two good examples of this jug, 203mm high, lightly coloured in pale manganese, pale yellow and blue feather-edging in the City Museum and Art Gallery, Stoke-on-Trent *3185 & 3860* (see page 192). Another version coloured only in underglaze blue on a pearlware body 203mm high can be seen in Merseyside County Museums *65.145.1.* A small version of the same jug with a rustic handle and richly coloured in green, blue, manganese and black, 150mm high, is in the Peter Manheim Ltd Collection, London.

Greenock Pottery

James Stevenson, formerly of the Clyde Pottery, established the Greenock Pottery on the Ladyburn at Crawfurdsdyke about the year 1818. The pottery imported ball clay from Dorsetshire and china clay from Cornwall.[1] White earthenware with underglaze coloured relief decorated designs was made here, as well as transfer-printed ware, and was usually stamped with the design of a ship inside an oval garter. In the National Museum of Antiquities of Scotland, in Edinburgh, there is a fine circular plaque with a relief decoration of Bacchus, Venus and Cupid in underglaze colours, incised on the back are the words GREENOCK POTTERY 1818.

After a few years Stevenson sold the pottery to the owners of the Clyde Pottery on the other side of the Ladyburn, so that he could devote himself to the retail side of the business. He exported quantities of ware to Newfoundland, for Greenock was an important market for the seal hunters, who, after unloading their oil and skins, returned across the Atlantic with cargoes of pottery.

---

1. J. Arnold Fleming, *Scottish Pottery,* Glasgow, 1923.

9. Commemorative jugs, mugs, busts and plaques of royalty and famous people

Commemorative subjects have long been used as decoration on British pottery. The makers of tin-glazed earthenware in the mid-seventeenth century made commemorative ware, the earliest London delft charger of this type is decorated with a handsome portrait of King Charles I and is dated 1653; from then on royal portraits are to be found on London and Bristol delft. These include Charles II, Queen Anne, William and Mary and George I, and from the nobility are portraits of the Dukes of Marlborough, Ormond and Albemarle.

At the same time, in Staffordshire, where tin-glazed earthenware was not made, the Tofts, Taylors and Simpsons and their contemporaries were making huge elaborately decorated slipware dishes with portraits of royalty as well as cavaliers and their ladies.

From the middle of the eighteenth century the makers of salt-glazed stoneware were decorating their wares with portraits that included Frederick, King of Prussia and Prince Charles Edward Stuart. The makers of relief decorated underglaze coloured earthenware were merely continuing in the same tradition when they used portraits of royalty and other famous people on their commemorative pieces.

The royal portraits include various representations of Louis XVI, Marie Antoinette and the Dauphin; George III and Queen Charlotte, George IV and Queen Caroline and oddly enough Charles I. Portraits of other famous people include Oliver Cromwell the Protector, Henry Brougham and Thomas Denman (Queen Caroline's defenders at her trial), Charles James Fox, David Garrick and Sarah Siddons; even Josiah Wedgwood himself appears on a plaque decorated in relief underglaze colour.

The portraits often bear little resemblance to the actual likeness of the person named — the same portrait is also often used to portray different people. The matter of making use of one portrait to represent different people was nothing new, the habit dates back at least to the *Nuremberg Chronicle* of 1493, where 1809 illustrations, mainly portraits, were printed from only 645 separate wood blocks. Such duplication in the field of commemorative pottery continued well into the 1840s when a Staffordshire figure of George Washington also served as a model for Benjamin Franklin.

Among the sources the potters turned to for their designs were prints and engravings from contemporary books and the popular journals of the day such as *The Pocket Magazine* and *The European Magazine* where portraits of famous people were often illustrated. Medals, the glass paste portraits of the Tassies and the jasper ware portrait medallions of Wedgwood and others were frequently copied.

The relief underglaze coloured portraits were sometimes faithful copies from these sources, but more often were simplified and relatively crude representations of the originals. Other liberties were taken, such as in the case of Catherine the Great on page 125, where the Empress is made to look much younger than on the Wedgwood medallion from which it was copied.

27. Charles I plaque c.1820
The crowned monarch holds the sceptre in his right hand and the orb in his left, resting on a pedestal. He is shown wearing yellow and orange robes trimmed with blue and ochre. The pedestal is blue and he stands on a green base surrounded by three small classical figures and set within a yellow frame of simulated rope pattern with an inner beaded border. The frame which has a modelled bow at the top is after a design by Hackwood for Wedgwood. The background is uncoloured. The plaque is attributed to Sunderland. It may well have been made by Dixon, Austin & Co., for two of the small classical figures also appear on watch stands made by the same firm, in which case it must have been made between the years 1820-26. A little late one would think for a bi-centenary commemoration of the king's birth. The plaque is of very good quality, the colours are as intense as on the figures of the Seasons from the Garrison Pottery (see page 103). It is one of a pair with Oliver Cromwell. 248mm high. *Warrington Museum and Art Gallery. RA 794.*

Engraving of Charles I

The engraving of Charles I is by Charles Grignion after a design by Samuel Wale. It is one of the many illustrations for *A New Universal and Imperial History of England* by George Frederick Raymond, which was dedicated to the Prince of Wales and published in 1787. *By permission of the British Library.*

Samuel Wale (d.1786) was a Professor of Perspective and Librarian to the Royal Academy. He provided most of the illustrations for Raymond's *History*. He exhibited at the Royal Academy between 1769 and 1778. Charles Grignion (1717-1810) was trained by H. Gravelot. Grignion's most famous work was an edition of Gray's *Poems* (1753) wherein he engraved a series of designs by R.Bentley.

Charles I plaque c.1800

One of a pair of plaques (the other is Cromwell) richly decorated in yellow, blue, ochre and manganese with a little dark green. The king, in royal regalia, wearing a yellow robe and blue cloak is standing by a pedestal with his hand on the orb and his right hand holding the sceptre. The background is painted with delicate sprays of flowers in ochre, blue and green. This plaque was probably made at the time of the bi-centenary of the monarch's birth (b.1600). 189mm high. *Wolverhampton Museum and Art Gallery. E.137.*

This relief portrait has obviously been adapted from the engraving shown above.

Engraving of Oliver Cromwell

The engraving of Oliver Cromwell is by Charles Grignion after a design by Samuel Wale. It is one of the illustrations from *A New Universal History of England* by George Frederick Raymond, published in 1787. *By permission of the British Library.*

Emperor Joseph II of Austria plaque c.1790 *opposite left*

The head and shoulders of the Emperor are in relief on an oval, yellow-framed plaque. His hair is coloured manganese brown and he is wearing a yellow uniform with a blue sash. 178mm high. *The Royal Pavilion Art Gallery and Museums, Brighton. HW 186.*

The rough treatment of the paint and the coarse texture of the unpainted background suggest that this piece may have been made at one of the Scottish East Coast potteries. The Willett Collection Catalogue calls this plaque 'Admiral Duncan' — a popular figure in Scotland, but it does not resemble him, and in fact the plaque is a copy of a blue or green jasper-dip cameo of the Emperor Joseph II of Austria listed in Wedgwood's 1788 Catalogue. It was modelled from an engraving done by Jacob Adam at Vienna in 1783. The Scottish potters were as likely as their English counterparts to make a portrait of one notable serve for another.

Holy Roman Emperor Joseph II (1741-90) was the son of Francis I and Maria Theresa. He made many political reforms in Austria, abolishing serfdom and was liberal in his attitudes to dissenters, giving freedom of worship to the Protestants and the Greek Orthodox church.

Wedgwood portrait medallion *opposite right*

Blue jasper cameo portrait of the Emperor Joseph II of Austria. *Courtesy Trustees of the Wedgwood Museum, Barlaston, Stoke-on-Trent.*

Oliver Cromwell plaque c.1800

The pair to the Charles I plaque overleaf, showing the Protector in Puritan costume with a blue cloak and breeches and an ochre tunic and black hat, standing with his arm outstretched. The background is painted with sprays of blue flowers with manganese and ochre. 182mm high. *Wolverhampton Museum and Art Gallery. E.133.*

The relief portrait has obviously been adapted from the engraving shown above.

In the *Earle Collection of Early Staffordshire Pottery*, there is a large oval plaque 261mm x 355mm with both Charles I and Cromwell in the centre with Oenone and Cupid to the right and Venus and Cupid to the left, with a snake in the foreground.

124

Catherine the Great and Peter III plaques c.1796

This flattering relief portrait of the Empress of Russia is after a jasper ware medallion listed in Wedgwood's oven book 21st August 1779 and again in the 1787 Catalogue. This portrait was adapted from a medal by T.Ivanov (1762). The other plaque is presumably depicting her unloved consort, who was murdered in 1762, so it is said, at Catherine's instigation. The garments are picked out in blue, their hair in manganese brown and they are both wearing small Russian crowns coloured green. 146mm high *Courtesy Sotheby's.*

These plaques were probably made for the Russian trade in the year the Empress died.

Wedgwood portrait medallion 1776
Blue jasper cameo portrait of George III modelled by William
Hackwood in 1776 after a wax portrait by Isaac Gosset. *Courtesy
of the Trustees of the Wedgwood Museum, Barlaston, Stoke-on-Trent.*

There are other cameo portraits of George III more like the one
on the Pratt ware tea-caddy, in particular a wax portrait by
Henry Burch Junior in the collection of H.M. the Queen at
Windsor Castle; and a jasper ware portrait set against a lavender
pink dip background in the Fogg Art Museum, Harvard
University.

George III tea-caddy c.1790
A large and handsome tea-caddy with bust portraits in relief of
King George III (1738-1820) on both sides. The portraits, after a
Hackwood cameo, are finely modelled and coloured in green,
ochre and blue. They are framed within uncoloured beaded
borders. Below the portraits are satyr-like masks set between
Prince of Wales' feathers and a green garland. The King is
wearing an ochre coloured uniform with a blue sash and
epaulettes. There is a markedly blue-tinged glaze over the cream
coloured body of the ware. 166mm high.
Courtesy P.K. Hill Collection.

The relief may have been after a portrait by Allan Ramsay, from
which the image on the coinage was taken. There are numerous
engravings after Ramsay's painting, one by W.Woollett and
another by W.Walker dated 1777. Also the various Wedgwood
jasper cameos are very similar to this tea-caddy portrait and it is
perhaps more likely that one of them provided the inspiration for
this underglaze coloured version.

Wedgwood portrait medallion 1779
This double portrait medallion of George III and Queen
Charlotte is attributed to William Hackwood. There is a similar
likeness in wax of the King and Queen by Isaac Gosset. It was
mentioned in Wedgwood's oven book 23 June 1779 and listed in
his catalogue in the same year. *Courtesy of the Trustees of the
Wedgwood Museum, Barlaston, Stoke-on-Trent.*

These likenesses are clearly not the inspiration for those of the
French royal family shown on mugs, jugs, flasks and plaques on
pages 129-131.

George III commemorative plaque c.1790

A curious plaque decorated with somewhat incongruous applied relief images. It is edged with blue and an uncoloured beaded border. Across it a horseman gallops preceded by some hounds and a hare. There are also two cherubs engaged in various activities and some trees. The colouring, which is particularly pleasing, is limited to green for the foliage, blue for the border and brown with touches of yellow. On the background are painted flights of brown birds. At the bottom of the design the characters $_{G R}^{111}$ are firmly stamped from printers' type. This is probably an apprentice piece, but a very competent one. 235mm wide. *Courtesy P.K.Hill Collection.*

George III and Queen Charlotte plaque c.1786

A small, crudely modelled plaque with portraits of the King and Queen, the yellow letters $_{G_R C}$ in relief between their heads. Their garments are coloured in manganese brown and they wear yellow crowns. The busts are enclosed in a roughly moulded green rococo border with two large manganese flowers below the portraits. 127mm high. *Harris Museum and Art Gallery, Preston. 251 H.531.*

George III and Queen Charlotte tankard c.1790
The side of the pearlware tankard showing a moulded portrait of George III set within an oval medallion edged with an acanthus leaf border and against an orange-peel textured background. The top border is a serpentine blue ribbon entwined with vine or ivy leaves and the flared lower part of the piece is uncoloured with vertical ribs. It is exactly the same design as that used for the Royal Sufferers and Duke of York tankard opposite. 153mm high. *Delhom Gallery and Institute, Mint Museum, Charlotte, North Carolina.* The other side of the tankard shows the relief portrait of Queen Charlotte.

Louis XVI and Marie Antoinette tankard c.1793
The side of this pearlware tankard showing Louis XVI, a relief portrait after a commemorative medal, enclosed within a medallion edged with fleurs-de-lis. There is a moulded leaf border at the top, and at the foot of the tankard is a border of alternate acanthus leaves and a tall lily-like plant. At the front of the piece and again below the handle are acanthus leaves in relief outlined in blue. The rest of the colouring is restricted to green, brown and yellow. 155mm high. *Delhom Gallery and Institute, Mint Museum, Charlotte, North Carolina. 79.310 EPyS.* The other side of the tankard, shows the relief portrait of the Queen.

The Royal Sufferers and Duke of York jug 1794

The two small pearlware jugs are illustrated here to show both sides. The one showing the Duke of York's portrait in a medallion bordered with leaves and fruits being more strongly coloured. Louis XVI and Marie Antoinette with the Dauphin between them are in a similar medallion. Below handle and spout are acanthus decorations outlined in blue. The vine and ribbon border round the neck is adapted from one of Hackwood's border designs and is painted orange and green. The fluted bottoms of the jugs are treated differently, one with a simple horizontal blue line and the other with the flutes picked out with alternate blue and orange vertical lines. The jug on the right has a moss rose painted beneath the spout. The colouring on both jugs is confined to blue, orange, yellow, green and black with a little pale manganese. 115mm high. *Private Collection.*

A sparsely coloured version of this jug is in the Huntly House Museum, Edinburgh, but there is no real evidence that it was made in Scotland. Another colourful small jug with similar portraits is marked HAWLEY and can be seen in the Yorkshire Museum (see page 73).

A jug sold at Sotheby's in 1971 had the title 'The Royal Suffers' (*sic*) pencilled in beneath the three profiles and on the other side a named portrait of the Duke of York.

A similar jug in the Victoria and Albert Museum *C.63.1952* is captioned 'La Fayette' in place of 'Duke of York' 187mm high. In fact it must be the Duke of York, because the bas relief bears a close resemblance to a contemporary engraving by I.Pass.

As Louis was executed in January 1793, and the Queen and the Dauphin in the following November, the likelihood is that the first of these jugs was produced in 1794, though it is possible that they were made during their imprisonment. The naming of the portrait La Fayette in place of Duke of York may have been done for the North American trade. The Marquis de la Fayette was a great hero both in France and in North America, because of the assistance he gave to Washington's army. Liberal in his views, he nevertheless made strenuous efforts to save the lives of the French king and queen.

Frederick Augustus, Duke of York (1763-1827) was a soldier whose humanity and bravery earned him the love of all who served with him. He bore not the slightest resemblance to La Fayette.

These subjects are sometimes described as being portraits of King George III and Queen Charlotte, with Frederick Prince of Wales, with Admiral Nelson or the Duke of Cumberland on the reverse side. The Wedgwood cameo of George III and his queen show this to be a mistaken attribution.

Ribbon and ivy border design c.1780

This border design is a detail taken from a page from William Hackwood's sketchbook dated 1799 (see page 25) though the border had been used in relief on pottery before that date. *Courtesy of the Trustees of the Wedgwood Museum, Barlaston, Stoke-on-Trent.*

129

Contemporary engraving of the Duke of York, by I.Pass c.1794
The title describes him as Commander-in-Chief of the British and Hanoverian Troops. *National Portrait Gallery.*

Nothing seems to be known of this engraver. A Dutchman William Pass who was an engraver, settled in London in 1621, so perhaps I.Pass may have been a descendant.

His ROYAL HIGHNESS the

DUKE of YORK

Commander in Chief

of the British and Hanoverian Troops.

The Duke of York and Royal Sufferers Spirit flask c.1794
This flask, made to carry a quarter of a pint of spirits has portraits of the ill-fated French Royal family on one side and the Duke of York on the other. They are set within medallions bordered with dark green leaves. The edges of the flask are feathered in burnt orange and the figures are coloured in manganese, blue and orange. 120mm diam. *Private Collection.*

The Royal Sufferers and Duke of York tankard c.1794

This large tankard has the usual portraits set against an orange-peel textured background within medallions edged with green acanthus leaves alternating with tiny orange leaves. At the top there is a serpentine blue ribbon border entwined with green vine leaves, set against an uncoloured orange-peel textured background, under a scalloped edge. The piece is brown banded at the top and bottom. The flared lower part has uncoloured vertical ribs and there is a very deep foot rim. The plain loop handle is joined to the body with an elaborately moulded acanthus border — the same acanthus decoration but edged with brown appears on the opposite side of the tankard. 153mm high. *Private Collection.*

The Royal Sufferers and Duke of York mug c.1794

The reverse side of this smaller mug showing the portrait of the Duke of York unframed below a border of green cat's claw decorations. The foot of the mug is bordered with stiff leaves, edged with green. It is brown banded at top and bottom. The loop handle has a thumb-rest, moulded with an acanthus pattern edged with brown. Under the handle is a moulded acanthus decoration, repeated on the opposite side of the mug. 114mm high. *Private Collection.*

Medal designed by Benjamin Duvivier 1781

Profile portraits of Louis XVI and Marie Antoinette on a medal issued by the State Legislature of Burgundy. *City of Manchester Art Galleries.*

There are numerous underglaze coloured plaques, mugs, flasks and jugs with similar portraits. The profile portraits of the two bareheaded adults with the child between them is a copy of two of the heads from the medal designed by Benjamin Duvivier and struck to celebrate the birth of the Dauphin in 1781. When the underglaze coloured version was modelled the head of the king has been thrown back in a more heroic attitude, to make it easier to introduce the child's head. A Wedgwood portrait medallion of Louis XVI, copied from the Duvivier medal was issued in 1782.

Louis XVI plaque c.1793

A portrait in full relief showing the King with manganese brown hair and wearing a blue and orange shirt under a burnt orange coat. The portrait is set within an orange beaded border with a simulated brown ribbon at the top. 197mm high. *Harris Museum and Art Gallery, Preston. H.529.*

At the Harris Museum this portrait plaque is said to represent Frederick Louis, Prince of Wales, eldest son of George II.

Queen Marie Antoinette plaque c.1792

A relief portrait bust set within a yellow beaded border. The Queen's dress is coloured in orange, yellow and green and trimmed with ermine. 182mm high. *Glaisher Collection, Fitzwilliam Museum, Cambridge 751.*

Dr Glaisher described this plaque as representing Princess Charlotte Augusta Matilda, Princess Royal and eldest daughter of George III.

The source of these plaques must have been a pair of jasper ware Wedgwood portraits modelled by William Hackwood in 1778, after a pair of terra cotta portrait medallions by Jean Baptiste Nini which were modelled in 1774. The Hackwood portraits are illustrated in *Wedgwood: the Portrait Medallions* by Robin Reilly and George Savage, London 1973.

The Royal Sufferers plaque c.1794

Louis XVI wears an ochre coat with a blue sash and Marie Antoinette and the Dauphin are dressed in blue. Their eyes and eyebrows are also outlined in blue. The background is painted with sprays of flowers in blue, green and yellow. The frame is ochre with a blue rim and a brown band inside with a blue ribbon bow at the top. 260mm high. *Harris Museum and Art Gallery, Preston. 229 (H.393).*

Charlotte Corday c.1793
An engraving by John James Hinchcliff after a painting by Denis-Auguste Raffet of Charlotte Corday on her way to the guillotine. *Private Collection.*

Charlotte Corday bust c.1793 *top left*
This well-modelled bust shows the murderess with ashen face and staring blue eyes. Her shoulders are draped in an ochre shawl, ermine spotted in brown. She is mounted on a small circular socle, set on a rectangular tapered base decorated with a brown band and a border of stiff green leaves. 280mm high. *Courtesy Sotheby's.*

On July 13th 1793, Marie Anne Charlotte Corday d'Armont, a supporter of the Girondins, having conceived the idea that Marat was their main persecutor, carried out her self-imposed mission to kill him. She drove a kitchen knife into his side, as he sat in a hot bath, trying to alleviate the pains of the intolerable disease which was slowly reducing him to a state of putrefaction. It almost looks as though she had done that bloodthirsty monster a good service. Four days later, Charlotte Corday went fearlessly to the guillotine.

Charlotte Corday bust c.1793
Another bust from the same mould of Charlotte Corday with horrified, even more heavily outlined, staring eyes. She wears a yellow shawl patterned in black with ermine. The bust is mounted on a circular socle coloured yellow, orange and blue, the base of which is moulded with a pattern of green grasses. 299mm high. *Courtesy Sotheby's.*

'Boney and John Bull' jug c.1815

This rather crude jug is unusual in that the relief decorations are all sprigged on to the body and not moulded in the usual way. A prancing, caricatured figure of Napoleon in pugilistic attitude, having had his sabre knocked out of his hand, is faced with the resolute figure of John Bull, holding a cutlass in his right hand. Napoleon is dressed in ochre jacket and blue breeches, John Bull in blue jacket and ochre breeches; both have black hats and black boots or shoes. Napoleon's sabre is flying through the air (further round the jug) and on the reverse side is a sprigged-on ship of war running before the wind. The jug is brown banded with a simple repeat bell decoration pencilled in brown round the top. The style of this design is very much in the manner of Isaac Cruikshank, George Cruikshank's father, who drew many cartoons on this subject. 142mm high. *City of Manchester Art Galleries. 1923.918.*

Napoleon and John Bull jug c.1795 *top left*

This creamware jug is transfer printed in terracotta with a caricature very much in the manner of Isaac Cruikshank and was probably the inspiration for the relief decorated jug with the same subject. 137mm high. *Central Museum, Northampton. D25/1946.*

Bust of Napoleon Bonaparte c.1802

The hair is coloured manganese brown and he is wearing a blue uniform coat with yellow facings and epaulettes. The bust is mounted on a waisted socle, ochre banded at top and bottom and with coloured relief trophies of war on the front. The impressed letters BONAPARTE filled in with brown are on the front of the base. 223mm high. *City Museum and Art Gallery, Stoke-on-Trent. 3317.*

The bust must have been made during the period of peace before the signing of the Treaty of Amiens. After 1803, he signed himself 'Napoleon', dropping the Buonaparte.

Weavers' Arms jug c.1816

A very crisply moulded creamware underglaze coloured jug of squat shape with a bearded satyr's head under the spout. On the sides are the Weavers' Arms supported by griffons with orange faces, orange and green wings and yellow and green bodies. The lions' faces in the actual coat of arms are uncoloured, except for manganese whiskers. The blue chevron has Tudor roses on it. On a scroll beneath is 'Weave Truth with Trust' and round the top of the jug is an uncoloured relief lacy border with the words, in brown impressed capital letters 'May the Lost Rights of Briton (sic) Soon be Restored'. The jug has an uncoloured fluted base and there is yellow and orange mantling above the coat of arms. The handle is an elaborate upswept scroll with acanthus moulding. 133mm high. *The Royal Pavilion Art Gallery and Museums, Brighton. HW 563.*

In the early years of the nineteenth century, the introduction of machinery to the manufacture of cotton and wool products resulted in the ruin of many small traders and the pauperization of the families connected with them. This change from handicraft to mechanized industry resulted in the Luddite Riots, when the workers smashed the weaving frames throughout north and midland counties. These riots must have been the inspiration for the designs on this jug. The slogan probably refers to Lord Liverpool's repressive legislation. The riots began in Nottingham in 1811 and over the next few years spread to Derbyshire, Leicestershire, Lancashire and Yorkshire. In 1816 the riots were resumed, this time the cause being the depression that followed the end of the Napoleonic Wars. Firm repressive measures finally put a stop to the movement.

Queen Caroline plate c.1820
A plate with a relief bust of Queen Caroline, wearing one of her elaborate feathered hats. This example is decorated in overglaze enamel colours with a border of crowns, Prince of Wales' feathers and flowers in relief round the rim. 165mm diam. *Private Collection.*

Caroline had an unhappy marriage to the Prince of Wales, who deserted her within a year of their wedding in 1795. She lived abroad for many years but on the death of George III she returned to London amid popular rejoicing. She was excluded from the coronation in 1821 and died broken-hearted in the same year.

We have not found the engraving on which this portrait is based. There is a drawing by George Cruikshank, engraved by J.Chapman entitled 'Brougham announcing the abandonment of the Bill to the Queen'. She is depicted wearing the same hat as is shown on this plate.

Queen Caroline plate c.1820
A small creamware plate with a relief portrait of Queen Caroline in the centre and a relief floral border decorated with somewhat arbitrary patches of blue and ochre. 90mm diam. *Courtesy John May.*

Henry Brougham plate c.1820-30
A small plate with a relief portrait in the centre, face and head uncoloured. He wears a blue coat and a yellow waistcoat. The rim is decorated in relief with a border of roses and leaves in yellow and green. The portrait on this plate is very like an engraving by R.Page, published by J.Robins, Albion Press, London and dated 1820. 133mm diam. *Sheffield City Museums. K1937-29.*

Henry Brougham, as her attorney-general, defended Queen Caroline during her trial in 1820. He was not elevated to the peerage until 1830, the same year he was elected as M.P. for Knaresborough, and later for Yorkshire.

Thomas Denman plate c.1820
An underglaze coloured plate with a portrait of Thomas Denman who was solicitor-general to Queen Caroline in 1820. The head is uncoloured, but there is a border of blue, green and ochre roses in relief round the rim. The portrait is after an engraving by R.Page, the features are the same but Denman is wearing a stock and a high collar in the engraving. 174mm diam. *Merseyside County Museum. 28.62.4.*

Denman was responsible for the withdrawal of Lord Liverpool's bill of pains and penalties against Queen Caroline. He stoutly supported her innocence before the House of Lords in 1820. In 1831 he drafted the Reform Bill and in 1834 he was made Baron Denman of Dovedale.

Queen Caroline jug c.1820

A full bodied pearlware jug with a splayed foot and scalloped rim with a blue edge, has a spout decorated with a horned satyr's head with horns, eyebrows and ears all picked out with manganese. Below this there is a large acanthus leaf coloured green. The semi-scrolled handle with incised leaf decoration and a brown husk pattern down the centre also has a large green acanthus leaf beneath it. 'QUEEN CAROLINE' is in raised capital letters on both sides of the top of the jug, below the scalloped edge. On either side there is a profile portrait of the Queen in slight relief, set within a circular medallion with a plain raised rim. The Queen is wearing an elaborate blue hat trimmed with green feathers over a brown head scarf. Her yellow coat has a blue turned-up collar. The face is uncoloured except for brown eye and eyebrow and a row of brown curls. On either side of the medallion there is a relief decoration of flowers, yellow roses on one side and yellow thistles on the other, both with green leaves and brown stems. The jug is banded in brown above and below the portraits and round the foot.

The base of this jug has a raised foot rim and within this is stamped

WARRANTED
WINCHESTER
MEASURE

enclosed within a typographic border made up of diamond shapes. 151mm high. *Private Collection.*

For the measurements of liquids, the old 'wine gallon' (231 cu.ins.) was in use in England until 1824, when in the Weights and Measures Act of that year the Imperial Standards were legalised. Before that the Winchester quart, Winchester gallon, bushel, etc., were so-called because the original measures had be deposited at Winchester in the time of Henry VII. This jug, when filled to the brim holds exactly two pints. The likelihood is that such jugs were used in public houses.

The portrait on this jug is very like an engraving by Woolnorth, dated 1820, after a painting by Wageman. In this engraving Queen Caroline is wearing a similar feathered hat and a ruffled collar. She had a weakness for elaborate feathered hats which can be seen in paintings of her by Sir Thomas Lawrence and by Lawrence's former pupil, Samuel Lane.

It is possible that this jug was made by one of the Scottish East Coast potteries, though some authorities think this unlikely.

There is a creamware jug of a similar shape with the same satyr spout and similar handle in the Royal Scottish Museum, which was made by Reid's Pottery Musselburgh and which was dated 1822. The same portrait appears on one of a pair of plates made by Robert and George Gordon of Prestonpans.

Brougham and Denman jug c.1820

This enamel coloured jug, smaller but comparable to the Queen Caroline jug has a moulded portrait of Thomas Denman on one side and Henry Brougham on the other, each set within a raised and beaded border of an oval frame, flanked with sprays of roses and thistles and with a satyr mask below the spout. Below the scalloped rim and above the portraits are the inscriptions

H.BROUGHAM ESQ M.P. and T.DENMAN ESQ M.P. in incised capital letters. The jug has a simulated bamboo handle. 120mm high. *Courtesy Mr and Mrs J. Orange.*

There is a similar example in the Fitzwilliam Museum, Cambridge *1124.1928.* It may have also been made with underglaze coloured decoration.

Sarah Siddons plaque c.1790
This relatively large plaque, painted in underglaze colours shows the famous actress with a brown blob on her cheek, flanked by jewel-like decorations. The elaborate coiffure she is wearing is very like that she assumed for a part in *The Tragedy of the Grecian Daughter* which can be seen in an engraving by J. Caldwell in 1798. 216mm high. *The Royal Pavilion Art Gallery and Museums, Brighton. HW 368.*

Sarah Siddons, who was born in 1755, was the daughter of the actor Roger Kemble. Her first London triumph was as Isabella in Garrick's production of *The Fatal Marriage.* She continued to act with success, particularly at Covent Garden, giving her final performance as Lady Macbeth in 1812. Reynolds painted her as the Tragic Muse. She died in 1831. There is a variant of this plaque in John Hall's *Staffordshire Portrait Figures.*

A portrait plaque of David Garrick, facing to the left is set in an oval frame of leaves and flowers surmounted by three putti. It is possibly earlier than the Siddons plaque. Garrick (1717-79) was the greatest comic and tragic actor of his time. 197mm high. Illustrated in John Hall's book.

The bust of an unnamed actor c.1810
The man has brown hair and exaggeratedly large raised eyebrows; his cheeks are blobbed with ochre. He wears a blue jacket and a white waistcoat, spotted in green and ochre. The splayed base is striped in the same colours. 203mm high. *Courtesy Sotheby's.*

This bust may be intended to represent Charles Mathews the Elder (1776-1835). He was a popular actor on the York circuit, so it is possible that one of the Yorkshire potteries

produced this bust. More likely, however, is that it represents T.P.Cooke (1786-1864), who after serving in the navy, had a great success on the stage, specialising in naval parts and playing the original William in *Black Eyed Susan.* The base of the bust looks as though it had been modelled on a ship's capstan.

Lady Godiva plaque c.1810 *opposite*

This fully modelled naïve portrait of the celebrated equestrienne shows her holding an ochre coloured bridle and modestly wearing a long yellow shift with a dark blue sash. The colouring is otherwise limited to brown for her ladyship's hair, eyes and eyebrows and for the horse's eye and hooves. There is a blue circle inside the uncoloured rope border and the horse wears a blue plume. The plaque is lettered in brown 'LADEY GO DIVER'. 120mm diam. *Private Collection.*

Lady Godiva (d.1067) the pious wife of Leofric, Earl of Mercia, rode naked through the streets of Coventry, her husband having light-heartedly promised to remit a tax he had imposed on the people of Coventry if she would undertake such a brazen act. She took the precaution of telling the townsfolk to stay within their houses and not to look out of the windows. The famous 'Peeping Tom' who disregarded this injunction was struck blind.

28 & 29. George III and Buonaparte jug 1802-3

This jug is decorated with two portrait medallions, one on either side, representing George III and Napoleon, though neither bear much likeness to the subject. Both are crowned with laurel leaves, and the jug must have been made after the Peace of Amiens. Above the portraits are initials G on one side and B on the other enclosed by a decorative design of crossed cornucopias. 230mm high. *Courtesy G.F. Arnold.*

Charles James Fox c.1800
An engraving by I.W.Cook after a portrait by Sir Joshua
Reynolds. *Private Collection.*

Charles James Fox plaque c.1806
The portrait on this plaque of a well-nourished man in civilian
dress, wearing a blue coat is after a portrait by Sir Joshua
Reynolds, which was later engraved by I.W.Cook. There is a
very similar enamel coloured relief decorated plaque with a
portrait of C.J.Fox (1749-1806) with the name incised under it.
This was no doubt made to commemorate Fox's death in 1806.
The portrait is surrounded by a laurel wreath. 125mm diam.
Courtesy Sotheby's.

Fox was one of the most famous statesmen of his day and the
great adversary of William Pitt the Younger; he advocated the
cause of Admiral Keppel in 1779. Plaques attributed to Keppel
show a face very similar to this, but potters used one face for
another with complete abandon.

Bust of Alexander Pope c.1790-1800
The poet has manganese coloured hair and his eyes are heavily
outlined in blue. He is wearing a manganese shirt with green
drapery over his shoulders edged with blue and white. 210mm
high. *The Royal Pavilion Art Gallery and Museums, Brighton. HW 952.*

Alexander Pope (1688-1744) was an intimate of the literary figures
of the time, including Addison, Wycherley and Swift. His *Rape of
the Lock* was published in 1712. Translations of the *Iliad* and the
Odyssey followed. His *Dunciad,* originally published anonymously
in 1712 was attacked by numerous writers, the final volume not
appearing until 1742. His health was bad, due it is said, to
overworking as a child. As he grew older he became more
quarrelsome. In his lifetime he was regarded as a great poet.

Jasper ware cameo portrait of (?) Edmund Burke c.1790
This portrait, although attributed to Wedgwood, is not actually
listed by the firm. *Courtesy Robin Reilly.*

A portrait of a gentleman jug c.1795
A fine pearlware jug with a bust portrait of a gentleman, after a
Wedgwood medallion. He is wearing an ochre jacket with a yellow
collar and a frilled stock. His brown hair is dressed *en queue*. The
bust is flanked by trees with ochre trunks and green foliage. The
jug is banded in brown at top and bottom and has a border of
small triangular leaves at both top and base of the neck. 140mm
high. *The Royal Pavilion Art Gallery and Museums, Brighton. HW 437.*

Edmund Burke c.1790
An engraving by H.Robinson after a painting by Sir Joshua
Reynolds. *Private Collection.*

This portrait jug was attributed by the original compiler of the
Willett Collection Catalogue as being of the Marquis de la
Fayette, but bears no resemblance to any contemporary portrait
engraving. The Wedgwood jasper medallion on which this relief
portrait is clearly based is given in *Wedgwood: the portrait medallions*
by Reilly and Savage as being of Edmund Burke (1729-97). Robin
Reilly in a letter to us written on May 9th 1983 said in reference to
this jug that he now entertains the gravest doubts about the
attribution to Burke. Certainly it is more like Burke than La
Fayette, but the wax portrait by T.R.Poole of Burke in the
Victoria and Albert Museum shows an older man with a more
prominent nose and a different hair style.

Edmund Burke was a popular figure in his day — at one time
secretary to the Marquis of Rockingham, he was Member of
Parliament from 1765-80, representing Bristol in the last seven
years. In 1774 Richard and Judith Champion the owners of the
Bristol Pottery, presented him with the most extravagantly
decorated porcelain dinner service that the Bristol Pottery ever
made. Burke's *Reflections on the French Revolution,* published in 1790,
in which he expressed his horror of that event, ran through eleven
editions and his fame spread across Europe.

Sir Francis Burdett c.1810

This small equestrian figure of the politician, shows him seated on a rearing horse; he is wearing a black hat and boots, a blue coat and yellow breeches. Below the horse's belly and framed within ears of corn is the inscription in capital letters impressed from printers' type

S + F
BURDETT
BRITAINS + FRIEND

102mm high. *The Royal Pavilion Art Gallery and Museums, Brighton. HW 502.*

Sir Francis Burdett (1770-1844) was M.P. for Westminster from 1807-37. He was against the war with France, corruption in Parliament and flogging in the army. He was imprisoned twice on political charges, the first time on April 6th 1810, when he was committed to the Tower on the Order of the Speaker for breach of privilege, and the second time in 1820.

Josiah Wedgwood plaque 1795-1815

A circular plaque with a bust portrait of the potter in profile, his brown hair *en queue,* wearing a yellow jacket, an ochre waistcoat and white cravat. He is flanked by painted sprays of flowers and surrounded by a beaded and lined border. This plaque is remarkably like the Joachim Smith cameo portrait of Wedgwood. There are no firm grounds for thinking that this plaque was made by the Wedgwood firm. By the time of his death in 1795, Wedgwood must have been one of the most revered figures in the potteries, so it is quite possible another potter made use of the cameo portrait for a commemorative piece. 140mm high. *Courtesy Sotheby's.*

Josiah Wedgwood cameo 1773

A white cameo portrait on black jasper dip of Josiah Wedgwood in his forty-third year, by Joachim Smith, made as a partner to the cameo of Thomas Bentley. This portrait must have been the inspiration for the underglaze coloured relief plaque of Wedgwood. Impressed on the back in capital letters is the word WEDGWOOD, which is also incised in a cursive hand in upper and lower case letters. 126mm high. *City of Manchester Art Galleries. 1906.134.*

10. Commemorative jugs, mugs, busts and plaques of naval and military subjects

Wars breed heroes and patriotic fervour and during the time of the production of relief decorated, underglaze coloured earthenware, Britain was, for most of the time, at war. The makers of this type of pottery were not slow to see the possibilities of a market for their wares.

Britannia was a favourite subject with the Pratt ware potters (including the Pratts themselves). Designs adapted from contemporary prints of 'The Sailor's Return' and 'The Sailor's Farewell' were extremely popular. Trophies of war and relief portraits of Admirals and army commanders decorate many pieces. The most commemorated, quite naturally, as he was the most popular hero of the time, was Admiral Lord Nelson, whose image can be found on plaques, mugs, jugs and flasks, as a full length standing figure, or as a portrait head and shoulders. Other Admirals to be found include Rodney, Howe, Duncan, Jervis and Keppel; among the Captains are Cook, Berry, Collingwood, Hardy, Trollope and Taggs. They are often shown wearing hats, though paintings, engravings and cameo portraits of the period usually portray these sitters bareheaded.

Many of the portraits that appear on relief decorated plaques are difficult to identify from contemporary paintings or engravings. Keppel had a broken nose, Howe a craggy face, Duncan was heavily handsome, St. Vincent had a large nose and a firm mouth. Three-quarter face portraits on plaques have been attributed to all these Admirals. Obviously one was very like another as far as the potters were concerned. The rather full face in Plates 30 and 31 suggests that the original was Keppel (anyway he was the first in chronological order) and the others were merely adapted from him.

Among the army commanders are the Duke of York, the Duke of Cumberland, General Eliott, Lord Wellington and General Hill.

Military subjects

For most of the eighteenth century Britain was at war. The Boston Tea Party in 1773 resulted in the American War of Independence. France soon joined in on the American side and though Britain made peace with the American colonies in 1783, the war with France dragged on with one brief respite until 1815.

Our main successes were at sea and from Rodney to Nelson our naval commanders were duly celebrated in Pratt ware. Of the military commanders General Eliott, who most gallantly defended Gibraltar from 1779 to 1783 appears to be the first to be commemorated in a well-modelled, if somewhat colourless flask.

The Duke of York's successes in the Netherlands as the Commander of the British forces under Prince Coburg in the campaigns of 1793-4 inspired an attractive series of jugs portraying both commanders. The Duke of Cumberlands's brutal defeat of the Highlanders at Culloden was recalled half a century later with an equestrian portrait of the Duke on one side of a jug, backed up with a scene of Hercules slaying the Hydra.

Admiral Lord Rodney mug c.1785
A creamware mug in the form of the Admiral's head, his shoulders coloured green forming the foot of the mug. His hair is pale manganese brown and there are ochre patches on his cheeks and in the detailing round the mouth. A yellow band runs round the top, below the green rim and on it is lettered 'Success to Lord Rodney' in relief. 110mm high. *Courtesy Leonard Russell.*

Admiral Rodney mug c.1785
A creamware mug in the form of the Admiral's head. The foot of the mug is formed by his collar, cravat and the tops of his shoulders. His hair and cravat are mottled in black. LORD RODNEY in raised capital letters can be seen round the top of the head. The loop handle at the back is decorated with laurel leaves and the shoulders are washed with green. 108mm high. *Crown Copyright, Victoria and Albert Museum. II 279.*

George Brydges Rodney, first Baron Rodney was born in 1719 and entered the Navy in 1732. He was promoted Captain in 1742, Rear Admiral in 1759 and Admiral in 1778. He resigned his command of the West Indian fleet to Hood, owing to ill health in 1781, but the following year rejoined Hood and together they defeated the French under Admiral de Grasse off Domenica. Samuel Hood, first Viscount Hood, was born in 1724 and entered the Navy in 1741. He was Commander on the North American Station 1767-70.

The Peace of Amiens in 1802 must have been the inspiration for a handsome jug with classical portraits of George III and Buonaparte, both crowned with laurel leaves. Within a year we were at war once again and a caricature of Buonaparte appeared on a Pratt jug showing him being defied by a bellicose John Bull.

The very fully modelled jug with portraits of Lord Wellington and General Hill must have been made before Wellington was elevated to the Dukedom. This jug frequently appears with enamel colouring.

Apart from the few army commanders that we have mentioned, various jugs and plaques were made showing scenes of military reviews and cavalry exercises, some based on engravings from *The Sporting Magazine.* One of these jugs has an unnamed equestrian portrait of the Duke of York on one side. The formation of the 'Volunteers' was commemorated with both figures and jugs, and there are jugs and plaques with a dashing scene of a mounted hussar jumping over a gun crew who are in some disarray.

Captain Cook plaque c.1785

An oval plaque with the bust of Captain Cook moulded in relief after the painting by William Hodges. His cheeks are coloured with ochre and his hair is manganese brown. He wears a blue coat, an ochre waistcoat and is encircled by an ochre beaded border with a blue line within. The scrolled ornament at the top and bottom of the frame is coloured blue. The name COOK is incised beneath the bust. 202mm high. *Harris Museum and Art Gallery, Preston. 231 H 530.*

Captain James Cook (1728-79), one of the most celebrated navigators of all time, was born at Marton in Cleveland, Yorkshire. At an early age he went to sea in a Whitby collier and learned his trade in the hard school of the North Sea, coasting and voyaging to Norway and the Baltic. In 1755 he joined the Royal Navy and was soon appointed Master of a succession of vessels. He became engaged in survey work, establishing a reputation not only as a navigator but also as a mathematician and astronomer. There is no space here to record the achievements of his circumnavigations. On his third and last great voyage he was killed in a scuffle with some natives at Hawaii. This plaque was no doubt made within a few years of his death, possibly by one of the Yorkshire potteries as a tribute to a great Yorkshireman.

Engraving of Captain Cook c.1776

An engraving by J.Basire of William Hodges' portrait of Captain Cook which appeared as a frontispiece to Cook's *Voyages* (1777). This was no doubt the source for the jasper ware cameo. *National Portrait Gallery, London.*

James Basire (1730-1802) was the son of Isaac Basire. He began his professional career as an engraver of maps. In 1760 he became the engraver to the Society of Antiquaries. From 1771-78 William Blake was his apprentice. Basire also engraved several portraits of eminent people, including this portrait of Captain Cook after William Hodges.

Jasper ware medallion of Captain Cook c.1780

This cameo portrait is attributed to Flaxman. He must have taken the likeness from the portrait by William Hodges, who was with Cook on his 1772-75 voyage. The underglaze coloured plaque is clearly based on the Wedgwood medallion. *Courtesy of the Trustees of the Wedgwood Museum, Barlaston, Stoke-on-Trent.*

145

Admiral Duncan bust c.1798

The Admiral, brown haired and dressed in a blue uniform with ochre epaulettes and waistcoat, is mounted on a waisted socle, uncoloured except for some trophies of war in relief, coloured in green and ochre on the front. 197mm high. *The Royal Pavilion Art Gallery and Museums, Brighton. HW 188.*

White glass paste portrait of Admiral Duncan

Profile bust portrait facing to the left of the Admiral, by James Tassie, modelled from life. It is inscribed on the truncation 'ADMIRAL/VISC. DUNCAN 1797' and '*Tassie F.*' The opaque white glass paste portrait is mounted on a blackened glass ground. 102mm high. *National Maritime Museum, London. C.8118.*

James Tassie (1735-99) was born at Pollokshaws near Glasgow. After first working as a stonemason, he studied drawing and modelling at the Foulis Academy in Glasgow. He travelled to Dublin in 1763 and there met Dr Henry Quin who showed him how to make casts in a white glass paste. Tassie improved on this material and after three years in Dublin he moved to London where he soon established himself. Over the years he made some 20,000 copies of gems and portraits of famous people. At some late stage he must have been joined in his business by his nephew William Tassie (1777-1860) who, in 1798, actually signed with his initials a similar paste portrait of Admiral Duncan. William Tassie succeeded to the business on the death of his uncle in 1799.

Admirel (sic) Duncan and Homage to Ceres jug c.1798
On this crisply potted version, quite a different shape from the usual Duncan jugs, Admiral Duncan is shown wearing a blue uniform and a black hat, the sash across his chest bears his name in capital letters.

In the sea, as well as the two dolphin's heads is the head of Mercury (or at any rate a small head wearing a winged helmet). On the other side of the jug are the two classical ladies often found on a Duncan jug. They have been adapted from Flaxman's bas relief 'Offering to Ceres' and with them is lying a large spotted hound. The plain bands on the jug are brown as is the outlined acanthus leaf below spout and handle. The leaf border at the top is outlined in orange, and the acanthus border round the foot of the jug is left uncoloured. 159mm high. *National Maritime Museum, London . W2225.*

Admiral Duncan flask c.1798 *opposite page*
Spirit flask decorated with a bust profile portrait of the Admiral wearing an ochre uniform with a black hat on his brown hair. The white sash across his chest carries his name in raised lettering. The wavy sides of the flask are followed by a border of acanthus foliage outlined in green. 170mm long. *Crown Copyright, Victoria and Albert Museum. C.75 1952.*

This likeness is almost certainly from a profile engraving by William Ridley (1764-1838) which appeared in *The European Magazine,* February 1798, and was after a glass medallion by James Tassie, modelled from life, in the previous year. Ridley engraved illustrations for a number of books, and his engravings also appeared in *The Evangelical Magazine.*

Adam Duncan (1731-1804) was commissioned a Naval Lieutenant in 1755. He was at the blockade of Brest in 1759, served in the West Indies in 1762 and sat on the court-martial of Admiral Keppel in 1779, to whom he gave much support. He was made an Admiral in 1795 and was Commander-in-Chief of the North Sea fleet from 1795 to 1801. In 1797 he defeated the Dutch Admiral de Winter off Camperdown and in the same year was raised to the peerage.

Captain Trollope and Admiral Duncan jug c.1798
This small, rather gritty coarsely potted creamware jug with a slightly blue tinted glaze has a bust of Captain Trollope on one side, wearing a yellow uniform trimmed with orange and with his name CAPTAIN TROLOP (sic) on a white sash across his chest. On the other side of the jug there is a portrait of Admiral Duncan. For a picture and a full description see page 112. It is probably a product of one of the Scottish East Coast potteries. 139mm high. *Private Collection.*

Captain Henry Trollope (1756-1839) had served under Admiral Duncan. In 1796 in HMS *Glatton,* off Hellevoetsluis, he had attacked and beaten off six French frigates, thus ensuring the safety of a convoy of merchantmen. He served with distinction at the battle of Camperdown for which he was knighted. In 1805 he was refused a pension. In 1812 he became an Admiral, in 1831 he was awarded the G.C.B. and sadly in 1839, at the age of eighty-three, he committed suicide.

Another Duncan jug, with the same portraits, has Trollope's name replaced by Captain Taggs (or Taggart, the lettering is unclear). This jug is very similar in shape, colouring and border decorations. Clio, the Muse of History, is seen to the right of the portrait (as on the Duncan jug marked W.DANIEL (see page 43). 162mm high. *Crown copyright Victoria and Albert Museum C.62.1952.* Further examples of Admiral Duncan jugs can be seen at the Royal Pavilion Art Gallery and Museums, Brighton, *HW 194,* and the Royal Scottish Museum, Edinburgh, *1902.162.*

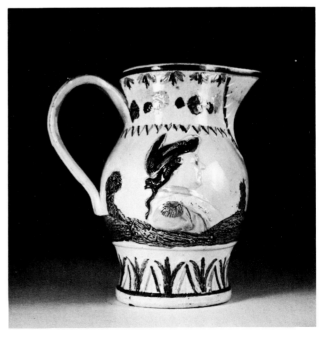

Admiral Keppel c.1780
An engraving by J.Chapman after Sir Joshua Reynolds' portrait of the Admiral, painted in 1776. *National Portrait Gallery, London.*

Admiral Augustus Keppel (1725-86) was a grandson of the Earl of Albemarle. He was educated at Westminster School and entered the Navy in 1735. Five years later he accompanied Anson on a voyage round the world. By 1754 he was a member of the court-martial of Admiral Byng, and in turn was court-martialled himself in 1779 for his conduct against the French Fleet off Ushant, when he was Commander-in-Chief of the Grand Fleet. The quite unwarranted charge of cowardice in the face of the enemy was dismissed and in 1782 he became First Lord of the Admiralty, being created Viscount in the same year.

The court-martial aroused strong feelings of support for Keppel from the populace. Josiah Wedgwood, writing to his partner Bentley on February 25th 1779 says 'But why do you not send me his head when it is advertised every day in shade — etching and wax, by Mrs Harrington. Pray send me one of each by the first coach; we should have had it a month since and advertised it for pictures, bracelets, rings, seals, etc., and after presenting a ring or polished seal of him to each of the thrice worthy court-martial...' A month later Wedgwood wrote to Bentley saying 'A bust of Admiral Keppel will be very acceptable too, though we are making one by the last print. We had a gentleman here last week who knows the Admiral and says the print is like him but has not so martial an air as the original carries and we have set his head more upright and opened his eye a little wider upon this intelligence.'[1] The same gentleman remarked that the bas relief was a very good likeness of the Admiral.

The Wedgwood jasper cameos of Keppel are in profile, showing clearly his broken nose. The Pratt ware plaques were almost certainly after Sir Joshua Reynolds' portrait of Keppel which was painted in 1776.

1. Keele University Archives. 18878-26.

Turner pitcher moulds c.1780
Pitcher moulds of boy with eagle impressed TURNER, 45mm high *TMMS/410* and the figure Air with the word 'AIR' incised on the back 98mm high *TMMS/233. Courtesy Spode Museum, Stoke-on-Trent.*

30. Admiral Augustus Keppel (?) plaque c.1780-1810

A three-quarter view bust portrait, attributed by the Museum because of its provenance to being of Admiral Keppel. The bareheaded, blue-coated Admiral is framed in a medallion surrounded by a blue border and set within trophies of war and strongly coloured in blue, ochre, black and brown, with manganese stars at the bottom. 217mm high. *National Maritime Museum, London. M64/42.*

This plaque was bought at Sotheby's in June 1934 by Colin Keppel, a descendant of the Admiral's. Though the subject should date the plaque c.1780, the style and colouring suggest it was made at least twenty years later.

31. Admiral Keppel plaque 1810

An almost surrealistic circular plaque, pierced for hanging, framed in yellow with brown bands at the edges and displaying an incongruous mixture of sprigged decorations. The head of an Admiral at the top, below which is a black eagle with a cherub on its back (after a Turner mould) and to the right a classical lady in a yellow dress flying through the air, her blue scarf blowing out behind her symbolising Air (also after a Turner mould), form the main decoration framed with formalised vegetation at each side and below the figures patches of cobalt, green and ochre finish the design. Incised on the back of the plaque, which must have been an apprentice piece are the words

C S Walton
Bottom of (*illegible*)
July 10th 1810
egle (*sic*) and child

159mm diam. *City Museum and Art Gallery, Stoke-on-Trent. 186.P39.*

Admiral Earl Howe (?) plaque c.1794

A circular plaque shows the Admiral facing to the left, where he looks, in fact, very like the Reynolds portrait of Admiral Keppel. The figure has black hair and is wearing a blue uniform with yellow epaulettes and is set within a laurel wreath, decorated in ochre and green. 27mm diam. *City Museum and Art Gallery, Stoke-on-Trent. 3285.*

The ambiguity in these pottery images was to the potter's advantage because it meant he could attach any name he liked to these vague portraits. Earl Howe, after a distinguished Naval career was First Lord of the Admiralty from 1783 to 1788. He commanded the Channel Fleet in 1790 and in 1794 won the great victory of the glorious 1st of June, capturing six French ships off Brest. Howe was not too popular in the Navy, partly because of his failure to give adequate credit to the various distinguished officers who served under him.

As a proof that Richard Earl Howe was a popular public figure in his day, in addition to the Dunkarton engraving his portrait appeared in *The Pocket Magazine* in October 1794 in an engraving by G.Murray after a drawing by M.Brown. In the following April 1795 another portrait engraved by Orme was published in *The European Magazine and London Review.*

Admiral Howe c.1795

An engraving by R.Dunkarton after John Singleton Copley's portrait of Admiral Howe 1794. *National Portrait Gallery, London.*

Robert Dunkarton was born in London in 1774. He studied under the engraver William Pether. His mezzotints date from 1770 to 1811, the year in which he died.

Jasper ware portrait medallion of Sir John Jervis, First Earl of St Vincent 1798

This portrait modelled by John de Vaere is obviously the forerunner of the underglaze coloured plaque. *Reproduced by courtesy of the Trustees of the British Museum. 1909 12-1 152.*

There is a similar cameo portrait of the Admiral impressed ADAMS in the Schreiber Collection at the Victoria and Albert Museum *II 555.*

Admiral Sir John Jervis, a renowned disciplinarian, was Commander-in-Chief in the Mediterranean when he defeated the Spaniards off Cape St Vincent in 1797. He was created Earl St Vincent in the same year. Nelson served under Jervis and in 1798 was dispatched by his Commander to Aboukir, resulting in Nelson's great victory at the battle of the Nile.

Jervis was a Staffordshire man, born at Meadford a mile or so from the potteries on January 16th 1735, so he enjoyed considerable local popularity, which accounts for the many versions of the Jervis jug. He died in 1823. The jug was made in a white stoneware body with a smear glaze of the Castleford type and also in a porcelain body (the only Pratt type jug that we have seen made of porcelain see page 152).

A smaller version of this jug 128mm high with rather stronger colouring than the one illustrated over the page is in the Victoria and Albert Museum *C443.1940,* and another in the Royal Pavilion Art Gallery and Museum, Brighton. *HW 195.*

A particularly brilliantly coloured version is in the City Museum and Art Gallery, Manchester *1947.616* and a crudely painted version where the Admiral's name is spelt GARVILLE is in the Merseyside County Museum *2376 M.* Another version 188mm high can be seen at the Castle Museum, Norwich *158.23.18* where the spelling is LORD GARVIS and is placed on a scroll above the Admiral's knees. In this jug the lower border is uncoloured.

John Jervis, Earl of St Vincent, K.B.

An engraving by J.Cochran after the painting by J.Keenan. *Private Collection.*

John Jervis, Earl of St Vincent plaque c.1798

A small, fully modelled pearlware plaque, framed with a translucent yellow border, showing the Admiral in blue naval uniform with ochre epaulettes. His elaborately dressed hair *en queue* is coloured a greeny-grey, the same colour as the rosettes at the corners. Made after the defeat of the Spaniards off Cape St Vincent in 1797. 89mm high. *Private Collection.*

This portrait is after the Wedgwood jasper ware medallion, modelled by John de Vaere in 1798.

151

32. Admiral Jervis jug c.1798

This creamware jug has a three-quarter length relief portrait of the Admiral, dressed in ochre tunic with a blue cloak and breeches and a black hat. He holds a speaking trumpet in his right hand, and is flanked by two naval vessels and the faces of two dolphins. Above the Admiral's head is a border of gun barrels and ramrods in blue and orange. The Admiral's name and title spelt 'LORD JARVIS' appears on two scrolls on either side of him. The design appears on both sides of the jug, but the name and scrolls are omitted from the verso. The top of the neck of the jug is green banded and decorated with a border of pendant narrow pointed leaves, coloured alternately in green and yellow. A similar border appears around the lower part of the jug. The spout has a blue feathered edge where it joins the body and the plain loop handle is enriched with a blue outlined acanthus leaf. 153mm high. *Private Collection.*

33. Admiral Garvis (sic) jug c.1798

Pratt type jug in porcelain. The glaze is a marked greenish colour, which suggests it might have been made in Liverpool. *Private Collection.*

If this is so, our dates are wrong by three years, for the Herculaneum Pottery only began making porcelain in 1801. There is a similar porcelain jug in the Sheffield City Museum, Weston Park.

152

Lord Jervis jug c.1798

A larger, pearlware version of the Jervis jug coloured mainly in blue and a dark orange with manganese brown and a few touches of mossy green in the sea. The Admiral has a brown hat, dark orange breeches and a blue tunic over which he is wearing a white cloak. On one side only there are small scrolls on either side of his head bearing the words in relief 'LORD' and 'JARVIS' (*sic*).

The handle is of an upswept scroll type with a thumb-rest and is decorated with brown pencilled strokes. The jug is brown banded top and bottom and there are brown flecks on either side of the spout in place of the usual feather edges. 190mm high. *Private Collection.*

There is also a version of this jug in white smear-glazed stoneware where 'Lord Garvis' (*sic*) is lettered on a scroll in front of his legs. It is decorated with a little pale green on the leaf border and banded in dark blue in the Castleford manner. 115mm high.

There is an unusual Admiral 'Garvis' jug with a portrait of Admiral Duncan on the other side, coloured only in green, blue and manganese in the National Maritime Museum, London.

Admiral Nelson and Captain Berry jugs c.1798 and c.1905
These must be the most common of all the underglaze coloured
relief decorated commemorative jugs and are to be found with
both cream and pearlware bodies. They were made in at least
three sizes. The one on the right may be one of the Leeds
Pottery jugs reissued by W.W. Slee and made by the Seniors
(see page 68), from the end of the nineteenth century.

The profile bust of the Admiral is shown usually wearing a
blue uniform and a black cockaded hat trimmed with yellow. A
similar portrait of Captain Berry is on the other side of the jug,
both portraits flanked by ships of the line. Apart from blue or
brown lines round the top and sometimes the foot, these jugs are
decorated with only a simple border of upside-down fleurs-de-
lis, sometimes picked out in colour below the top rim. Round
the neck of the jug the names of Nelson and Berry are moulded
in relief, sometimes accentuated by the application of brown or
black painting over the lettering. 160mm high. The two other
sizes are 191mm and 127mm high. *Private Collection.*

A version of this jug is in the Willett Collection at the Royal
Pavilion Art Gallery and Museum, Brighton *HW 207.* Another
one can be seen in the Victoria and Albert Museum *3632.1901.*
A larger version, showing a longer bust is in the Dover Museum
0.417 (197mm high). Other examples can be seen in the City
Museum and Art Gallery, Stoke-on-Trent, and in the Nelson
Museum at Monmouth. There are also examples in the Abbey
Museum, Kirkstall, which houses a mould from which they
could have been pressed.

Lord Nelson was featured by many potters, not only on jugs and
mugs but on cameo portrait medallions and in the form of busts
and standing figures. In Pratt ware he appeared in relief on jugs,
mugs, flasks and plaques; he was also shown as a head mug and
as the bowl of a pipe. Such details of his career that we give here
may be a help in dating the various pieces.

In July 1797, in attempting to take a treasure ship at Santa
Cruz Horatio Nelson (1758-1805) lost his right arm. (This loss is
an aid to dating some of the Nelson jugs and plaques). On
August 1st 1798 he won a great victory over the French at
Aboukir Bay and was created Baron Nelson of the Nile. In 1799,
after subduing the Neapolitan Jacobins, Nelson was made Duke
of Bronté, he was created Viscount Nelson in 1801 and
promoted Vice-Admiral. On October 21st 1805, off Cape
Trafalgar he was shot by a musketeer from the French ship
Redoubtable and lived just long enough to hear the conclusion of
his most famous victory.

Captain Edward Berry (1768-1831) who served with Nelson
between 1796 and 1805, was Nelson's First Lieutenant in *The
Captain,* after Nelson had left the 74-gun *Agamemnon* in 1796. In
1797 Nelson referred to Berry as 'my right hand' when at a levée
at St James's Palace the king commiserated with him for the loss
of his right arm. In 1798 Berry was Nelson's Flag Captain at the
battle of the Nile. Berry conveyed the news of the great victory to
England where he was knighted on December 12th, 1798. He
continued to serve with the Admiral until Nelson's death, being
his Flag Captain at Trafalgar. Nelson, in his Norfolk accent,
always referred to Berry as 'Sir Ed'ard'. Berry later became a
Rear Admiral.

Admiral Nelson and Captain Hardy jug c.1805 or c.1905

This adaptation of the Nelson and Berry jug was probably made after the Admiral's death at Trafalgar (or a hundred years later). The portrait of Captain Hardy is identical to the portrait of Captain Berry. The lettering is somewhat clumsily painted and the painting is altogether crude. The mould from which the jug was taken was very worn, the top relief border being almost non-existent. Doubtless there was considerable demand for this jug after the Admiral's death, or it may have been made to celebrate the centenary of the event. 160mm high. *From the Collection of the Laing Art Gallery. Reproduced by permission of Tyne and Wear County Council Museums. E.2429.*

Sir Thomas Masterman Hardy was an old messmate and friend of Nelson's and an officer in whom he had complete confidence. Hardy had been taken prisoner in 1796, but had escaped and was back in service by the time of the battle of Cape St Vincent (February 14th 1797). Nelson put him in command of *Vanguard* following Berry's departure for England after the battle of the Nile. He was serving in the *Victory* at Trafalgar when Nelson was killed. In 1806 he was created baronet and towards the end of his life he was made Governor of Greenwich Hospital. He died in 1837. There is another version of this jug in the National Maritime Museum, London and another in the Nelson Museum at Monmouth.

A version with Captain Collingwood's name painted over Berry's is in the National Maritime Museum, London *W.222.2.*

Nelson pipe c.1802

A most idiosyncratic pipe with the Admiral's coat and hat in white, the latter tall as a bishop's mitre and serving as the bowl. On the front and back of the hat are the words 'Nelson' and 'Forever' on scrolls, also on the front are clasped hands (the same little hands that are on the Nelson celebration jug on page 161). His hair is a greenish brown and his uniform is trimmed with brown. The stem is looped and decorated with a green leaf behind the inside curl of the pipe stem, which is decorated with floral sprigs in orange and brown. The mouthpiece is ochre coloured. 245mm long. *National Maritime Museum, London. W.129.*

In the same museum is another version of this pipe, differing only in the colouring. The hat is ochre coloured, the Admiral wears a blue uniform and the stem is dotted all over with blue and brown. *SS 362.*

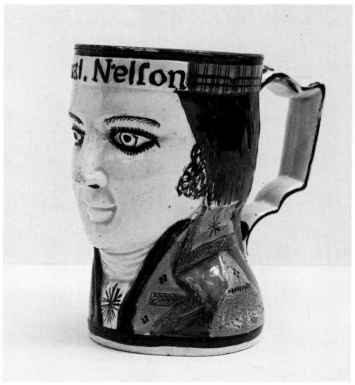

Admiral Lord Nelson mug c.1799 *two views*
Mug in the form of Nelson's head with brown hair drawn back to a *queue* at the back, at the base of the handle. He is wearing an ochre uniform with yellow epaulettes and other details. The handle is decorated with a chain of ochre star-like flowers with brown stalks. The lettering round the top is in dark brown. Underneath the base the initials 'A G' are pencilled in brown. 109mm high. *Courtesy Elias Clark.*

Admiral Lord Nelson mug c.1799
Mug moulded in the form of the Admiral's head, similar to the Rodney mug, but like the one above, lettered ADMIRAL NELSON round the top in relief lettering. There are ochre blotches on the cheeks and he wears an ochre coloured uniform with a dark blue collar. 117mm high. *National Maritime Museum, London.*

Another similar mug can be seen in the City Museum and Art Gallery, Stoke-on-Trent; and another version of this mug, 127mm high, is in the Royal Pavilion Art Gallery and Museum, Brighton *HW 208.*

Nelson was promoted to Rear-Admiral after the battle of St Vincent and raised to the peerage in November 1798.

Nelson plaques c.1798 *opposite page*
A small oval plaque with a full length standing portrait of Lord Nelson wearing an orange coloured uniform jacket with the right sleeve empty, and blue trousers. Set within a moulded yellow and blue-ringed frame. The whole is rather crudely painted. 86mm high. *National Maritime Museum, London. SS 3171.* This is flanked by two glass paste plaques of the Admiral. One of these shows him with a cutlass in his right hand and the other with an empty right sleeve. In both cases he holds a trumpet, a symbol of victory, in his left hand. 65mm high. *National Maritime Museum, London. WB 2 & WB 3.*

Admiral Nelson jug c.1800
This elegant, small pearlware jug has a scroll handle with slight blue decoration. The full-length figure of the Admiral shown without his right arm, is seen standing in front of naval trophies, wearing a blue uniform coat and a black hat trimmed with yellow. On either side of the figure is a branch of laurel in green and ochre and beside that a ship of the line with pennants flying; the same design is repeated on the other side of the jug.

There is a narrow brown band round the top of the jug below which is a border of draped and tasselled material on which rest pairs of doves, picked out in ochre and blue. Below this is another brown band and then an uncoloured border of demi-florets. The same design of florets, only interspersed with an upright fern-like leaf is repeated round the foot of the jug above a narrow brown band. The colouring is sparsely but effectively carried out. 130mm high. *Private Collection*. A larger version of this jug (191mm high) can be seen in the National Maritime Museum, London *SS 153*.

Engraving of Admiral Lord Nelson 1799
Engraving by William Barnard (1774-1849) published in 1799 of Lemuel Abbott's three-quarter length portrait of Admiral Nelson. *National Portrait Gallery*.

Barnard was a mezzotint engraver who was Keeper of the British Institution. Lemuel Abbott (1760-1803) whose fame mainly rests on his portraits of Nelson, studied under Frank Hayman.

The engraving after a painting by Lemuel Abbott, shows the Admiral without a hat standing in a comparable position with his hand resting on a sword. Abbott also painted a three-quarter length portrait with the Admiral wearing a hat, his head and shoulders in just the position shown on the jug.

HMS Victory plaque c.1805

This small plaque, a companion to the Trafalgar Memento plaque, shows a man-of-war under sail, as seen from the starboard quarter. This cannot be taken as an accurate representation of the *Victory*, but the same ship is to be found on various jugs and flasks of the period, clearly taken from the same source. The plaque is coloured with orange, yellow and manganese only and is set within a beaded frame. 101mm high. *National Maritime Museum, London. W 14.*

Transfer printed and underglaze coloured relief decorated flask c.1800

A flask decorated with an underglaze blue transfer design of flowers, in the centre of each side is a standing figure of Admiral Nelson, sprigged on in relief and decorated with ochre, yellow, blue and black. The same figure appears on the jug opposite. Under the foot of the flask are the initials D R pencilled in blue in a fat face italic. These are probably the initials of the recipient (for it looks like a 'gift' or a tourist trophy) and have nothing to do with the maker, who remains anonymous. 210mm high. *Crown Copyright, Victoria and Albert Museum. 3633.1901.*

Trafalgar Memento plaque 1805

This oval plaque, commemorating the battle of Trafalgar, is a design that also appears on a black basaltes cream jug. It shows a pyramid and a crocodile, presumably symbolising the battle of the Nile, a fort representing the battle of Copenhagen and the word 'Trafalgar' on a blue scroll. There is also a shield and a cannon and two crossed flags reversed in sign of mourning. The whole design is set within a double-beaded border, palely coloured in green, yellow and blue. 102mm wide. *National Maritime Museum, London. L7 (71).*

Nelson celebration jug c.1802

A very handsome large jug decorated with the standing figure of the Admiral below the spout, with the word 'NELSON' lettered above his head; on one side is a tableau of the standing figure of Britannia, wearing a blue robe and flanked by a hussar and a foot soldier. There is a lion at Britannia's feet and uncoloured clasped hands above her head. On the verso is the stern view of a man-of-war under sail, the same that appears on a small plaque. On either side of the neck of the jug is a group of trophies of war, including crossed cannon, a drum, flags, etc. Below the neck and on the lower part of the jug are borders of leaves with green edges and orange veins, with uncoloured acanthus leaves surrounding the foot.

The jug is coloured in green, blue, manganese brown, ochre and yellow. 220mm high. *National Maritime Museum, London. L17 (2).*

In the same museum there is another jug of this size, with similar decoration but lacking the trophies on the neck and the word 'NELSON' on the front (see page 160). Also in the National Maritime Museum there is a small version of this jug only 127mm high. *L.16 (59).*

There is a small jug in the Nelson Museum at Monmouth decorated with green relief acanthus pattern, with orange and brown bands round the rim and foot. This jug is lettered

AD,L

LORD, NELSON

A pair of plaques, one showing a bust of Nelson and the other Lady Hamilton wearing a feathered head dress and a green décolleté dress, were sold at Sotheby's on October 13th 1969. Both plaques have moulded borders coloured with green and ochre. 267mm high.

Nelson Celebration jug c.1802
Another version of this jug, lacking the trophies on the neck. *National Maritime Museum, London.*

Turner mould c.1790
A master pitcher mould of Britannia flanked by a cavalryman and an infantryman and with a lion at her feet. Impressed TURNER on the front and incised *N.1.* 80mm high. *Courtesy Spode Museum, Stoke-on-Trent. TMMS/S.*

34. Nelson Celebration jug c.1802
The side showing Britannia, of the jug illustrated on page 159.
220mm high. *National Maritime Museum, London. L.17 (2).*

Men-of-War jug c.1800
A jug of slightly unusual shape, with an upswept handle the point terminating in a hound's head. The main decoration consists of three men-of-war in line astern, outlined in black and with orange sails, under a blue rococo cloud. There is a rich border round the neck, of vine leaves and grapes with brown festooning stems and small ochre fronds round the top, with blue bands round the head and foot of the jug and down the edges of the handle. On the other side is a Bacchanalian scene of cherubs cavorting with a goat (see page 201). 116mm high. *Wakefield Art Gallery and Museums. 167.*

'Jemmy's Return'
An engraving by Robert Sayer, published in 1786, was accompanied by a set of verses called 'Jemmy's Return'. This illustration shows a weeping lass who had been wedded to another but four weeks before her lover's return.

The sailor and his lass, flanked by a three-masted ship and a ketch with verses beneath from *The Song of Auld Robin Gray,* are to be found on a transfer-printed creamware teapot marked WEDGWOOD & CO which was made at Ferrybridge between 1798 and 1804. This is in the Yorkshire Museum.

The Sailor's Return and Farewell plaques c.1790
A pair of oval plaques with piecrust borders, showing these familiar scenes. 159mm high. *Courtesy Sotheby's.*

The Sailor's Return and Farewell jug c.1790

The largest and smallest jugs of a very handsome set, octagonal in shape particularly well made and crisply moulded, with a markedly bluish glaze. Of the colours used in the decoration the blue is very dark in tone, the orange and yellow rather opaque, the green is distinctly greyish and the manganese pale. The familiar scenes of the departing sailor and his lass waving goodbye with his ship in the background and the returning sailor consoling his girl who has wed another in his absence are enclosed in oval medallions with beaded borders, so crisp that they might have been sprigged on, but are in fact moulded. The beads are alternately blue and orange. The background behind the figures has an orange-peel texture. Round the foot of the jug is an upstanding border of oak leaves in relief with alternate ovals of ochre and green painted over their edges. A brown band encircles both the feet and top of the jug. Below this top rim is a repeat pattern of ears of corn interspersed with narrow pointed green leaves. The square-topped chamfered handle is secured to the jug with a simulated riveted strap and a blue bell and dot motif occupies the centre strip of the handle. Below the spout is a bunch of freehand flowers and leaves, precisely painted in ochre, blue and green. 180mm high. (The smallest jug in the set is only 123mm high.) *Private Collection.*

The Sailor's Return and Farewell jug c.1800

This large jug has similar scenes to those shown on the jugs above, but they are not enclosed in any kind of border. It is obviously from a rather worn mould. The colours used are green, brown, orange-yellow and blue. The jug is actually made of a red bodied clay covered with a white slip (revealed by a chip on the foot). This is the only Pratt type jug we have come across made with this sort of body, though the example of the same jug in the Merseyside County Museum and Art Gallery is made of a buffish clay covered with a white slip. 186mm high. *Royal Ontario Museum, Toronto, Canada. 910.104.2.*

Similar jugs are in the Victoria and Albert Museum *C.64.1952*, the Royal Pavilion Art Gallery and Museum, Brighton *HW 292*, and in the Merseyside County Museums *M.2375.*

The design also appears on a white stoneware body, on a jug in the Yorkshire Museum, coloured blue on the neck with blue bands and green lines.

Contemporary prints of this popular subject had appeared for many years in the street literature of the day.

163

General Eliott flask c.1786

This must be one of the earliest commemorative pieces to be decorated with underglaze colour. It is made of a somewhat rough, almost stoneware body and the portrait is in quite high relief. The painted decoration merely consists of flecks of blue, ochre and yellow on the background. 160mm high. *Courtesy John May.*

General Sir George Augustus Eliott (1717-90) became famous as the gallant defender of Gibraltar in the siege of the Rock by the Spanish which lasted from July 1779 to February 6th 1783. The defence was brilliantly carried out by General Eliott, culminating in the repulse of a massive attack and the annihilation of the heavily armoured gunships moored within half a gunshot of the walls. This was achieved by Eliott's use of red hot shot. By noon on September 14th, every ship had been blown up or burnt to the water-line. Before Christmas Lord Howe had won a great victory at sea over the superior forces of the Spaniards and Gibraltar was relieved. In 1783 Eliott was made a K.B. and in 1787 was created Baron Heathfield of Gibraltar.

General Eliott portrait engraving 1786

This line engraving was published by S.W.Fores at the Caracature (sic) Ware House No.3 Piccadilly, London. A Wedgwood jasper medallion of General Eliott said to be adapted from a drawing by G.F.Koehler and engraved by W.Angus had been issued in the previous year. Clearly this line engraving shown here was also after Koehler's drawing. *National Portrait Gallery, London.*

Military Review jug c.1790-1800 *two views opposite*

A jug with the horsemen in different positions. One is galloping with his sword raised and pointing backwards in the 'cut two against the infantry' position which is illustrated in *Rules and Regulations for the Sword Exercises of the Cavalry*, London, 1796. In the background is an encampament and the much smaller figure of a cavalry officer with his sword held upright, sits firmly in his saddle as his horse rears up on its hind legs. On the other side of the jug is the mounted figure of the Duke of York. This jug has no colouring on the neck or lower part, which are both decorated in relief with stiff or curved acanthus leaves. These two jugs are similar in style and modelling to the Prince Coburg-Duke of York jugs, both have double scroll handles, attached to the top by a circular pad with a scalloped edge. 159mm high. *Private Collection.*

'Sword Exercise Cut I'
Engraved by John Scott after Samuel Howitt. From *The Sporting Magazine*, June 1799. *By permission of the British Library.*

The designs on these Military Review jugs seem to have been based on a set of six engravings by John Scott after paintings by Samuel Howitt, titled 'Sword Exercises for the Cavalry', which first appeared in *The Sporting Magazine*. In November 1799 they were advertised to be published separately as a set '2/6d plain or 3/6d coloured, Six Highly Esteemed Engravings', to be sold by J.Wheble, bookseller, 18 Warwick Square, St Paul's, London. John Scott was employed by the engraver and printseller Robert Pollard. He worked for various contemporary magazines.

Military Review jug c.1790-1800 *two views*

On one side a cavalry officer, wearing the cocked hat of the Horse Guards, rides between two oak trees with his sword held upright. On the other side the horse rears up on its hind legs as the rider points his sword forward. In the background a flag waves over an encampment and another much smaller figure of a cavalry officer on a white horse gallops in the opposite direction. There is an uncoloured relief repeat pattern of oak leaves and acorns under the top rim of the jug and above the equestrian figure there is a relief pattern of gun barrels and ramrods. The bottom part of the jug is uncoloured and has a relief decoration of encircling bull rushes. 159mm high. *Private Collection.*

A similar jug 178mm high can be seen in the Royal Pavilion Art Gallery and Museums, Brighton. *HW 245.*

The Duke of Cumberland jug c.1796

This jug is decorated with a spirited relief portrait of the mounted figure of William Augustus, Duke of Cumberland (1721-65), son of George II. The Duke, sword in hand and wearing a blue uniform is seated on a white horse prancing over a green sward with trees in the background. The top of the jug is finished with a feather-edged scalloped border and there is a band of acanthus leaves round the top of the body of the jug. The lower part is decorated with upright stiff green leaves. The handle is in the form of a snake with a dolphin's head. On the other side of the jug is a mythical scene of Hercules slaying the Hydra. 153mm high. *Courtesy Beaumont Varcoe Collection.*

There are numerous equestrian paintings and engravings on which this design might have been based. George Stubbs painted the Duke reining in his horse, and B.Green made an engraving of the painting. The nearest resemblances to the prancing horses were a painting by D.Morier and an engraving by J.E.Ridinger. A mug of the same design is in the Willett Collection at the Royal Pavilion Art Gallery and Museum, Brighton.

'Butcher' Cumberland, as he came to be called, achieved fame and notoriety after the 1745 rebellion, because of his brutal treatment of the Highlanders at Culloden in 1746. It is possible that this jug was made to commemorate the fiftieth anniversary of the battle.

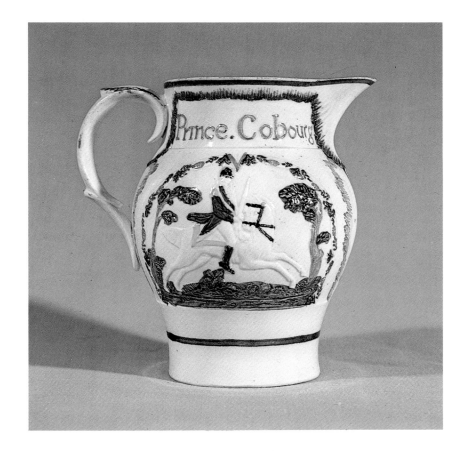

35. Prince Coburg and Duke of York jug 1793
The other side of the jug shown at the bottom of page 168. *Private Collection.*

36. Military Review jug 1790-1800
This jug differs from the other military review jugs in having two extra figures standing by a gun with a ladder. It is difficult to decide what they are intended to represent. The border round the bottom is very colourfully painted in bright orange, blue and yellow, the top border is green and yellow. 230mm high. *Courtesy G.F. Arnold.*

HIS ROYAL HIGHNESS FREDERICK DUKE OF YORK
Commander in Chief of the British Forces on the Continent.

Published Sep 20th 1794, by John Fairburn, No 146 Minories London

Equestrian portrait of the Duke of York
An engraving by John Fairburn and published by him in 1794 from 146 Minories, London. *National Portrait Gallery, London.*

Duke of York circular spirit flask c.1795-1800
The flask is decorated with a relief picture of the Duke of York, mounted on a prancing white charger with a flowing brown tail. He wears a blue coat and yellow breeches and his hair, hat, horse's hooves and bridle are all picked out in manganese. The trees in the background are ochre and green. 125mm high. *Crown Copyright, Victoria and Albert Museum. C.44.1967.*

Duke of York and Prince Coburg jug 1794
A pearlware jug with mounted equestrian figures of the Duke of York on one side and Prince Coburg on the other. Each figure is set within an arch of floral forms. Both riders are wearing blue tunics and are galloping over dark green grass with trees in the background. The jug is banded with dark blue lines at rim and near the foot. Below the top band and under the spout and handle is a line of blue feather-edging and under that are the names of the generals in raised lettering coloured orange. There is an acanthus motif outlined in orange below the spout and the double scrolled handle. 146mm high. *Private Collection.*

A pearlware version of this jug with a very blue glaze is in the Victoria and Albert Museum 146mm high *C.66.1952.* Another version, pressed from a well-worn mould and crudely painted, the names inexpertly pencilled on letters that are barely in relief, 181mm high is in the Museum and Art Gallery, Glasgow. *38.10js.*

The portrait of the Duke is probably taken from a mezzotint by an unknown artist, published by John Fairburn. A smaller etching of the same subject also exists.

From 1793 to 1795 Frederick Augustus, Duke of York and Albany (1763-1827), second son of George III, commanded the British in Flanders. His contingent of 10,000 men was part of the army of Prince Josias of Saxe-Coburg. The Duke of York's popularity was due, not only to his ability as a soldier, though he did much for the army, but to the fact that he was a keen sportsman and was reputed to be a very amiable man and as compassionate a victor as was his commander.

The Duke of York and Prince Coburg jugs were probably made to celebrate the victorious campaigns of 1793. There was less to celebrate the following year, when Prince Coburg, after the Austrian reverse at Fleurus, decided to evacuate the Netherlands and the Duke of York's troops fell back and embarked for home.

168

Loyal Volunteers jug c.1803

A cream coloured earthenware jug with L^{L}VOL^{N}TEERS, lettered on both sides. Three soldiers wearing fur-crested helmets and presenting arms stand or kneel on one side of the jug and three soldiers with their arms in the firing position decorate the other side. There is an uncoloured acanthus border round the base of the jug and a band of stiff pendant narrow leaves enrich the neck above the lettering, these are coloured ochre and green. The top rim and the bottom of the jug are brown banded and a brown edged acanthus design is placed beneath the handle and under the spout. The handle is a plain loop with an acanthus moulding at the top. 155mm high. *Private Collection.*

This jug reflects the enthusiasm for the Volunteer forces, which in 1794 had been raised to counter threats of invasion. At the Peace of Amiens in 1802 the 340,000 Volunteers then serving were disbanded, but when the renewal of war in the following year seemed likely, they were recalled. Enoch Wood was connected with the formation of the Burslem Volunteers in 1798 and again at the time of their recall in 1803.

In 1803 an Act of Parliament was passed enabling His Majesty to call out anyone fit to bear arms. However the spontaneous enthusiasm of the populace anticipated the Act and a compulsory call-up was rendered unnecessary by the fact that half-a-million men volunteered. In the Potteries, a force of 1,400 men was raised under the banners of the Lane End Volunteers, commanded by Major William Turner, the Longport Volunteers, including the Tunstall and Burslem levies and the

Hanley and Shelton Volunteers, including the Stoke, Penkhull and Fenton Volunteers.

In 1808 the Volunteer forces were replaced by the much stricter, better disciplined Local Militia. This indicates that the jug must have been produced between 1794 and 1808, and most likely in 1803. Presumably the abbreviation L^L stands for Loyal. It has been referred to by some authorities as the 'Liverpool Loyal', 'Leek Loyal', and 'Leeds Loyal'.

A similar jug was marked LEEDS POTTERY impressed on the base, which perhaps gives some credence to the 'Leeds Loyal' attribution. The other side of the jug is illustrated with its mould on pages 28 and 29 and a version of it is also shown in the page from W.W.Slee's catalogue c.1913-18 on page 67.

A pair of Loyal Volunteers c.1800

Two figures, one representing a Foot Volunteer with a musket at his side and the other a Horse Volunteer with a cutlass. They are dressed in orange tunics edged with blue, cross banded with yellow straps; yellow breeches, manganese brown fur-crested helmets and brown boots. They are mounted on uncoloured circular bases with a thin blue line top and bottom enclosing a rouletted border and an incised Greek key pattern. 229mm high. *The Royal Pavilion Art Gallery and Museums, Brighton. HW232 & a.*

There is a smaller figure of a Volunteer in the same museum 152mm high *HW 233.* Another of the larger figures can be seen in the Harris Museum and Art Gallery, Preston.

37. Capture of the cannon plaque 1795
The same scene as on the jug on the opposite page, of a hussar mounted on a white horse jumping over a field gun, with the gun crew scattered in disarray. Coloured rather sparingly with a manganese feather-edged border. 157mm diam. *Courtesy Earle D. Vandekar.*

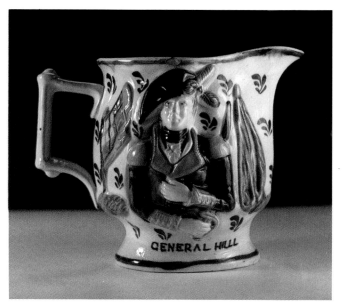

38. Lord Wellington and General Hill jug c.1810
The side of the Wellington and Hill jug showing the portrait of General Hill. 120mm high. *The Royal Pavilion Art Gallery and Museums, Brighton. HW 138.*

Capture of the cannon jug 1795

This pearl ware jug is decorated on both sides with the same scene, showing a hussar wearing a cylindrical white hat with a plume, his horse leaping over a field gun, with the gun crew scattered in disarray. There are brown bands at the top and bottom of the jug, below the top band there is a border of pendant stiff green leaves and round the foot a border of smaller uncoloured leaves. The plain loop handle has an acanthus leaf motif under the top part where it joins the body and the spout is outlined with blue feather-edging. 143mm high. *Private Collection.*

This jug is sometimes referred to by Scottish authorities as the 'Prestonpans' jug. This seems a little far-fetched as that battle was fought some seventy years before.

A very crude version of this jug can be seen in the Victoria and Albert Museum *C73.1952.* There is also a larger version 197mm high in the Pavilion Art Gallery and Museums, Brighton. *HW 246.*

There is a somewhat similar jug in America with identical scenes, inscribed THOMAS Thorley 1795.

Lord Wellington and General Hill jug c.1810

A very fully modelled jug with relief portraits of Lord Wellington on one side and General Hill on the other, with their names and titles impressed below the portraits. Versions of this jug are often seen in overglaze enamel colours. The jug is noteworthy for the strength of the modelling, which is in greater depth than on any other Pratt jug that we have seen. 120mm high. *Private Collection.*

Lord Wellington and General Hill jug c.1810

A similar jug from the same mould attractively painted in blue, yellow, green and black with little manganese brown leaf sprays scattered over the body of the jug. *The Royal Pavilion Art Gallery and Museums, Brighton. HW 138.*

The reverse side of the jug shown opposite is from the same mould as the other one illustrated on this page. It is attractively painted.

Wellington was created Viscount Wellington in 1809 and was not elevated to the Dukedom until 1814, so this jug was almost certainly made between those dates. General Rowland Hill was, with Wellington, one of the two most popular soldiers in the Army. He was much loved by his troops, and this gained him the title of 'the soldiers' friend'. Lord Hill (he was created Baron Hill in 1814) fought in many engagements and with much distinction. At Waterloo he led the famous charge of Sir Frederick Adam's brigade, against the Imperial Guard. In 1842 he was made a Viscount and died the same year.

Waterloo jug c.1815
The decoration shows a cavalry officer waving his sabre and reining in his horse, set beneath a tent like canopy. On the other side is a group of trophies of war. On the front of the jug under the spout the initial W N and the date 1815 are pencilled. 162mm high. *City Museum and Art Gallery, Stoke-on-Trent. 2345.*

The horseman is sometimes referred to as the Duke of Wellington, though on a smaller, lustre and enamel coloured version in the Burnap Collection of English Pottery in the William Rockhill Nelson Gallery in the Atkins Museum, Kansas City Missouri, he is described as George III and the initials G.R. on the jug substantiate this.

Military figure c.1800-20
A most unusual figure, over a foot high, of an officer, possibly a light dragoon, wearing a blue uniform jacket with ochre facings, epaulettes and star. His helmet is black and ochre, his breeches and sash are white and he is wearing black boots. His eyebrows are dotted in the same manner as on the Toby jug on page 84 and the colours are of the same rich intensity, so it is possible that it was made at the same pottery. The figure is mounted on a stepped square base, moulded in relief with a border of uncoloured stiff leaves, and edged with blue. 367mm high. *Courtesy Jonathan Horne.* This figure has recently been acquired by the Museum and Art Gallery, Doncaster.

11. Sporting and rustic jugs, mugs and plaques

By far the largest group of Pratt pieces are those with non-commemorative subjects. These include a great many decorated with sporting scenes and pictures of rural life of the time. Towards the end of the eighteenth century there was a growing interest in sporting subjects; to cater for this taste *The Sporting Magazine or Monthly Calendar of the Transactions of the Turf, Chace (sic) and every other Diversion interesting to the Man of Pleasure and Enterprise* was first published in 1792. It remained virtually unchanged until 1831 when it became *The New Sporting Magazine.* The sports and pastimes it publicised are often very distasteful to our present day sensibilities. Bull, bear and badger baiting, cockfighting and all the more usual activities of fox, hare and stag hunting, as well as horse racing were all illustrated. These engravings provided the potters with a ready-made gallery of subjects with which to decorate jugs, mugs and tea-caddies.

On most occasions the mould maker used engravings from the popular magazines as pictorial references, just as an illustrator today might work. From sporting prints after the paintings of such artists as Samuel Howitt, Corbould and Sartorius, or even little wood cuts by the Bewicks, they would take a dog from one, a horse from another and perhaps landscape details from a third, and with these elements they would compose their scenes.

In addition to racecourse and hunting scenes, groups of musicians, men drinking, couples eloping to Gretna Green, and placid scenes of cows in farmyards (no doubt made to embellish the walls of dairies) were all made with underglaze colouring. Rural landscapes with peacocks and birds feeding their nestlings are also common subjects. A design of children playing, dating from at least as early as 1795 must have been extremely popular for it is to be found on all manner of objects including jugs, mugs, teapots and tea-caddies, bowls plaques and spirit flasks (see page 188).

Woodcut decoration
Racing cut used as a chapter heading and on the cover of *The Sporting Magazine* in 1793, drawn and engraved by John Bewick, the younger brother of the great engraver Thomas Bewick of Newcastle. *Private Collection.*

Stag hunting jug c.1800
Three views of the jug showing its crisply moulded frieze of the hunting scene, coloured in yellow, ochre and brown. Round the neck is a broad border of yellow acorns with green leaves and brown stems. The base of the jug below the figures is moulded with uncoloured basketwork. The rim and the handle are edged with brown. 161mm high. *Wolverhampton Museum and Art Gallery. E 106.*

Hunting jug c.1820
A small jug with a hunting scene of dogs chasing a stag, a horse being led by its rider with a dead stag at his feet. The neck is decorated with an unusual vine border and there is a painted floral pattern on the upswept loop handle. Painted in the usual underglaze palette. 122mm high. *The Nelson-Atkins Museum of Art, (Burnap Collection) B626 (BI.899). Kansas City, Missouri.*

Modern jasper ware border design
This acorn and oakleaf border decoration was originally designed for use on Wedgwood jasper ware. It was probably the inspiration for the border on the stag hunting jug. This design is still in use on Wedgwood jasper ware today. *Courtesy Josiah Wedgwood and Sons Limited, Barlaston, Stoke-on-Trent.*

Shooting jug c.1828

A white full-bodied, rather squat shaped jug with relief scenes of boys holding guns with dogs and game. The neck is decorated with a trailing vine pattern in blue and green. The lower part of the jug is moulded in relief but uncoloured. 191mm high. *The Nelson-Atkins Museum of Art, (Burnap Collection) B.638 (BI 898) Kansas City, Missouri.* In the same museum there is a similar jug with lustre decoration and overglaze enamel coloured.

Shooting jug 1828

A similar jug to that described above, but with the following inscription lettered on it:

ELIZA GATTY / AGED 86
SAMUEL GATTY / AGED 88
1828 / CORBY / LINCOLNSHIRE

Inside the jug there is a large brown frog. 165mm high. *The Nelson-Atkins Museum of Art (Burnap Collection) B.633 (BI 900) Kansas City, Missouri.*

175

39. Sporting jug c.1795
This very large jug is a finely potted example of Pratt ware, from a fairly new mould, showing the typical underglaze palette, with classical borders of acanthus leaves and hyacinth bells. The moulded handle is unusually elaborate. 210mm high. *Private Collection*. (See page 183 for the other side.)

Horse Racing jug c.1800

The design shows two jockeys on galloping horses, one animal coloured brown, the other spotted with the same colour. On the other side (see page 33) the two horses are standing in the enclosure, one mounted, one awaiting saddling. Both scenes are set within an oval frame with a lozenge border. There is a stiff leaf border at the bottom and a border of pendant bunches of leaves set between triangles round the top of the neck, overpainted with orange and blue ovals. This is a crudely painted jug, pressed from a worn mould. The handle has been modelled as if it had been made in two separate parts held together with a simulated strap. 157mm high. *Courtesy Beaumont Varcoe Collection.*

Horse Racing jug c.1800

A larger version of the jockeys on galloping horses jug, showing rather a different style of painting. 178mm high. *Nelson-Atkins Museum (Burnap Collection) B.629 (BI 904). Kansas City, Missouri.*

Horse Racing jug c.1800

A nicely painted small jug with a simple loop handle is moulded with much the same design as those above. This jug has an almost similar foot rim to the jugs marked PRATT (see page 18). 140mm high. *The Royal Pavilion Art Gallery and Museums, Brighton. HW 1059.* There is a mug in the same museum with a similar design, 127mm high.

The horses in this design are almost identical to those in a small woodcut by John Bewick that appeared several times as a headpiece to 'The Racing Calendar' in issues of *The Sporting Magazine* during the 1790s.

40 & 41. Woodcock Shooting jug c.1795
On one side of this jug a man in a blue coat and yellow breeches holds his shot gun at the ready as he watches his pointer; on the verso the dog has put up a flight of brown birds and the man with his gun to his shoulder is firing at them. The neck of the jug is decorated with a border of oak leaves and acorns. The lower part of the jug has a border of un-coloured wide curved leaves with unserrated edges. The border has been adapted from jasper ware pieces marked ADAMS of the 1787-1805 period.

The double scroll handle of the jug is joined to the body at the top with a boss in the shape of an open flower. 153mm high. *Private Collection.*
The shooting scene has been copied from a painting 'Woodcock Shooting' by Samuel Howitt (1765-1822). This was later reproduced in 1807 by Daniel Orme, as one of a series of sporting prints.

Woodcock Shooting jug c.1795
A larger variant of this jug with spotted dogs in different attitudes, though the figures of the men are very similar in appearance and colour. There is an uncoloured border of curved acanthus leaves around the neck of the jug and a gilded band at the base where it joins the body just above an uncoloured border of small acanthus leaves. The lower part of the jug is decorated with large straight, stiff leaves, outlined in manganese brown. The same type of double scroll handle as the other Woodcock Shooting jug. 203mm high. *The Royal Pavilion Art Gallery and Museums, Brighton. HW 1084.*

Shooting and hunting jug c.1795
A sportsman with his gun pointed downwards is walking with three pointers; on the other side three huntsmen, one jumping over a four barred gate, are with a pack of hounds in pursuit of an orange fox which is moving up hill. There is an orange band top and bottom of this jug and below the top band is a small neat relief border of laurel leaves and fruit, uncoloured but for a green band running through the centre of it. The rosettes at the base of the neck are alternately coloured blue and yellow. 155mm high. *Private Collection.*

Sporting jug c.1795
The jug is decorated with men and hounds in a rural landscape with rocks and foliage. On one side a man is seated holding a dead hare in his lap and another man is shooting at a bird. The border round the top of the jug is of pendant green fern-like leaves. The plain loop handle terminates in a leaf shape. The colouring is pale green, blue and manganese very subtly combined. 148mm high. *Crown Copyright, Victoria and Albert Museum. C.214.1938.*

Coursing jug c.1795 *two views*

A full-bodied pearlware jug decorated on one side with a beater in a blue coat standing behind some green bushes, waving his hat and a stick to put up a hare; in the foreground two spotted greyhounds leap away in pursuit. On the other side, the chase is over. The huntsman is carrying the dead hare back to his waiting horse while two tired greyhounds limp slowly home.

The neck of the jug is decorated with a vine border in blue, black and green. The lower part of the jug is fluted and

uncoloured except for a blue band near the foot. A crudely outlined acanthus leaf below the spout and another below the plain loop handle have been gilded and there are the remains of a gilt band at the bottom of the neck. 153mm high. *Private Collection.*

A larger version, 190mm high is in the Royal Pavilion Art Gallery and Museum, Brighton. *HW 1153.*

Pointers jug c.1810

A rather clumsily shaped pearlware jug with a single fully modelled pointer on one side about to put up a partridge which is crouching under a bush. The dogs are spotted in brown and burnt orange and there is a wash of mossy green over the ground and on the ivy or hop border round the top of the jug. Round the rim there is a blue and orange repeat pip-shaped moulding. Beneath the spout there is a painted decoration of a star in blue, brown and green. There is a plain brown band about half an inch from the bottom of the jug. 140mm high. *Private Collection.*

There is also a smaller version of this jug 126mm high. A similar jug 140mm high is in the Nelson-Atkins Museum of Art, (Burnap Collection) *B.634 (BI 897),* Kansas City, Missouri.

Hunting jugs c.1795

Two versions of this large jug from the same mould show very different treatment in the way they have been painted. The relief decorations are of horsemen at full gallop with a pack of hounds in pursuit of a hare; the horses are light brown, dark brown, white and a purply manganese. The horsemen wear blue jackets, yellow breeches, black boots and hats, the hounds are spotted in ochre and manganese on a green landscape with trees. The borders at the tops of the jugs are of pendant acanthus leaves either richly coloured in blue, green and orange or lightly outlined in green. The border round the top of the body of the jug is of alternate acanthus and stiff leaves, either white or outlined in blue and orange. The bottom border of broad stiff pointed leaves is lightly outlined in blue, green and orange. The double scroll handle is 'fastened' with a double simulated strap. There is an acanthus thumb-rest at the top of the handle which is edged with blue and a feathered-edged acanthus moulding of the same colour appears on the neck under the handle and bordering the spout. 205mm high. *Private Collection.*

Huntsmen resting plaque c.1790

A rectangular plaque, somewhat warped in shape, showing a scene of huntsmen being served drinks in the garden of a public house, the colours are restricted to green, orange, ochre and yellow and the scene is set within a yellow and orange frame. 152mm high. *Courtesy Elias Clark Collection.*

There is another plaque from the same mould in the Royal Pavilion Art Gallery and Museum, Brighton. *HW 1133.*

The Meet, hunting jug c.1790

A small pearlware jug decorated with a scene used by John Turner c.1775-90 on a series of stoneware jugs and mugs. The colouring on this jug is a dark mossy green, brown, blue, black and ochre. There is an ochre band at the top and bottom. The jug is decorated with uncoloured acanthus leaves around the bottom and a narrow border of small laurel leaves round the top below the ochre band. A strip of widely spaced florets decorates the base of the neck. On the other side is an incongruous scene of the Judgement of Paris. 121mm high. *Courtesy Beaumont Varcoe Collection.*

Sporting jug c.1795
This very large jug has on one side a mounted horseman with a
hunt servant on foot carrying a net. A spotted long-haired
retriever sits waiting and watching some birds crouching under a
tree. On the other side a huntsman has shot a snipe which is
falling to the ground, another man is seated on a log with three
excited retrievers. The huntsmen are dressed in blue coats and
yellow breeches. A classical border of alternating acanthus
leaves outlined in blue and orange hyacinth bells decorates the
neck of the jug below a brown band at the top. At the base of the
neck there is a border of small pointed leaves in orange and blue,
beneath a brown line and at the foot of the jug there is a border
of upright acanthus leaves outlined in orange below which is a
brown line. The handle is elaborately scrolled. 210mm high.
Private Collection. (See page 176 for the other side.)

There is an untypical jug in the Merseyside County Museum,
Liverpool, with a hunting scene of small figures in full cry in
pursuit of a fox (the scene at its highest not exceeding 50mm)
which seems out of scale in its smallness to the size of the jug.
Another interesting and unusual factor is that the body of the jug
appears to have been dipped in white slip before being painted
and glazed, almost giving it the appearance of tin-glazed
earthenware. 178mm high. *54.171.503.*

Hunting and Shooting jug c.1795
The description and reverse side of the jug are on page 179.

Gretna Green Marriage plaque c.1800
An oval plaque with a detailed scene of the blacksmith's forge with the ceremony being performed. The frame is brown and there are brown buildings and green trees in the background. A marked bluish glaze is used. 197 x 233mm. *City Museum and Art Gallery, Stoke-on-Trent. 574.*

Pitcher mould
An unmarked pitcher mould of the Gretna Green marriage ceremony, probably made by John Turner. 102mm wide. *Courtesy Spode Museum. J/SWWN.*

Gretna Green Marriage jug c.1790
A fine quality jug depicting the marriage ceremony at Gretna Green, decorated at the top and bottom with curved leaves. 180mm high. *Courtesy Sotheby's.*

This jug is the same shape and with similar colouring to the jug with the scene of the grooms carousing (see page 196).

Gretna Green, the first village beyond the Scottish border, was notorious as the destination for English couples who made many runaway elopements in order to be married there. Under Scottish law, it was sufficient for the couple to state that they wished to be married in front of witnesses, be they blacksmith, ferryman, toll-keeper or anyone else. Up until 1754, when Lord Hardwick's act abolished English clandestine marriages, it was possible for any couple to be married in the Fleet Prison in London. From that date onwards they had to go beyond the borders and Gretna Green was the nearest point in Scotland. Up to two hundred couples were married in Gretna Green each year until 1856 when Scottish law established that one of the couple had to have had three weeks' residence in Scotland before a marriage could take place.

Gretna Green Marriage jug c.1790
On one side of this strongly coloured jug the marriage ceremony at the Blacksmith's forge at Gretna Green is shown and on the other side Toby Fillpot. 143mm high. *Crown Copyright, Victoria and Albert Museum. C.61.1952.*

Jugs of this kind with a scene of the Gretna Green blacksmith's forge backed by Toby Fillpot were attributed to the Prestonpans pottery by J. Arnold Fleming, writing in 1923 in his book *Scottish Pottery.*

The Grey Goose nursery rhyme jugs and mug c.1800

The decorations on these pieces illustrate a traditional nursery rhyme. The jug on the left shows Old Mother Slipper-Slopper unleashing the savage-looking spotted dog, while John stands agape, pitchfork in hand. The relief borders are the same as the jug in the centre but treated differently in the colouring. The jug has a plain loop handle. 129mm high. *Private Collection.*

There is a particularly crisp version of this jug, very delicately modelled and coloured in green, blue, manganese and yellow in the Victoria and Albert Museum. *C.77 1952.*

On the jug in the centre, the farmer dressed in a spotted smock, is seen stick in hand, hat flying off behind him, in pursuit of the fox (tail just visible) that is carrying off his goose.

Round the neck below the top band there is a repeat border of horizontal bell-shaped florets with long stamens, and below that a wavy ribbon and ivyleaf border. Below the neck is a border of insects with yellow wings, green bodies and uncoloured antennae and round the foot is an uncoloured repeat of stiff triangular leaves. The spout is outlined with a feather edge in blue and the double scroll handle has a thumb-rest at the top and the scrolls are joined by a simulated strap. There is a capital 'T' pencilled on the base of the jug. 129mm high. *Mattatuck Museum, Waterbury, Connecticut X70472.*

In the mug the borders have been reduced to the chain of bell-like florets at the top and triangular leaves at the bottom. Inside the mug a large brown frog or toad is crouching. 114mm high. *The Royal Pavilion Art Gallery and Museums, Brighton. HW 1330.*

There is a small mug, 120mm high, in the Museum and Art Gallery Stoke-on-Trent *35.P.62* inside of which is a hand-written note attributing it to Lakin and Poole. There is another mug with the same design in a creamware body with a bluish glaze in the City Museum and Art Gallery, Manchester *1922.1613.* It is attributed to Enoch Wood.

Pastoral dish c.1790 *opposite*

An oval dish decorated in relief with figures of two shepherds, each with a spotted dog and two girls picking fruit. At either end there are two large vine leaves in relief, their stalks forming a delicate handle. Figures of uncoloured sheep wander across the centre of the dish. There are two cupids, sitting in orange trees, the sun, the moon and seven stars and a flying bird scattered across the sides of the dish. The foliage is mossy green and the figures are coloured in burnt orange and blue. 292mm x 355mm. *Crown Copyright, Victoria and Albert Museum. II 303.*

'Midnight Conversation' tankard c.1785-90 *two views opposite*

A tankard decorated with scenes in relief decorated in underglaze brown, ochre, green and blue. The design was probably inspired but certainly not copied from Hogarth's 'A Modern Midnight Conversation' engraved in March 1732/3, in which the artist illustrated a group of well-known tavern personalities in St John's Coffee House, parodying a Dutch tavern scene.

The rest of the tankard is patterned with fantastic birds, animals and fishes with plant forms. The letter 'N's' in the title are the wrong way up. 153mm high. *Delhom Gallery and Institute, Mint Museum, Charlotte, North Carolina.*

187

Mischievous Sport and Sportive Innocence jug c.1795
Both sides of one of a set of ovoid shaped jugs, made in at least three sizes. There is a chainlink border at the top with florets and leaves and a border of acanthus leaves at the foot. 150mm high. *Private Collection.*

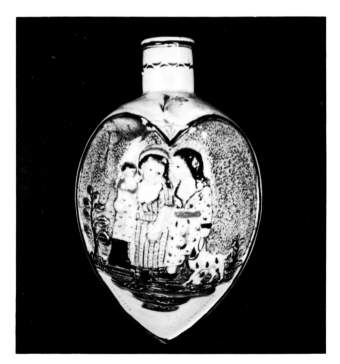

Mischievous Sport and Sportive Innocence flask c.1795
This heart-shaped spirit flask will hold half a pint of spirits. The orange-peel textured background has been coloured with cobalt. The other colours used in the decoration are dark brown, orange and green. 145mm high. *Private Collection.*

Mischievous Sport and Sportive Innocence mug c.1795
The same designs with similar borders as those found on the jugs are to be found on mugs of at least two sizes. This one is 110mm high. *Private Collection.*

The original drawings for Mischievous Sport and Sportive Innocence were probably done by Lady Templetown or Lady Diana Beauclerk, for they both specialised in drawing children. The same designs appear in engravings by F. Bartolozzi. Though both ladies worked for Wedgwood, we have not yet found a jasper ware piece with these designs.

Though these subjects appear on all manner of objects from plaques to teapots, the earliest dated piece we have been able to find is a tea-caddy, illustrated with a teapot on page 230. The words SPORTIVE INNOCENCE are impressed from the printers' type on either side of a heart-shaped medallion which encloses a design of two sedate little girls, one standing holding a doll and the other a dog by its lead. On the other side one child, holding up a gruesome mask, frightens her companion who falls back in alarm; the lettering reads MISCHIEVOUS SPORT.

There is a jug 181mm high, with these designs in the Nelson-Atkins Museum of Art (Burnap Collection) *B.628 (BI.903)* Kansas City, Missouri; and another in the Castle Museum, Norwich *358.25.96*. One of these jugs was exhibited at a Scottish Arts Council Exhibition in Edinburgh, where it was attributed to Gordon's Bankfoot Pottery at Prestonpans c.1790. A nicely modelled bowl in the Huntly House Museum, Edinburgh *HH 2353.7.62* has the familiar groups set against a yellow background and the medallions are enclosed with green leafy forms, 120mm high. The same designs appear on a flat circular disc with radiating branches of green and orange leaves and fruits leading to the outer edge. 165mm diam. This can be seen in the Royal Pavilion Art Gallery and Museum, Brighton *HW 1568*, where there is also a flask with the same designs *HW 1597*. Another flask can be seen in the Museum and Art Gallery, Stoke-on-Trent *4599.35*.

Toby Fillpot jug c.1790
Jug of compressed ovoid shape has a relief of Toby Fillpot, dressed in an orange coat and blue waistcoat and yellow breeches, seated at a table, holding a jug of ale with a good head on it. The borders at the top and bottom are composed of stiff green leaves. 149mm high. On the verso is a scene of Diomedes with the Palladium (see page 206).

Another version is on a rather squat rounded jug with a full spout marked FERRYBRIDGE, with a group of huntsmen on the reverse side (see page 76).

Toby Fillpot jug c.1790
This is on the other side of the Gretna Green Marriage jug (shown on page 185). The Toby figure is again based on the mould by John Turner. 143mm high. *Crown Copyright, Victoria and Albert Museum. C61.1952.*

Toby Fillpot pitcher mould
Master pitcher mould by John Turner showing Toby Fillpot based on Dighton's engraving, impressed TURNER. Purchased by Spodes in 1829 at the sale of Turner's property. *Courtesy Spode Museum, Stoke-on-Trent.*

Printed for & Sold by CARINGTON BOWLES,

TOBY FILLPOT.

Nº 69 Sª Pauls Church Yard LONDON.

Dear Tom this brown Jug that now foams with mild
(In which I will drink to sweet Nan of the Vale) Ale.
Was once Toby Fillpot a thirsty old Soul
As e'er drunk a Bottle or fathom'd a Bowl.

It chanced as in Dog-days he sat at his ease,
In his Flow'r woven Arbour as gay as you please,
With a Friend and a Pipe, puffing Sorrow away,
And with honest old Stingo was soaking his Clay.

His Body when long in the Ground it had lain
And time into Clay had resolv'd it again
A Potter found out in its Covert so snug,
And with part of fat Toby he form'd this Brown Jug.

Toby Fillpot engraving

'The Brown Jug' a print published by Robert Dighton in 1761 to illustrate a poem about Toby Fillpot, showing a fat man seated at a table with foaming jug of ale, was the inspiration for a relief design by Turner, copied by the Pratt ware potters in many versions.

The subject is reputed to be a Yorkshireman called Henry Elwes, who was said to have drunk 2,000 gallons of ale.

Toby Fillpot plaque c.1790

A large and bizarrely decorated plaque with Toby Fillpot in the centre dressed in a dark blue coat and waistcoat with yellow breeches. He is surrounded by the same figures that are on the plaque below, but they are less well defined. Blue scrolls or leaves have been pencilled in on the background between them. The outer rim of the plaque is banded in blue with a husk border. The predominating colour is a greyish blue. Diam. 261mm. *Courtesy Leonard Russell.*

Toby Fillpot plaque c.1790

This circular plaque gives substance to the theory that these plaques were used for trial runs for moulds later to be incorporated into the reliefs on jugs, mugs, etc. In the centre is Toby Fillpot (after the Turner design) surrounded by four utterly irrelevant relief decorations and a few floral forms thrown in for good measure. At the top a putto is seated on a duck's back, to the left is a dancing putto, to the right a man seated on an upturned barrel and at the foot a classical group depicting 'The Marriage of Cupid and Psyche'. All painted in the usual underglaze colours and set within a wide ochre frame. 228mm diam. *Courtesy Sotheby's.*

Parson, Clerk and Sexton jug c.1790 *two views*
Another version of this jug, lightly coloured in pale manganese brown and yellow with blue feather-edging and pale green leaves. 203mm high. *City Museum and Art Gallery, Stoke-on-Trent. 3185.*

Comparable jugs were made in Glasgow (see page 119) and at Bovey Tracey in Devon (see page 107).

Parson, Clerk and Sexton jug c.1800
A very small jug decorated in brown, green and blue only with the same figures as on the larger versions of the same subject. The acanthus border round the top of the body of the jug is a dark green. It is very unusual to find this subject on a jug of this shape. 115mm high. *Courtesy Jonathan Horne.*

The Parson plaque c.1790
This richly coloured plaque has the same standing figure of the Parson, as on the 'Parson, Clerk and Sexton' jug. The man is wearing a blue coat, green waistcoat, orange breeches and yellow and white striped stockings. The rococo frame is coloured in two shades of green, with a blue feathered inner edge with a ring of manganese dots inside it. The figure stands against an orange-peel textured background, patterned with brown dots. The initials I.W. or J.W. are incised on the back. 159mm high. *Harris Museum and Art Gallery, Preston. 232 (H.220).*

Vicar and Moses plaque c.1790
The figures are wearing manganese coloured hats, blue coats and yellow breeches. They are standing on a patch of green and Moses is carrying a lantern, coloured blue and green. The frame of the plaque is yellow. This is after the well-known Ralph Wood design. 138mm high. *The Royal Pavilion Art Gallery and Museums, Brighton HW 808.*

193

Peacock jugs c.1800

This is a series of jugs of compressed ovoid shape; they were certainly made in three sizes. The groups of peacocks are different on each side of the jug and are set within a leaf bordered 'sunburst' oval medallion. Under the rim is a border composed of a fruiting vine; the lower part of the jug is waisted and decorated in relief with tall upright acanthus leaves alternating with a stiff lily-like plant on a long straight stalk. This acanthus and lily border occurs on ADAMS marked jasper ware of the 1787-1805 period, and a very similar border can be seen on a Wedgwood flower basket dated 1810, illustrated in *Early Wedgwood Pottery*, Barlaston, 1951.

Round the bottom of the jugs is a relief rope or guilloche border. The manner of the painting varies greatly from jug to jug and different styles of handles are used. The three sizes are 123mm, 153mm and 200mm high. *Private Collection.*

This design was also made in fine white smear-glazed stoneware enamelled with blue lines in the Castleford manner. Underglaze coloured versions of this jug can be seen in the Victoria and Albert Museum *3652.1901* and in the Merseyside County Museum Liverpool *54.171.837;* this specimen has an unusual beaded rim.

The Archery Lesson jug 1794

Detail of the archery scene on a Turner stoneware jug dated 1794. See page 27 for the photograph of the master mould of this scene. *City Museum and Art Gallery, Stoke-on-Trent. 3195.*

There is a full-bodied underglaze coloured jug decorated with an archery scene of the same three figures copied from the relief design by John Turner. The subject may have been inspired by a print called 'Archery at Hatfield House', which was popular at the time. In the print, however, there are five standing figures and a lady seated in the foreground. The underglaze coloured jug has a ribbon and vine or ivy leaf border round the neck and a plain fluted lower part. Though we have never seen an example of this jug, it was illustrated in Reginald Haggar's *English Country Pottery*.

42 & 43. Toper and Smoker jug c.1795

A pearlware jug with a prominent spout and very fully modelled figures. On one side the man is drinking outside an inn (the same figure as on one side of the Parson, Clerk and Sexton jug see page 192) he looks somewhat befuddled, one of his stockings has fallen round his ankle and he holds up a little brown jug. On the other side a horseman reclines on a grassy bank while his horse grazes under a tree. These figures are set against an orange-peel textured background framed within a half circle, edged with acanthus leaves. The neck and base are both fluted and decorated with stiff straight leaves at top and bottom. The handle is held in position with a simulated strap and a leaf-shaped terminal decorates the lower end of it. 190mm high. *Private Collection.*

A similar but crudely painted version is in the Victoria and Albert Museum *C.442.1940.* The figure of the toper can also be found on stoneware pieces marked ADAMS. c.1800.

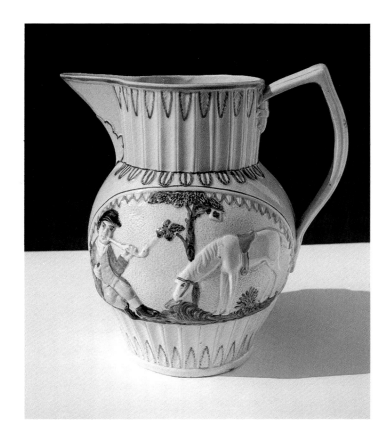

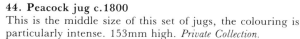

44. Peacock jug c.1800

This is the middle size of this set of jugs, the colouring is particularly intense. 153mm high. *Private Collection.*

Coloured glaze plaque by Ralph Wood c.1780
Three men grouped round a brown barrel, one drinking and
wearing a yellow jacket and hat, another smoking a pipe and
wearing a grey jacket, the third slumped forward with his head
resting on his arms wearing a green jacket and yellow trousers.
The surrounding foliage is green and yellow and there are traces
of gilding. 203mm high. *Courtesy Sotheby's.*

This subject is the basis for the designs on numerous underglaze
coloured relief moulded pieces. It was almost certainly inspired
by paintings by Adriaen Brouwer. One called 'The Slaughter
Feast' has in the foreground a drunken peasant in a similar
position resting his head on his arms on top of an upturned
barrel.

Grooms Carousing plaque c.1790
This is based on the coloured glaze plaque by Ralph Wood. Two
of the figures are wearing blue jackets, the third is slumped over
a manganese coloured barrel. Above their heads within the
arched frame is a decoration of flowers coloured with green and
orange; the plaque is edged with blue. 108mm high. *Courtesy
Elias Clark Collection.*

Grooms carousing jug c.1790
One of a set of richly coloured jugs. The scene is based on the
relief plaque by Ralph Wood. The jugs are decorated at the top
and bottom with curved leaves alternately coloured blue and
orange. On the reverse side of these jugs is Lady Templetown's
design 'An Offering to Peace'. 180mm high. *Private Collection.*

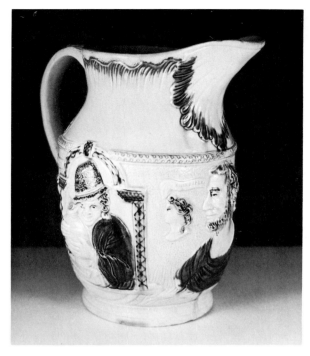

Shakespeare jug c.1790

Under the spout is a relief portrait of the Bard, with 'Shakespeare the Poet' on scrolls on either side of the head, which is flanked by two smaller unnamed portrait heads. Relief portraits of 'The Miser' and 'The Spendthrift' are in frames on either side of the jug. These portraits are similar to paintings by Teniers and Brouwer. The colouring is limited to a pale manganese brown, and pale yellow with blue feather-edging. 203mm high. *City Museum and Art Gallery, Stoke-on-Trent. 2346.*

A version of this jug is heavily and crudely coloured in blue with a clumsy attempt at feather-edging. Additional colours used are manganese, ochre and green. The jug is in the Royal Pavilion Art Gallery and Museum, Brighton. *HW 941.*

The Miser jug c.1795-1800

This ovoid shaped jug was made in various sizes. The design shows a fully modelled head and shoulders of a man, apparently counting money, set within an arched medallion bordered by stiff leaves, coloured in brown, blue green and orange. There is an acanthus leaf under the spout and inside the handle, which is vertically striped in blue and orange. The same portrait appears on both sides of the jug.

This design of the Miser looks as if it was based on a painting by David Teniers the Younger in the Louvre called 'A Man with a glass of beer'. 159mm high. *Private Collection.*

A larger version of this jug is in the Huntly House Museum, Edinburgh, it is a finely potted specimen with little colour, the portraits picked out with fine dark lines, otherwise the colours are limited to two shades of green and brown. 190mm high. *HH 2353.8A.62.* A rather crudely painted Miser jug with a whitish body and a colourless glaze is in the Art Gallery and Museum, Glasgow. 159mm high. *38.10jh.* (Attributed by Arnold Fleming to Prestonpans.) A medium sized jug, strongly coloured in blue, ochre and manganese is in the Victoria and Albert Museum *C.76.1952.* Another good example is in the City Museum, Stoke-on-Trent. 194mm high. *3170.*

Miser and Spendthrift plaques c.1790
A pair of very good quality pearlware plaques with portraits of the Miser counting his money and the Spendthrift. The frames are outlined in blue and detailed in orange with a green bow at the top where they are pierced for hanging. The Miser wears a brown hat and the other man a blue cloak fastened at the neck. Vases of flowers are sprigged on either side of the portraits in a somewhat haphazard manner. 220mm high. *Crown Copyright, Victoria and Albert Museum. 3676-7. 1901.*

The Connoisseur plaque c.1785-90
A circular pearlware plaque with two men in relief, one holding a jug, the other a tall glass, at which he is looking with some eagerness. Both figures are dressed in dark blue coats and dark manganese brown hats. There is no other colouring. The plaque has been attributed to Ralph Wood. 190mm diam. *Courtesy Peter Manheim Ltd., London.*

Dairy farming plaque c.1800
Two cows and a cowherd in relief coloured in ochre, pale yellow and pale manganese brown, stand in a green meadow under blue clouds. The scene is enclosed within a yellow frame surmounted by the head and wings of an angel. 153 x 140mm wide. *The Royal Pavilion Art Gallery and Museums, Brighton. HW 1336.*

Dairy farming plaque c.1800
A similar plaque to the one on the left. Cows spotted in blue, brown and yellow stand with a dairymaid behind them on an orange base. The scene is surrounded by a blue frame and topped by the head and wings of an angel. 153 x 140mm wide. *The Royal Pavilion Art Gallery and Museums, Brighton. HW 1337.*

Cow and Bull plaques, c.1820
A pair of oval plaques, heavily painted in ochre and dark green. There are green trees in the background. The cow has a spotted head and is framed in yellow and blue, the bull is framed in ochre and blue. 156 x 184mm wide. *The Royal Pavilion Art Gallery and Museums, Brighton. HW 1339.*

12. Classical and non-figurative jugs, mugs and plaques

In the latter half of the eighteenth century, sophisticated taste leaned heavily on classical antiquities, inspired by the excavations at Herculaneum and Pompeii. Various books were published illustrating the artefacts discovered. Sir William Hamilton, the British Ambassador to the court at Naples commissioned a book on his own collection. It was called *Etruscan, Greek and Roman Antiquities,* and written by Pierre François Hugues (called d'Hancarville) with engravings by F.A. David. It was first published in Naples in 1776-9 and later in Paris in 1785. A copy of this book was in Josiah Wedgwood's possession and was clearly the inspiration for many of his classical designs. Wedgwood actually sent Henry Webber, one of his most talented designers, to Rome to study classical sculpture in the 1780s. Webber was instructed to bring back to Staffordshire drawings that might serve for ceramic designs. Wedgwood stipulated that the drawings were to be his, but that Webber could make copies of them for his own use. Ultimately some of these designs appeared on relief decorated underglaze coloured jugs, including various adaptations of classical scenes such as Hercules slaying the Hydra or wrestling with the Nemean Lion, the Judgement of Paris, or putti carousing among fruiting vines. These scenes are sometimes found on one side of a jug with a completely different and unconnected subject on the other side. The Judgement of Paris, for instance, is sometimes backed with a hunting scene and the gambolling putti by a line of sailing ships. It is possible that these jugs were made in stock sizes and shapes, the separate sides of the mould being interchangeable from one jug to another.

In addition to pieces decorated with figures and animals, some are enriched with floral forms or quite abstract raised patterns.

Many of the jasper ware designs made at Etruria were copied by the makers of relief decorated underglaze coloured earthenware and among the designers of these reliefs who worked for Wedgwood were John Flaxman from 1775, William Hackwood who had joined the firm as a boy in 1769, and Henry Webber who worked in the studio at Etruria from 1782-94. Hackwood eventually became chief modeller and remained with the firm for sixty years.

Two titled ladies, Elizabeth Templetown and Diana Beauclerk provided many drawings of children which were subsequently modelled by Hackwood. Lady Templetown, formerly Elizabeth Boughton, married Clatworthy Upton in 1769. Upton was created Lord Templetown in 1776. Lady Diana Beauclerk, eldest daughter of the third Duke of Marlborough designed various classical scenes, usually incorporating children, for Wedgwood. She was a talented draughtsman and much admired by Sir Joshua Reynolds. Her work was collected by Horace Walpole. She was also a more than adequate portrait painter and she illustrated Dryden's *Fables.* First married to Viscount Bolingbroke in 1757, she was divorced in 1768 and married Topham Beauclerk, a friend of Dr. Johnson's.

William Hackwood spent much of his time adapting antique busts and bas reliefs, but he also did original work including many portrait medallions (including one of Josiah Wedgwood).

Hercules slaying the Hydra jug c.1796

Jug with a large spout and handle painted with a scale pattern with a dolphin's head as a terminal. A lively scene of Hercules holding three of the hydra's heads on a chain is bordered by acanthus leaves at the top and stiff leaves at the bottom. There is a feathered decoration suspended from a wavy line below the rim. On the verso is a mounted figure of the Duke of Cumberland (see section on commemorative jugs). 190mm high.
Courtesy Beaumont Varcoe Collection.

This representation of the second of the labours of Hercules shows the Greek hero attempting to chain up the nine-headed monster in the marshes of Lerna near Argos. Though this design is always referred to as 'Hercules slaying the Hydra' there are only three of the monster's heads clearly visible, so it may represent the triple-headed monster Geryon, whose disposal was his tenth labour. The arrows dipped by Hercules into the blood of the Hydra ever afterwards inflicted fatal wounds.

Boys with goat jug c.1800

This jug is of a rather unusual shape. It has a scene of four naked boys playing with a goat, one tumbling over its back; after a relief by François Duquesnoy.

There is a rich border of vine leaves and grapes in blue and green with brown festooning stems and small ochre fronds at the top. The upswept handle terminates in a hound's head. There are blue lines round the top and foot and down the edges of the handle. On the other side is a panorama of three men-of-war in line astern under a rolling blue cloud (see page 162). 116mm high. *Wakefield. Art Gallery and Museums.*

This design also appears on both white and buff-coloured stoneware jugs. One 241mm high is impressed ADAMS on the base. *City Museum and Art Gallery, Stoke-on-Trent. T3.120B.*

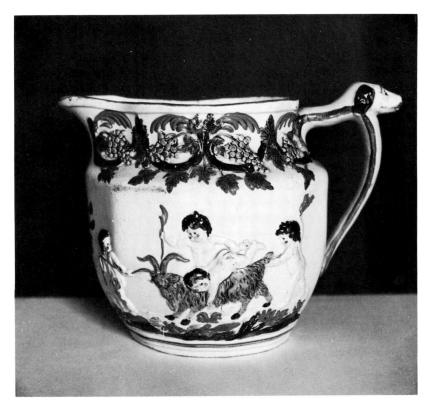

An Offering to Peace jug c.1790
The largest of a series of three richly coloured jugs, relief moulded and decorated at the top and bottom with curved fluting and leaves alternately coloured blue and burnt orange. This side shows a group of two girls in classical draperies coloured in blue and orange with a child and a dog or sheep standing between two trees. This is after a design by Lady Templetown, that was modelled by William Hackwood and used on Wedgwood creamware and jasper ware vases and plaques. On the other side is a group of three grooms drinking and smoking (see page 196). 180mm high. The smallest jug of the series is 120mm high. *Private Collection.*

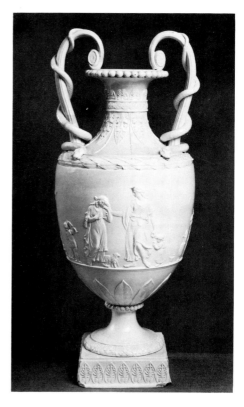

Creamware vase c.1785
This Queensware vase is decorated in relief with Lady Templetown's design 'An Offering to Peace' modelled by William Hackwood in 1783. This same design was used on jasper ware plaques and was borrowed by the makers of Pratt jugs as well. This vase clearly shows some of the border motifs also adopted by the makers of relief decorated underglaze coloured earthenware; the acanthus leaf, laurel and anthemion. Even the flower in relief on the upper terminal of the handle appears on a Pratt jug marked WEDGWOOD (see page 51). This creamware vase is also marked WEDGWOOD. 368mm high. *Crown Copyright, Victoria and Albert Museum. C.799.1935.*

An Offering to Ceres jug c.1798

This design appears on numerous Pratt jugs, with a portrait of Admiral Duncan on the other side. Below the brown-banded rim of the jug is a repeat pattern of half vine leaves in brown and below this is a green border of grapes and vine leaves. At the base of the neck is a narrow border of stiff leaves, alternately coloured ochre and green. The two female figures (sometimes called Flora and Pomona, or Peace and Plenty or Spring and Summer) have been adapted from part of a green jasper ware plaque entitled 'An Offering to Ceres' designed and modelled by John Flaxman in 1779. The design also appears on Copeland stoneware.

Round the foot of the jug is a brown band and an uncoloured border of splayed fronds, alternating with stiff triangular leaves coloured in brown. The plain loop handle has a trailing pattern of leaves on it. 195mm high. *Courtesy Beaumont Varcoe Collection.*

Copeland pitcher mould

Intaglio mould, incised 'Copeland' on the back of one of the figures, from the 'Offering to Ceres' design. 102mm high. *Courtesy Spode Museum, Stoke-on-Trent.*

Offering to Ceres plaque c.1795

An oval plaque, edged with a wavy blue feathered border; the figure on the left wears an ochre coloured skirt and a blue spotted over-dress. The other figure wears a blue spotted dress and carries a yellow sheaf of corn. The sprays of flowers are painted in blue, ochre and green. 133mm high. *Courtesy Elias Clark Collection.*

Bacchus and Pan plaque c.1800
A classical group with two other figures in addition to the two drunken gods and a donkey. The plaque is lightly coloured with some blue drapery and a yellow border. 146mm high. *City Museum and Art Gallery, Stoke-on-Trent. 457.P.41.* This design is after a relief sculpture by François Duquesnoy entitled 'Drunken Silenus'.

Boy with dolphin plaque c.1800
A deeply moulded relief figure of a boy astride a dolphin, with flying drapery, coloured in ochre and green and framed with blue lines. 127mm diam. *Courtesy Elias Clark Collection.*

45. Bacchus with nymphs plaque c.1800
A classical group of a carousal, richly coloured.
The plaque has a blue and ochre border.
Bacchus wears a pinkish orange coloured cloak
and has at his side an orange and black spotted
lion on a green sward; the other drunken figures
are in relief against a dark blue sky. 185mm
high. *Courtesy Elias Clark Collection.* This may
well have been made at one of the Scottish East
Coast potteries.

46. Boy and dolphin plaque c.1800
Deeply moulded relief of the figure of a boy
astride an ochre coloured dolphin with blue flying drapery behind him. The plaque is framed
in yellow with brown lines. 127mm diam. *City
Museum and Art Gallery, Stoke-on-Trent. 456.P.41.*

Roman warriors jug c.1795 *two views*
A full-bodied jug with a mounted Roman warrior on a charging
horse and three other soldiers, one holding a flag. On the reverse
side are four Roman soldiers standing in conversation. There is
a border of vine leaves and grapes round the neck and the jug is
fluted at the bottom. This is a companion jug with the same
borders, to the 'Coursing' jug described on page 180. 157mm
high. *Courtesy Beaumont Varcoe Collection.*

Diomedes with the Palladium jug c.1795
This design was copied from a classical gem in the Chatsworth
Collection and shows the seated figure of Diomedes with the
Palladium in front of him. This was the sacred image of Pallas
(Athena).

   The stiff leaf borders at the top and bottom of the jug are
outlined in green below and above brown banding. On the other
side of the jug is the familiar figure of Toby Fillpot. 149mm
high. *Private Collection.*

Judgement of Paris jug c.1800

The design shows Paris sitting under a tree handing an apple to Aphrodite, whose attendant arranges drapery to cover her naked form. The colours used are blue, green, burnt orange and yellow. The jug is decorated with acanthus leaves round the bottom and a narrow border of small laurel leaves round the top below an ochre band. A strip of widely spaced florets decorates the base of the neck. On the other side of this jug there is a scene of huntsmen at a meet. 121mm high. *Courtesy Beaumont Varcoe Collection.*

The quarrel between Hera, Athena and Aphrodite was resolved by Hermes bringing the goddesses to Paris, the son of Priam and Hecuba, for him to judge which was the most beautiful. His preference was for Aphrodite. An ivory from Sparta shows Paris seated, holding the Apple of Discord, as the goddesses approach him.

Turner pitcher mould

Master mould for 'The Judgement of Paris' incised Turner on the back. 75mm high. *Courtesy Spode Museum, Stoke-on-Trent. TMMS/210.*

Spirit flask c.1795-1800

This pointed oval flask is decorated on one side with four cherubs holding bunches of grapes and gambolling with a very good tempered lion. On the other side is a landscape with a seated figure holding a cornucopia (possibly intended to represent Cybele) beside a seated lion and an attendant putto. The wreath of olive leaves and fruits in green which surrounds the scenes issues from a ram's head and is bordered by blue and brown lines. 192mm high. *Royal Ontario Museum, Toronto, Canada. 910.104.1.*

47. Peace and Plenty jugs c.1802
125mm and 185mm high. *Private Collection.*

48. American Eagle jug c.1815
This rather crudely modelled but richly coloured ogee-shaped creamware jug, based on a contemporary silversmith's design, is decorated in relief on one side with the American eagle surmounted by two olive branches. On the reverse side is a chrysanthemum-like flower. Round the top of the jug is a floral border incorporating passion flowers and on the front below the spout is a freehand painted whorl of petals enclosed in a strongly coloured pattern of green and blue stiff leaves. The rim and base are edged with dark brown. The handle has a moulded rope edge. 140mm high. *Private Collection.*

Another version of this jug, decorated in pale colours of green, yellow and brown, with a brown band at the base, is in the Glaisher Collection at the Fitzwilliam Museum Cambridge, *755.*

Peace and Plenty jugs c.1802

This series of jugs is known as 'Peace and Plenty' with finely modelled seated female figures set in semicircular frames against an orange-peel textured background. In most examples there is little or no colour in one background, but on the jug above this particular area is coloured a deep blue and the words PEACE and PLENTY are pencilled in black above the figures and the monogram 'J.P' is pencilled on the front. These would have been the initials of the recipient or owner of the jug and not the maker. The figures, dressed in high-waisted Regency gowns are comparable in their skilful modelling to many that appear on Wedgwood's jasper ware. The 'Peace' lady on the jug to the right holds an olive branch in her right hand, the 'Plenty' figure grasps a cornucopia filled with fruits and holds a sheaf of corn in her left hand.

'Plenty' is the reverse side of the 'Peace', in the colour plate. The different version of 'Peace' above clearly shows the orange-peel textured background. It is a crisply modelled jug. 185mm high. *Private Collection.*

Of the various Peace celebrations that were held during the time of the Napoleonic wars, the one most likely to have inspired the production of these jugs is the Peace of Amiens, which was concluded in March 1802. There was much rejoicing at what was thought to be the close of a long struggle, and the new French Ambassador was drawn in triumph through the streets of London.

Peace and Plenty mug c.1802

Creamware mug in the form of a cornucopia, with the tail forming a handle and with a moulded face on the front, flanked by laurel branches with green leaves and brown stems. Pencilled PEACE and PLENTY in brown around the foot, blue banded top and bottom. Below the top blue band there is an uncoloured border of fruits in relief. 120mm high. *City of Manchester Art Galleries. 1947.654.*

It is possible that these jugs were made at the Leeds Pottery. This was one of the relief decorated items produced by the Seniors at Hunslet and illustrated in Slee's catalogue of their wares produced during the first war. They may well have been made from one of the moulds from the old Leeds Pottery.

Plaque with two classical heads 1816

Two rather crudely painted girls' heads with manganese brown hair are set facing each other against a green background with painted flowers in ochre, blue and green between them. They are framed in an ochre yellow frame. On the back, incised and filled in with brown pigment is 'S.Mare (or Maze) Newcastle 1816'. 230mm wide. *Crown Copyright, Victoria and Albert Museum. C.394. 1918.*

This is perhaps an apprentice piece as no factory of the name of Maze or Mare can be traced either at Newcastle upon Tyne or Newcastle under Lyme: it is more likely to be from Staffordshire.

Plaque with classical head c.1810-20

One of a pair of plaques with a version of the same heads as on the S.Mare plaque. The colouring is confined to a rich dark burnt orange, a little blue on the background flowers and dark brown on the girl's hair. The frame, surmounted by a blue bow has a beaded edge coloured orange and a pattern of orange and blue blobs on the inner moulding. 260mm high. *City Museum and Art Gallery, Stoke-on-Trent. 117.P. 1960.*

Plaque with classical head c.1810-20

An oval plaque with the same head as the girl facing to the left as on the S.Mare plaque. Her manganese brown hair is falling to her shoulders in long tendrils and she is flanked by miniature portrait medallions with green rope-bordered frames. Other miniature portrait heads have been sprigged on above and below her. She has a clown-like ochre blob on the cheek. The simple moulded frame is lined with orange and blue. 184mm high. *Courtesy Sotheby's.*

Amphitrite plaque c.1800
Oval plaque with a relief design of the goddess with a dolphin, surrounded by a beaded border coloured in yellow, orange, green and blue; the outer rim is dark manganese brown.

Amphitrite has an orange body (obviously a long sleeved vest for modesty) as her hands and face are uncoloured. Her legs are dark blue and she is wearing a blue and green cloak draped over her shoulders and flowing behind her. The dolphin is dark blue. They are standing on an ochre and blue pedestal. The background is painted with sprays of flowers in orange, blue, green and manganese. In style and colouring this piece is reminiscent of the plaque at the top of page 191. The dark colouring and the treatment of the eyes is very much in character with pieces produced by the Hawleys. It is marked on the back in a cursive incised hand 'Hanna Marsh' and a rather enigmatic hieroglyph that might be interpreted as 'Oct 21'. 197mm high. *Courtesy Sheila & Edwin Rideout, Wiscasset, Maine.*

This figure is very similar to an early sixteenth century terracotta bas relief by Giovanna da Bologna.

Pomona plaque c.1790
An oval plaque with a half-length portrait of a girl, probably intended to represent Pomona, wearing a revealing dress and holding a bunch of grapes. The plaque has an orange chevron border within a yellow band with a brown beaded edge with scrolls top and bottom. 197mm high. *Courtesy Beaumont Varcoe Collection.*

Pomona was the Roman goddess of fruits, hence her doing duty for the classical figure of Summer in various groups of the Seasons. Ovid recounts how she was courted by sylvan deities and how Vertumnus the god of Autumn, won her. She is usually depicted as a beautiful girl with fruits in her bosom and a pruning knife in her hand.

Diana the Huntress plaque c.1795
An oval plaque of Diana, showing the goddess holding a bow in her right hand with a spotted hound at her feet. She is clothed in burnt orange drapery with blue ribbons and set within a burnt orange and blue border. 178mm high. *Fitzwilliam Museum, Cambridge. 726.*

The Roman goddess, in later times identified with the Greek Artemis, presided over the chase and the woodlands and was known as the goddess of the moon, of light and of childbirth. Her most famous shrine, set in a wooded grove was at Aricia, (near the modern lake Nemi) where she was worshipped with Virbius, a little known god of the forest and the chase. Diana's followers were mainly women.

Paris and Aphrodite plaque c.1790-1820

This underglaze coloured relief decorated plaque is very like one of the same subject said to have been designed by John Voyez for the Wood factory. An example can be seen in the Victoria and Albert Museum (C.36. 1930). The design shows Paris sitting under a tree, after the famous Judgement had taken place and holding out to Aphrodite the Apple of Discord. The lady stands naked except for a flowing cloak which does nothing to conceal her charms. Eros is seen clinging to her side. The group is set within a laurel leaf frame, the outer margin moulded with foliate scrolls. It is painted in the usual underglaze colours. 203mm high. *City Museum and Art Gallery, Stoke-on-Trent. 3280.*

Paris and Aphrodite plaque c.1790-1820

Another version of the same subject, also in a rococo frame, showing Paris dressed in blue and ochre spotted drapery with Aphrodite wearing a blue cloak. The figures are backed by green moulded trees and freely painted floral sprigs. 216mm high. *Yorkshire Museum.*

'Autumn' plaque c.1800

An oval plaque with an ochre frame showing a figure symbolic of Autumn, from a set of the Seasons. She is holding a sickle in her left hand and a yellow sheaf of corn in her right. She is wearing a dark blue dress with an ochre underskirt and shawl. She stands on a green mound and is flanked by an abstract motif and a basket of fruit. 305mm high. *Courtesy Sotheby's.*

There is a similar plaque in the Royal Pavilion Art Gallery and Museums, Brighton. *HW 1364.*

Lions plaque c.1800
A white bodied plaque with two reclining lions in relief, coloured with manganese manes and tails. 253mm x 311mm. *The Nelson-Atkins Museum of Art (Burnap Collection B.851 (BI 305) Kansas City, Missouri.*

Prometheus and the Eagle plaque c.1790
The design on this rectangular plaque is after an ivory carved by John Voyez, which is in the Holburne of Menstrie Museum in Bath. Prometheus lies fettered and naked on a blue cloak spread out upon a rock. The attacking eagle crouches at his side. The biscuit coloured plaque is painted with touches of blue, yellow, orange, green and brown. 172mm high. *Courtesy Leonard Russell.* There are several versions of this design, one set within an oval border.

The legend has it that after Prometheus had done various things to annoy the gods, including stealing fire from them, Zeus wreaked vengeance on him by chaining him to a rock and sending an eagle to tear out his liver. This part of his anatomy was as immortal as the rest of him and reconstituted itself as fast as the eagle could eat it. Even so, he must have been in some discomfort, and remained so until Hercules came to his rescue and released him. Scenes from this legend can be found on many forms of archaic art including many Greek vases dating from the latter part of the fifth century B.C.

Vine and scale pattern jug c.1805
A small cream jug moulded in relief and strongly decorated in blue, green and orange. The middle of the jug is covered in green vine leaves and blue grapes and decorated at the top with blue and orange stripes. The lower half of the oval shaped jug is decorated with a fish scale pattern, outlined in blue and orange. The top and base are rimmed with blue. 118mm high. *Private Collection.*

Striped jug c.1810
A full-bodied jug with a relief pattern of stripes in underglaze colours, framing on either side within an oval, a leafy bush in a flower pot. The neck is decorated with stars and under the rim on either side ar two half circles with trellis background. 153mm high. *Mattatuck Museum, Waterbury, Connecticut. X70467.*

Ivy border jug c.1800
This unusual, small pearlware jug has a carefully modelled circlet of trailing ivy leaves with tendrils and fruit round the main body, coloured in blue, green and manganese. This border must be based on a very similar one designed by William Hackwood and used on Wedgwood's jasper ware. The design can be seen in Hackwood's drawing book of 1799, which is now in the Wedgwood Museum. The acanthus border at the top of the jug is outlined with ochre and blue and there is a brown band round the foot above which is an uncoloured reeded border. The band of small triangular leaves round the top of the body of the jug has also been left uncoloured. The elaborate scroll handle has an acanthus leaf outlined in blue. 114mm high. *Collection of Mr & Mrs Robert Allbrook.*

Wedgwood jasper ware border
Wedgwood jasper ware ivy border decoration, originally designed by Hackwood which was probably the inspiration for the border on the jug above. *Courtesy Josiah Wedgwood and Sons Limited, Barlaston, Stoke-on-Trent.*

214

Swagged and tasselled mug c.1800
A small pearlware mug decorated with borders of stiff green leaves and swags of yellow bunting with green tassels. A similar design can be found on teapots marked ASTBURY and HAWLEY (see pages 36 and 76). 102mm high.
Courtesy G.F.Arnold.

Cottage cream jug c.1800
A cream jug in the form of a thatched cottage with a yellow roof and green and blue flowers and foliage. This must have been inspired by the earlier saltglaze and Whieldon-type cottage teapots, etc. and is a forerunner to all the 'cottage' tea ware made in the Art Deco period of the 1920s and 1930s. 95mm high. *City Museum and Art Gallery, Stoke-on-Trent. 1386.*

Miniature dish c.1800
A miniature dish with a design of fruit in high relief, decorated with blue, green, ochre and manganese. 112mm long. *Courtesy Constance Stobo Collection.*

Cabbage leaf jug c.1790
This relief moulded cabbage-leaf jug has a moulded border of small vine leaves below the rim set against an orange-peel textured background. The painted decoration of sprigs of flowers are quite independent of any moulding. In shape, with its

relatively long neck and large spout this jug is reminiscent of the porcelain cabbage-leaf jugs made at the Worcester factory and later at Caughley. It has a double scroll handle. The colours are limited to blue, orange and green. 200mm high. *Private Collection.*

215

Bacchus and Pan jug c.1790
A fine, early example of this design. Compared to that over the page, it is sparsely coloured. The cornucopia is lightly spotted in blue and ochre. Bacchus has manganese washed drapery over his shoulders and a yellow drape around his loins. The dolphin has a blue ridge on top of its head and the mouth is outlined in brown with yellow gills. The handle is in the form of a sealion or manatee with webbed feet, washed in manganese. The hair on both the gods is manganese brown, Bacchus has a vine circlet round his head and Pan wears the same round his loins. Bacchus sits on a white barrel, striped in brown and decorated with green foliage. The dolphin spout is complete. 322mm high. *Merseyside County Museums, Liverpool. 28.84.*

A Bacchus jug sold by Sotheby's on April 23rd 1981 was of particular interest as it had relief portraits of King George III and Queen Charlotte on either end of the barrel on which Bacchus is sitting.

13. Toby jugs, Bacchus jugs, Satyr mugs, etc.

Toby jugs decorated with coloured glazes were made by Ralph Wood in the 1770s; some of the same models continued in production until well into the nineteenth century, firstly in underglaze colouring and later in enamel colours. They not only came from the Wood factory but were copied by many other potteries. It is rare to find a marked specimen, but there is one with the typical coarse features of the most common of the Wood Tobys which is marked on the bottom with a large impressed crown (see page 85). This Toby is very strongly coloured under the glaze in cobalt blue, burnt orange and black.

Other Ralph Wood Toby jugs decorated with underglaze colours include the Thin Man, Martha Gunn (the Brighton bathing woman), and the Hearty Good Fellow.

The origin of Toby jugs has been discussed at length and inconclusively. It is quite possible that Aaron Wood, the brother of the elder Ralph Wood, the father of Enoch and a famous modeller, may have made the first of this type of jug. A likely inspiration is the print published in 1761 after a design by Robert Dighton. This engraving (see page 190) of a heavy bellied toper, seated with a foaming jug of ale in one hand and a churchwarden pipe in the other was used to illustrate a poem called 'The Brown Jug' which began with these lines:

> 'Dear Tom, this brown jug that now foams with mild Ale,
> (In which I will drink to sweet Nan of the Vale),
> Was once Toby Fillpot, a thirsty old Soul
> As e're drank a Bottle or fathom'd a bowl'.

and ends:

> ...His Body, when long in the ground it had lain
> And Time into Clay had resolv'd it again
> A Potter found out in its Covert so snug
> And with part of fat Toby, he formed this brown Jug...!'

These lines are worthy to be coupled with the words of the elder Ralph Wood:

> 'No art with potters can compare
> We make our pots of what we potters are'.[1]

The striking Bacchus jug, which may well have been modelled by John Voyez, was made by the Woods in coloured glazes. It has its appearance completely changed by the vigorous use of oxide colours.

In addition to the Toby jugs and Bacchus jugs, there are other anthropomorphic objects such as satyr mugs, in the form of the head of a satyr, sometimes with a large yellow or brown frog or toad inside. These originated in the Ralph Wood factory as probably did the Pope and Devil mugs, which, when viewed the right way up, showed the solemn face of a Pope wearing a papal crown, but when turned upside down revealed the leering face of the Devil. There were also teapots in the form of men and women.

---

1. These lines are inscribed on the front of an heirloom jug signed on the bottom 'T. Locker', illustrated in Frank Falkner's *The Wood Family of Burslem*, London, 1912.

49. Bacchus and Pan jug c.1800-20
The Pan side of the jug opposite. *Private Collection.*

50. Toby jug c.1790 *bottom left*
This typical Toby is wearing a white coat, edged with yellow and with yellow cuffs. The coat is patterned with blue stars and ochre dots. The same starry pattern is used on the jug he is holding. He is also wearing orange breeches, stockings with blue and ochre stripes and brown shoes and hat. There are orange blotches on his cheeks. He is set on a rectangular brown banded base with chamfered corners. 250mm high. *Courtesy Leonard Russell.*

51. Toby jug c.1790 *below*
This Toby is wearing a sponged pale blue coat with manganese cuffs and dark blue breeches. His vest is patterned in blue. He wears an orange hat and his shoes are manganese. 242mm high. *Courtesy Leonard Russell.*

There are many variations of these jugs both in the original coloured glazes and in underglaze colours.

Bacchus and Pan jug c.1800-20

This jug is based on a Ralph Wood model. Its vivid underglaze colours give it a very different appearance from the original coloured glaze decorated form. Bacchus is back-to-back with the god Pan and is holding a spotted cornucopia. A spotted leopard, balanced on his shoulder, forms the handle. The god is sitting on a wine barrel, striped in green, ochre, yellow and blue. He is draped in a lion skin and a blue garment that only partly covers his obese body. Pan has a garland of vines round his hips and is holding a goblet as well as his pipes. The figures are mounted on a circular base, lined in blue and with a spotted top. This is similar to the one with HAWLEY impressed on the base (see page 74). Frank Falkner suggests that though the original of this jug comes from the Wood factory, the influence is probably Continental. If it was designed by Voyez, this would not seem improbable. The spout is in the form of a dolphin, but unfortunately missing on this specimen. 290mm high. *Private Collection.*

A group of Toby jugs c.1770-1810

The Pratt ware Toby (1790-1810) on the left holds a brown tankard in his right hand. He wears a brown coat, ochre breeches, a white vest spotted with brown crosses, brown striped and speckled stockings, brown hat and shoes. The base with chamfered corners is painted with a brown line. 248mm high.

The Toby in the centre is a Ralph Wood model, c.1770-90 and is decorated with coloured glazes. He wears a pale green coat, yellow breeches, brown hat and shoes. Even in a black and white reproduction the contrast between the earlier style and the more robust underglaze colouring of the two Tobys on either side of him, shows up very well. 242mm high.

The Pratt ware Toby (1790-1810) on the right holds a brown jug in his left hand. He wears a blue and ochre patterned coat with yellow trimmings, blue breeches, ochre striped stockings and a spotted vest, a dark brown hat and ochre shoes. The shaped base is decorated with pale brown lines. 242mm high. *Courtesy Sotheby's.*

Toby jug c.1790
Front and side views of this attractive Toby. He is wearing an intense mustard coloured coat, blue breeches, orange and blue vest, brown striped stockings and brown shoes and hat. He is set on a rectangular brown-banded base with chamfered corners. 210mm high. *Courtesy Leonard Russell.*

Hearty Good Fellow jug c.1820
A small version of this well-known model is dressed in a blue coat, yellow breeches and with manganese brown shoes and hat. He holds a blue and white jug in one hand and a clay pipe in the other. His face is blobbed with yellow on the cheeks. The base and the handle at the back of the figure are sponged with yellow and blue. 215mm high. *Harris Museum and Art Gallery, Preston. 234. H.219.*

Hearty Good Fellow Toby jug c.1790
This well-modelled figure in rather muted colours, standing on a rocky base, holds a miniature Pratt jug with typical fluted decoration in his right hand and a pipe in his left. He is dressed in black shoes and hat, green coat, ochre patterned waistcoat, yellow breeches and white stockings. His hair is manganese brown. It is such a lively and competent piece of modelling, the original may well have been by John Voyez or the younger Ralph Wood. 305mm high. *Private Collection.*

There were several versions of 'The Hearty Good Fellow' in Captain R.K.Price's collection, including one in high temperature underglaze colours, wearing a burnt orange coat and green washed breeches and waistcoat. There was also a small example of the same figure 223mm high, with a white coat sponged with cobalt blue and burnt orange. Other versions have striped trousers in place of breeches.

There is also a white stoneware version of this jug impressed TURNER. Yet another version is dressed in a black hat, brown coat, black speckled waistcoat and yellow breeches. This last Hearty Good Fellow had the same dotted eyebrows as the Toby jug with the large crown impressed on the base. 293mm high.

Satyr mug c.1790

A mug formed as a bearded satyr's head crowned with a fruiting vine. The hair and ears of the satyr are coloured in shades of brown and the leaves and rustic handle of the mug are in different greens. The head is set on a green moulded base with a rope pattern round the edge. 101mm high. *Crown Copyright, Victoria and Albert Museum. II 288.*

Pope and Devil cup c.1780-90

A double-faced pearlware drinking vessel, the pointed end terminating in a papal crown with the Pope's face below it. The lower upside down face wears a leering expression and is fringed with dark brown hair, which forms part of the border round the rim of the cup which is decorated with a band of acorns and oak leaves and a brown line. The sides of the faces are moulded with acanthus leaves edged with yellow. The whole object is delicately painted with blue, orange, green, yellow and brown. 162mm high. *Reproduced by Courtesy of the Trustees of the British Museum. 1981 1-1 453.*

A very similar pair of these curious cups can be seen in the Victoria and Albert Museum. One of them is lettered inside the rim 'When Pope absolves the Devil smiles'. *II 305 & 306.* These were probably made about the time of the Gordon Riots when anti-popish feelings were running high.

Satyr jug c.1790

A small jug in the form of a smiling, bearded and horned satyr's head, his brow encircled with a wreath of fruiting vine. The head is mounted on a shell-shaped base and is coloured in manganese brown, green, ochre and cobalt. This jug is based on a Ralph Wood model, and in fact may well have come from the Wood factory. 100mm high. *Private Collection.*

Similar mugs, mounted on a waisted foot are to be found with large yellow toads squatting inside.

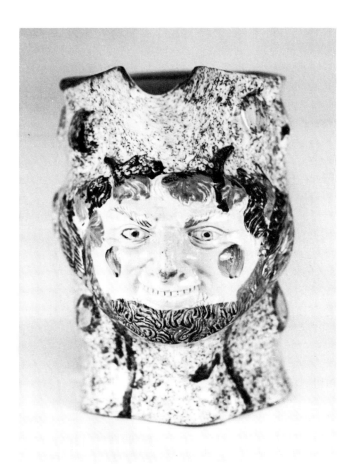

Pirate jug c.1800
A jug modelled in the form of a pirate's head, decorated in blue, black, orange and a little green. The handle is in the form of a snake painted with blue scales. 261mm high. *Courtesy Sotheby's.*

Satyr jug c.1790 *two views*
Jug in the form of a rough hewn log with a satyr's mask at the front and a crabstock handle at the back. The leering face with yellow blobs on the cheeks is crowned with green leaves and brown horns. The rustic body of the jug is lightly sponged with manganese with yellow and green ends to the lopped branches.

Side view of the jug illustrated above right. 159mm high. *Harris Museum and Art Gallery, Preston. 817.*

Martha Gunn Toby jug c.1790
This version of the Brighton Bathing Woman after a Ralph Wood model is decorated in underglaze colours. She is wearing a brown hat over a mob cap tied under her chin with a yellow edged kerchief. Her white dress is decorated with sprays of flowers and edged in ochre. On her feet are brown shoes and she holds a glass in one hand and a spotted jug of ale in the other. She sits on a square base which is lined in brown. 266mm high. *City of Manchester Art Galleries. 1923.924.*

Teapot in the form of a woman 1810-20
The body of the teapot is formed by the figure of a woman seated on a high-backed tub chair, her right arm forms the spout, her left arm with her hand on her hip forms the handle. Her white dress is spotted with ochre and trimmed with blue and her bonnet is tied with a blue bow. The crown of the bonnet forms the lid. The tub chair is marbled in brown and the circular base is edged with ochre. 216mm high. *Courtesy Sotheby's.*

This teapot has a partner in the form of a man wearing a broad-brimmed white hat, blue jacket with ochre collar and cuffs, yellow breeches and high brown boots. 228mm high. One of these was sold at Sotheby's on June 17th 1968.

14. Teapots and tea-caddies

Teapots with relief decoration and underglaze colours were made in cream coloured earthenware and pearlware by numerous potters in Staffordshire, Yorkshire, Liverpool and elsewhere. The same moulds were also used to produce black basaltes and white smear-glazed stoneware teapots.

Apart from the marked specimens seen earlier in the book, there are many teapots of equal interest and quality that were unmarked. Sometimes the pieces were inscribed with the name of some lady (the recipient of the gift, no doubt) and occasionally with a verse or motto. The decorations ranged from classical motifs, portrait medallions, formal landscapes and groups of musical instruments and floral forms, to specimens in the shapes of houses and castles and even a human likeness.

Very few underglaze coloured teapots seem to be dated, but there is one in the Pump Room Museum in Harrogate dated 1797. Most of the teapots illustrated here must have been made during the first decade of the nineteenth century.

Tea-caddies

The most common examples of relief moulded underglaze coloured tea-caddies are those decorated with Macaroni figures, clearly derived from some contemporary cartoon satirising the exaggerated hair styles of the time. Other tea-caddies were decorated with putti, portraits of royalty, classical figures, topers and Oriental scenes. There were also some double tea-caddies, some decorated with hunting scenes and others with more formal non-figurative designs, and quite elaborate examples where the two separate tea containers were mounted in intricately modelled stands with feet and handles.

Summer and Autumn tea-caddy c.1800
A tea-caddy with canted corners, decorated with a formal trailing leaf pattern. On one of the faces is a figure representing 'Summer' holding a swag of flowers (copied from one of Flaxman's 'Dancing Hour' girls, originally modelled by him in 1776). On the opposite side is another classical figure representing 'Autumn' holding in her draperies a mass of fruit or flowers coloured in ochre, green and blue. Spode also used similar designs. 127mm high. *Huntly House Museum, Edinburgh. HH 2353.458.62.*

225

Teapot with dolphin knob c.1790-1800 *above and below*
This boat-shaped teapot is decorated with borders of long straight leaves coloured in green and ochre, very like some of the borders on the teapots marked BARKER and HERCULANEUM (see pages 39 & 97). The handle with its upswept design is also similar to both these teapots. The dolphin knob is similar to the one on the BARKER teapot, and is coloured green and brown. The gallery round the lid is decorated with a chain of blue florets with orange centres. There is a moulded acanthus leaf at the base of the spout, oulined in blue and the lining or banding on the body of the pot is brown.

The central panel on one side has a relief decoration adapted from a Wedgwood jasper ware bas relief of Coriolanus with his wife and mother (listed in their catalogue of 1787). On the other side (shown below) there is a small decoration showing a boy with a dog. The teapot is unmarked. 190mm high. *Leeds City Art Galleries, Temple Newsam House. P10.22/36.*

Various relief decorated teapots are illustrated in the Leeds Pottery Drawing Books, and also in the Don Pottery book of engraved pieces. Most of these teapots have vertical sides.

Teapot with vine pattern c.1790

A finely modelled teapot, oval in shape, the side panels being bordered by long oval panels outlined in simulated rope and enclosing an upright flowering plant, at the base of which is a scrolled motif and two vine leaves.

The top border on the teapot consists of a shell pattern on an orange-peel textured background, alternating with a basic anthemion motif. The bottom border is moulded with acanthus leaves and an anthemion motif on an orange-peel textured background with radiating flutes painted with a simple plant form. The main panels are not modelled in relief, but are carefully painted with a vine pattern in blue and green. The semi-scrolled handle is slightly upswept. The spout has acanthus moulding round the base and the lid is surmounted by a 'widow' knob. The colouring is limited to blue, green and manganese brown. It has been attributed to Staffordshire. 158mm high. *Crown Copyright, Victoria and Albert Museum. C.220 & a 1914.*

'Love and Live Happay' teapot c.1805

A large teapot with a dolphin knob on the lid and an inscription on a medallion on the side 'Love and Live Happay' (*sic*). Above the medallion is a Prince of Wales' feathers motif. Coloured very nicely under the glaze in ochre, brown, green and blue. 188mm high. *Norwich Castle Museum, (Bulwer Collection). 371.*

Teapot c.1795-1800

A similar teapot of exactly the same basic shape and moulded decoration as the one opposite, except that instead of the cherub design, there is an urn sprigged on to the central panel. The ear-shaped handle is similar but the spout is quite different and rather more elegant. The knob (which may not be the original one) is also different. The painted decoration is done with a rather heavier hand in blue, brown and green with a few ochre or orange lines. The bands round the foot, top and lid are brown. 108mm high. *Royal Ontario Museum, Toronto, Canada. 950.157.130 a & b.*

Teapot c.1800

This attractively coloured but crudely painted teapot from a rather worn mould is basically the same shape as the one above and the delicate 'cherubs' teapot opposite with its slightly flared form. The small vertical convex panels decorated with trailing vines framing the main side panels are the same, but the main panel is decorated with a small oval medallion framed in dark blue, enclosing a woman's head facing to the left, silhouetted against a yellow background.

Round the top of the teapot is the same acanthus and bell-like flower border, but painted in blue and brown. The spout is a slightly different shape and is decorated with brown outlined stiff leaves. The handle is of a somewhat rococo form. Unfortunately the lid is missing. 105mm high. *Castle Museum, Norwich, (Bulwer Collection). 263.* Another example of this teapot is in the Merseyside Museum, Liverpool. *54.171.499.*

Teapot with a design of cherubs c.1800
A fine quality pearlware teapot, very light in weight, decorated with scenes in relief of a cluster of romping cherubs, coloured in green, ochre and brown. Round the top is a border of blue acanthus leaves alternating with orange bell-like forms. There are trailing vine borders down the chamfered corners. The teapot on the whole is sparely painted, the lines round the top and bottom being dark brown. The lid is surmounted with a knob in the form of a draped, seated female figure (known as the 'Widow'). It is attributed to Leeds, but looks more like a product of one of the Staffordshire potteries. 137mm high. *City of Manchester Art Galleries. 1947.647.*

Castle teapot c.1810
The body of the teapot is patterned with bricks in relief, coloured in ochre and it is edged with a blue band and green and yellow vegetation. The serpentine-sided gallery is vertically striped with yellow balusters interspersed with blue and yellow blobs. The top half of the spout is dark blue and the bottom part is ochre. The domed lid is blobbed with ochre and surmounted by a black and white spotted Dalmatian dog. The base of the pot is blue banded. 197mm high. *City Museum and Art Gallery, Stoke-on-Trent. 3230.*

Mischievous Sport and Sportive Innocence teapot c.1795
These familiar designs are used on either side of this teapot, with the addition of painted floral borders on the lid, spout and around the base. The domed lid is surmounted by a seated female figure (a version of the 'Widow') serving as a knob. 175mm high. *Mattatuck Museum, Waterbury, Connecticut. X70.486.*

Mischievous Sport and Sportive Innocence tea-caddy 1795
A nicely modelled square tea-caddy decorated with the same designs but coloured in pale blue and manganese only. It is decorated in addition with a small head at the top of each corner. 'Eliz.th Taylor Born March 18. 1795' is lettered around the top. 130mm high. *Fitzwilliam Museum, Cambridge (Glaisher Collection). 760.*

A comparable tea-caddy, the same shape but decorated with Cupids bird's-nesting (after a design by William Hackwood c.1777) inscribed 'Mary Podbury 1798', was sold at Sotheby's in 1968.

Tea-caddy 1796
Two views of a square tea-caddy decorated with blue feather-
edging and with putti holding garlands of flowers, or
bird's-nesting. The lid is surmounted with the small figure of a
lion. There are little busts at each top corner. The piece is
inscribed 'Saml. Harding 1796'. It is coloured only in shades of
blue and black. 130mm high. *Wolverhampton Museum and Art
Gallery. E.156.*

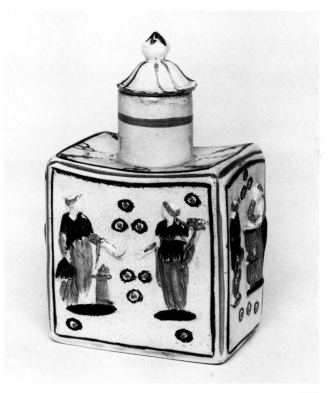

Classical figures tea-caddy c.1810
A tea-caddy, squarish in shape with a long neck and a pagoda-
topped lid striped in blue and orange has rather crudely painted
relief decorations of classical figures on each of the four sides.
Coloured in burnt orange, blue and black only. 129mm high.

The character of the creamware body, rough textured and rather
dark in colour, suggests that it may have been made at one of the
Scottish East Coast potteries. *Royal Scottish Museum, Edinburgh.
1973.132.*

Double tea-caddy c.1790 *above and opposite*
A tea-caddy in the form of a chest, divided into two compartments under a coffered lid with 'A B' incised underneath. It is decorated with a hunting scene on one of the long sides (shown opposite) and Toby Fillpot and a group of men attending a cockfight on the other. This scene was perhaps inspired, but certainly not copied from a Hogarth etching and engraving. Toby Fillpot is also to be seen on both ends of the chest with the two fighting cocks below him. On top of the lid is the bust of a hound with raised paws, to serve as a knob; and on one side of the lid is a seated figure of a gladiator with a dog and on the other a lady with a child. The chest is mounted on six capstan-shaped feet and the colours are confined to green, ochre, yellow and brown. 198mm long. *Northampton Central Museum. 1894D 210.*

Turner pitcher moulds
Master moulds made by John Turner of the cockfighting scene. The larger one is marked TURNER impressed. The small mould of the cock has the name 'Turner' incised on the back in a cursive hand. 85mm high and 30mm high. *Spode Museum, Stoke-on-Trent. TMMS/2.*

Hogarth's engraving called 'The Cockpit' was published in 1759 in two versions, one engraved by himself and the other engraved by T.Cook. The scene, in the Royal Cockpit, St James's Park, showed the blind Lord Albemarle Bertie being robbed of his winnings.

Toper tea-caddy c.1810
The fully modelled figure of the toper is dressed in a blue coat and ochre breeches and is repeated on both sides of the tea-caddy. There is a green leaf decoration on either side and the concave corners are striped in ochre and blue. 140mm high. *Huntly House Museum, Edinburgh. HH 2353. 414.62.*

Another version is in the Royal Scottish Museum *1890.657* and another can be seen at the Laing Art Gallery, Newcastle upon Tyne, *TWCMS.E.2430.* The latter is floridly coloured in blue and ochre with a dark bluish background.

233

Macaroni figures tea-caddy c.1790
On one side is depicted a gentleman in an exaggeratedly high wig with his servant standing beside him; on the other side a similarly caricatured lady and her servant. The figures are modelled in very full relief and painted in orange and blue only on one of the caddies and with the same colours and the addition of green on the other. The narrow sides of the tea-caddies are painted with sprays of flowers. There are variations in the dressing of the lady's wig, both in the arrangement of the curls and in the feathers that crown her head. In one she wears a simple 'Prince of Wales' feather arrangement and in another there are two separate groups of feathers. 120mm high.

A version of this tea-caddy can be seen in the Huntly House Museum, Edinburgh *HH 2353.413.62* where it is attributed to Gordon's Bankfoot Pottery at Prestonpans. It is strongly coloured in ochre and blue under a zaffre tinted glaze.

There is also an example of this tea-caddy in the Victoria and Albert Museum *C.34.1959* with the impressed mark LEEDS * POTTERY. As this one is markedly smaller than the general run of these Macaroni tea-caddies, and is also a very blurred impression, the likelihood is that a squeeze was taken from an actual tea-caddy instead of using an original mould, and that it was made by the Seniors in Leeds in the late nineteenth century.

Macaroni figures tea-caddy c.1780
This tea-caddy is decorated only in blue. The relief modelling is extremely crisp and it is probably the forerunner of all the polychrome underglaze coloured versions of the same design. This example has painted trails of leaves up the sides and is rather smaller than the more usual later versions. 112mm high.
Private Collection.

234

52. Ann Hudson's teapot c.1805

An attractively coloured teapot decorated with pendant green leaves and yellow and orange hearts and diamonds, with blue lines. This faceted straight-sided teapot has a swan knob on the lid and is lettered

'Ann Hudson
Love and Live Happy'

on the side. 158mm high. *City Museum and Art Gallery, Stoke-on-Trent. 717.* This same pattern was also made in a black basaltes body. There is an example in the Northampton Museum.

53. Double tea-caddy or vinaigrette 1793

This very fine double tea-caddy or vinaigrette, with two separate removable containers with lids, is delicately coloured with ochre lined green leaves and ochre, green and blue repeat patterns. The containers are separated by a loop handle and the front of the body of the piece is decorated with a putto holding swags of flowers in a pointed cartouche with a blue background. It is mounted on delicately modelled little feet. 'F.P. 1793' is inscribed on the base. This piece is somewhat similar in style to the Bradley & Co teapot on page 56. 242mm high. *City Museum and Art Gallery, Stoke-on-Trent. 3882.*

There is another similar tea-caddy or vinaigrette in the reserve collection at the City Museum, Stoke-on-Trent with a blue banded medallion on the front decorated with the relief of a kneeling classical female figure at an altar. 204mm high. *1113.*

235

Double tea-caddy c.1790
An oblong creamware tea-caddy decorated with hunting scenes set against an orange-peel textured background and coloured in green, blue, orange and brown. 'Mary How' is pencilled in an elegant script in orange on the base. 115mm x 145mm wide. *City Museum and Art Gallery, Stoke-on-Trent. 240.P.50.*

Double tea-caddy c.1790 *below*
An oblong creamware tea-caddy with two compartments. The screw tops are missing from the threaded necks. The sides are decorated with a continuous frieze of hunting figures in a treed landscape and the colouring is in green and brown only. 142mm long. *Crown Copyright, Victoria and Albert Museum. C.45.1967.*

15. Flasks, beakers, cornucopias and miscellaneous objects

A variety of vessels was made with relief decoration and underglaze colouring, many of them with the acanthus type borders so often associated with Pratt ware. Among these are vases, including spill vases and vases with masked faces, bowls, stirrup cups in the form of dog's and fox's heads and jugs in the form of bears. Sauce boats were made in the most fanciful shapes from ducks and swans and dolphins to mythical animals, part sheep part bird, or part fish part sheep. Three- and five-horned cornucopias were grouped to form flower vases and cache pots were made in various forms, sometimes with separate stands. There were also pepper pots, tobacco jars, small screw-topped containers and scent bottles in the form of mermaids. Cradles following the style of the early eighteenth century slipware productions and money-boxes in the form of cottages, churches and tall clocks as well as dovecots, bird fountains and feeders, pipes in the form of men dogs, monkeys and snakes and candlesticks supported by classical female figures, are all to be found.

In 1878 William Kent established a factory in Burslem where he made 'Old Staffordshire' style pottery produced from moulds made from original master moulds that he must have acquired. These pieces were all enamel coloured over the glaze. Several of the earlier cottages found in underglaze colouring were copied by the Kents; they cannot be mistaken for the early nineteenth century pieces as they are much heavier and the colouring of course gives them away.

The Kents also produced cow creamers, Toby jugs and many figures and animals, some of them in a Walton style and others like the later cottage ornaments. In 1955 they issued a catalogue listing some hundreds of their productions. The firm finally closed down in December 1962.

Clocks and watch stands

Towards the end of the eighteenth century, when time was of less importance than it is now and when the price of real clocks was too high for the average cottager, a popular ornament for the kitchen or parlour mantelpiece was the pottery model of a longcase clock. These rather crude productions took many forms. In the earlier models the bases were open. In the Manchester City Art Gallery, there is a collection of such clocks, some dated as early as 1794. There are two similar clocks in the Harris Museum and Art Gallery, Preston *270 (H223) & 812.*

Later versions, made for instance by Dixon, Austin in Sunderland and by J. Emery at Mexborough, elaborated the theme by flanking the clock with figures. Some of these have a hole where the clock face should be for the suspension of a watch. These were originally sold with a pottery watch to hang in the tower. These are now rarely found, though there is a complete one in the City Museum and Art Gallery in Stoke-on-Trent.

Some potteries made money-boxes in the form of a longcase clock and these had a slit at the top for the coins.

Winged dragon vase c.1790

A most unusual vase, mounted on a square, high, chamfered plinth. The body of the vase is a typical Ralph Wood shape, but the handles are in the form of orange-winged, brown-crested dragons with ochre necks and bodies. The shaped top is feathered in blue with an orange and blue motif in the centre. There is a blue line round the top of the body of the vase below which are looped ochre swags and blue and ochre stars. The bottom of the vase is moulded with acanthus leaves, every alternate one being coloured brown. There are small classical scenes in relief, coloured in manganese and blue on each face of the plinth between brown and blue lines; the splayed foot of the plinth is moulded with leaves alternately coloured green and brown. 242mm high. *Courtesy Leonard Russell.*

Vase c.1800 *top left*

A vase of flattened leaf shape standing on a waisted foot, the sides moulded with female figures after Flaxman's 'Sacrifice to Ceres'. It is feather-edged in blue at the top and round the rim at the base and with painted flowers in the usual underglaze colours. 178mm high. *Courtesy Brook-Hart Collection.*

Vase c.1800

This delicate, pearlware, ovoid vase has blue feathered edges at the top and foot, it is set on a brown banded rectangular base. The stiff leaves are outlined in green interspersed with blue flowers and there are brown painted sprays on the sides of the vase. 142mm high. *Harris Museum and Art Gallery, Preston. 233.(H.528).*

Bear jug c.1812

This pearlware bear jug is sponged in blue. The muzzle and collar of the creature are ochre coloured and it also has ochre claws; it holds in its arms a brown monkey wearing an ochre coat with a blue collar, surmounted with a bust of Napoleon. The detachable head of the bear forms a drinking cup. 247mm high. *City of Manchester Art Galleries. 1923.937.*

This jug is based on the earlier salt-glazed models made in Staffordshire and Nottingham from about 1730. The cobalt sponging replaces the shreds of clay which were applied to the salt-glazed jugs to simulate fur.

Dog's head stirrup cup c.1790

A very small stirrup cup in the form of a bulldog's head, wearing a melancholy expression with its eyes turned heavenwards. The face is yellow with a brown mouth, the eyes uncoloured except for manganese pupils. A white nail-studded collar, lined in grey forms the top of the cup. The underneath of the head is uncoloured. 73mm long. *Merseyside County Museums. M.2391.*

Oval bowl and cover c.1800

A creamware bowl, underglaze coloured and densely decorated with painted flowers and leaves. The lid is fully moulded with acanthus and other leaf decorations. A seated lion serves as a knob. The top of the bowl is rimmed with a blue band and the rest is coloured in blue, orange and green. 152mm high. *Royal Scottish Museum, Edinburgh. 1924.186 & A.*

Fox-Swan sauce tureens c.1790
One of a pair of sauce tureens modelled in the form of a fox's head joined to a swan, the neck of the swan serving as a handle. The fox is washed in ochre and the swan stroked in blue to simulate feathers with a good deal of the basic creamware showing through. The base of the tureen is washed in green. It stands on a leaf-shaped saucer, which is, in fact a flattened out swan with its head for a handle, decorated in blue and ochre. 122mm high by 178mm long. *Sheffield City Museums. K91.1.*

Sauce boat in the form of a duck c.1820
This duck has a yellow beak and yellow legs, its feathers are washed in pale blue, ochre and manganese. It is light in weight, but has a rather gritty creamware body. This originally came from the Fleming Collection and was attributed by J.Arnold Fleming to the Gallatown Pottery which was taken on by Archibald and Andrew Grey in 1810. It is difficult to see the justification for the attribution, but perhaps Mr Fleming had good reason for it. The piece is not marked. 195mm long. *Art Gallery and Museum, Glasgow 38.10.ki.*

A very similar fine pale creamware sauce boat can be seen at Temple Newsam, Leeds City Art Gallery *1928.99.* This piece is unmarked but attributed to the Leeds Pottery c.1780, for two blocks for this sauce boat were found on the site of the pottery by J.R.Kidson in the 1890s. There is another very similar sauce boat decorated in underglaze colours and inscribed 'M.L.' in the City Museum and Art Gallery, Stoke-on-Trent *1292.*

Sauce boat in the form of a swan c.1800
An attractive small pearlware object, the curved neck serves as a handle. The beak is brown and the wings are sponged in brown and ochre and partly washed in green. The glaze has a marked bluish tinge. 90mm high. *Huntly House Museum, Edinburgh. HH 2353.5.62.*

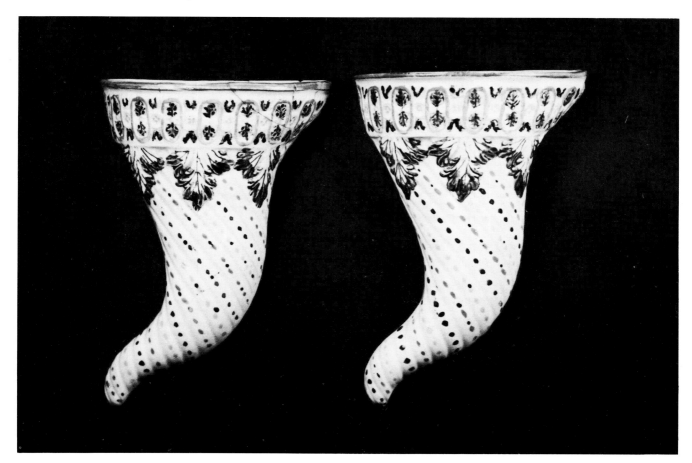

Cornucopias c.1800
A pair of delicately shaped cornucopias, diagonally decorated with incised lines, painted with rows of brown, orange and yellow dots. The rims outlined in burnt orange have linked chain borders with florets and leaves overpainted with vertical orange ovals. Below are large acanthus leaves the edges of which are painted green. 130mm long. *Private Collection.*

Flower pot and saucer c.1810
An oval flower pot with a jagged rim, feather-edged in blue and with stiff leaf decoration in ochre, brown and green. The same pattern repeated round the saucer. 180mm high. *Norwich Castle Museum. 345.35.96.*

'Neither fish, flesh, fowl nor good red herring' c.1795
A curious container in the form of a fabulous animal, the dorsal fin serving as a handle to the lid. It is delicately coloured in orange and manganese and mounted on a brown-banded oval base decorated with a border of orange leaves. 127mm long. *City Museum and Art Gallery, Stoke-on-Trent. 10H 1914.*

Parrot flask c.1790
A flask moulded with a decorative parrot in high relief on each side. The only colours used are blue, yellow and a pale green. 147mm high. *Courtesy Elias Clark Collection.*

Candlestick c.1800
Candlestick in the form of a female figure, nicely moulded and richly coloured, with her hands raised, clasping a sconce, decorated with brown leaves at the base and ochre leaves on the top rim. The figure is dressed in white with blue trim and with a brown spotted blue over-skirt and blue feathering at the foot of her dress. She stands on a shaped rectangular base with pendant stiff leaves, blue feathered at the top. The bottom of the base is brown sided. 252mm high. *City Museum and Art Gallery, Stoke-on-Trent. 244.P.49.*

Clock ornament c.1794 *left*
The whole model of the clock is washed in ochre except for the face and surround which have been left white. Branches of green leaves decorate each side. Above the face of the clock there is the profile of a man with brown hair and a blue coat. The edges of the clock are outlined with incised lines and coloured yellow. 262mm high. *City of Manchester Art Galleries. 1922.1536.*

Clock ornament 1794 *right*
A primitive model of a longcase clock with the date 1794 impressed above the clock face and a capital 'M' on the face itself, below the centre. Coloured in ochre and blue only, with leaves coloured in ochre and the impressed figures outlined in blue. There is a blue door and the panel below is outlined in blue. A frilly border, ochre edged, surmounts the clock face. 230mm high. *City of Manchester Art Galleries. 1922.1535.*

Clock ornament c.1800-20 *centre*
A smaller model of a longcase clock, picked out in puce, blue, green and yellow, with a little white dog lying at the foot. There are two cherubs in relief above the clock face and an urn in relief on the base, flanked by strips of leaves. The numbers on the clock face have been incised and then rather inaccurately painted not quite over the numbers. This is very like the centre piece from one of the clock money-boxes from the pottery that used the large impressed crown mark. 207mm high. *City of Manchester Art Galleries. 1922.1540.*

243

Blue and white jasper ware candlesticks c.1790
The two goddesses Ceres and Cybele, holding cornucopias forming candle sconces, in blue and white jasper ware designed by Henry Webber, who was head of the Ornamental Department at Etruria from 1782-94. Height of Cybele 312mm and Ceres 318mm. *Trustees of the Wedgwood Museum, Barlaston, Staffordshire.*

In November 1778 Bentley had sent some sketches of candlesticks to Josiah Wedgwood, to which Wedgwood

Ceres and Cybele candlesticks c.1800 *opposite*
These handsome underglaze coloured figures must have been inspired by the blue and white jasper ware candlesticks designed by Henry Webber for Wedgwood. It is interesting to see how the anonymous maker of this pair has simplified and adapted his bases and candle sconces with the stiff leaves and acanthus motifs that decorate so many underglaze pieces. It is unusual to find such carefully modelled little flowers as these on the bases.
  Ceres wears a diadem of yellow wheat ears and stands against a yellow wheatsheaf, she wears an orange spotted dress and her cloak is fringed with yellow. The leaves on the candle sconces are green, as is the acanthus border on the brown-lined plinth. The cornucopia is edged with brown with dark orange lines between the lobes. There are orange and yellow flowers and blue grapes below the sconce and similarly coloured flowers at her feet. 324mm high. *Royal Ontario Museum, Toronto, Canada. 965.19a.*

Ceres, identified with the Greek goddess Demeter was the mother goddess who governed the fruits of the earth, symbolised by the sheaf of wheat.

244

replied...'but I really despair of this article in pottery of any kind. In black it is too dismal...and in any other glazed ware it will be vulgar. Something pretty might be made in blue and white jasper, but would not that vulgarise the material?...If one may confess a disagreeable truth upon this subject, it seems to me that metal is the only proper candlestick material. Clay serves only to gratify caprice or poverty...'[1]

1. Keele University Archives. E.18859-26.

Cybele is wearing a dark brown mural crown, an orange spotted robe with a blue belt and yellow fringe above a green skirt. The cornucopia, flowers and bases are similar to those on the companion figure. She is accompanied by a brown lion. 324mm high. *Royal Ontario Museum, Toronto, Canada. 965.19b.*

Cybele was not only the mother goddess of Anatolia, primarily a goddess of fertility, but also a protector of her people, symbolised by the mural crown that she is wearing. She was also the mistress of wild nature, hence the attendant lion.

There is an illustration of a similar pair, slightly smaller and in enamel colouring on square marbled bases. These are illustrated in Godden's *An Illustrated Encyclopedia of British Pottery and Porcelain.* They are marked 'John Cartlidge at the Lodge in the plantation Cowbridge 1800'. An otherwise unrecorded potter, but there were Cartledges, or Cartliches working at Burslem around that time, but no John among them.

Watch stand c.1820

Watch stand supported on two back-to-back dolphins and mounted on a rectangular plinth with a relief figure of Cybele flanked by lions on the front. On one side is a free-standing figure of a female archer with a bow and arrow and on the other a man with a gun and a dog. The group is coloured in ochre, green and dark blue and mounted on a thin oval base. 229mm high. *Courtesy Sotheby's.*

Bird drinking fountain c.1810 *opposite*

An onion shaped object with a pipe projecting horizontally out of the back with a waterhole in it. On the front is a relief modelled face of a man and it is surmounted by a bird. The colouring is blue, green, yellow, ochre and brown. 140mm high. *The Royal Pavilion Art Gallery and Museums, Brighton. HW 1580.*

John Bull pipe c.1800-15 *opposite*

A pipe modelled in the form of a seated man wearing a tricorne hat with 'John Bull' impressed on it, a blue jacket with ochre collar and cuffs, yellow breeches, white stockings and brown shoes. A small lion rests beside him on a green mound base. 140mm high. *The Royal Pavilion Art Gallery and Museums, Brighton. HW 273.*

Pipe of bizarre form c.1800 *opposite*

This extraordinary construction consists of the pipe bowl made up of four grinning satyr masks, and the stem of one serpent swallowing another, with a dog rearing up in the middle. The dog's head is the mouthpiece of a whistle. It is speckled with black, blue and green and ochre and there is a mulberry-puce rim to the bowl. 253mm long. *City of Manchester Art Galleries. 1947.653.*

Fox and Goose pipe c.1795

Pipe in the form of a fox swallowing a goose. The head of the fox and the beak of the goose are coloured a brilliant orange. The rest of the bizarre object is sponged in ochre and blue. It is mounted on an octagonal green-washed stand decorated with stiff leaves in relief. 200mm long. *Courtesy Elias Clark Collection.*

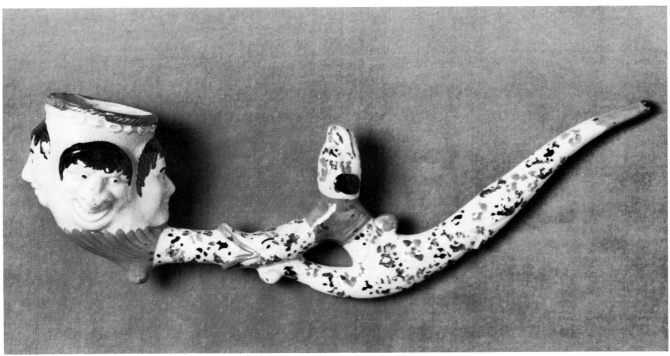

Martha Gunn pipe c.1795
A pipe modelled in the form of the seated bathing woman. She is wearing an orange bonnet and a dress spotted in blue and rests on a green-washed base. The bowl of the pipe is modelled as a head and the stem and mouthpiece is a combination of a snake and a dolphin, painted with touches of ochre and spotted in blue. 121mm high.
Courtesy Elias Clark Collection.

Bird feeder c.1810
A seed holder for attaching to a birdcage, decorated in blue, green and ochre. 102mm high. *Crown Copyright, Victoria and Albert Museum. C.81.1952.*

Bird drinking fountain c.1820
A hollow creamware vessel with a phallus pointing upwards and another pointing horizontally, to serve as a perch for the bird when drinking from the well in the pipe. The water is held in position by vacuum (on the old fashioned inkwell principle) as there is no other opening. A sprigged-on bunch of ochre, blue and green flowers decorates the front. The painted lines are brown. 165mm high. *Yorkshire Museum.*

Scent bottle c.1790 *side and front views*
A small scent bottle in the form of a man's head and shoulders. His hair is brown, he wears a blue jacket and there are two ochre spots on his cheeks. The height to the tip of the pewter top is 70mm. *Private Collection.*

There are other containers of unusual form; one in the shape of a clenched hand is in the British Museum; the flat circular disc at the wrist end unscrews on a clay thread. 82mm high. *1981,1-1,452.*

Snuff box c.1780-90
A small pearlware snuff box modelled in the form of a lady's head wearing a high, decorative, close-fitting cap, coloured in blue, orange and manganese. The screw-on base is missing. Unmarked, but probably made in Leeds. For a collection of similar containers, see Donald Towner's *Creamware.* 95mm high. *Wolverhampton Museum and Art Gallery. E.112.*

Pair of oval money-box groups c.1800
Oval money-boxes supported by flanking figures, coloured in burnt orange, green, blue, aubergine and black on a green-washed base. The money-boxes have a slit at the top and are decorated in high relief one side with a tulip-like flower and on the other by a naturally coloured bunch of grapes. 130mm high. *Courtesy Elias Clark Collection.*

This same basic oval shape decorated with grapes can also be found with a neck attached in the form of a flask.

Dovecot c.1800-20

A cruck-framed dovecot with shelves outlined in blue with thirty doves (originally there were thirty-three) perched on them. The birds are spotted in blue and yellow. The structure is surmounted by a large and quite out of scale fledgling dove. 329mm high. *City of Manchester Art Galleries. 1923.925.*

There is a slightly smaller version of this dovecot, coloured mainly in blue, in the same gallery, which must have been made by the same hand. One of these dovecots is illustrated in *Staffordshire Pots and Potters*. It was in Woolliscroft Rhead's own collection.

Tobacco jar c.1790 *two views*
On one side of this oval tobacco jar is the scene of the three grooms carousing (after the Ralph Wood original plaque). On the other side there is a group of oriental figures smoking pipes under an umbrella. The lid is decorated in relief with sprays of almond blossom and the finial is in the form of a man asleep on the top of two barrels. It is coloured in blue, brown, orange, ochre and green. 195mm high. *Brook-Hart Collection.*

Cradle c.1820
This large pearlware model of a cradle decorated in relief with a scene of women and children at play, is coloured in blue, orange, yellow and green with a simulated rope border round the edge. This piece is from the Glaisher Collection and was originally attributed by Dr Glaisher to Sewell and Donkin at St Anthony's Pottery, Newcastle upon Tyne. However there seems to be no good reason for thinking this is a Tyneside piece, it·is much more likely that it was made in Staffordshire. 312mm long. *Fitzwilliam Museum, Cambridge, (Glaisher Collection). 1095.* These cradles were made in various sizes, sometimes empty and sometimes with a sleeping child modelled within.

Barnburgh Church c.1820

This is a slab-built piece, made no doubt by a local potter and probably unique. It is a large, crude and somewhat fanciful pearlware model made to illustrate the legend of 'the cat and the man' that is still talked of in the village of Barnburgh in Yorkshire. The walls of the model church are outlined to imitate stones and the windows are coloured under the glaze in yellow, green, ochre and blue with black surrounds. Round the top fifteen corbels are represented by small human heads coloured with blue and black. The tail of a cat and a single cloven hoof on the roof of the church porch are indications of where the cat and the devil once stood, the footprints inside the porch show that Sir Percival Cresacre also once stood there, but all the figures are now lost. 407mm high. *Museum and Art Gallery, Doncaster. 140.78.*

The legend has it that Sir Percival, in 1477, returning to Barnburgh Hall was set upon by a wild cat in High Melton

Woods: the frightened horse threw his rider and bolted. The knight had a running fight through Harlington to Barnburgh church porch, where he sought refuge. The cat pursued him, but was crushed to death as the exhausted knight fell to the floor on top of it. There he was found by one of his servants, who heard this horrific tale from the dying man.

The model, with its ochre-knobbed spire, lacking its weathercock, bears little resemblance to the pretty square towered Barnburgh church, but clearly the legend was the inspiration behind it.

The source of the legend itself was obviously the beautiful wooden effigy of a knight lying in this church. He is lying with his feet on a lion (or cat) and holding his heart in his hands. He was an ancestor of the Sir Percival Cresacre of the legend and from his armour can be dated between 1335-50; too late for the last Crusade. Perhaps he died at the battle of Crecy in 1346?

Model of a church c.1820
The walls of the main body of this building are painted in ochre with white lines between to simulate stones. The tower is blue and ochre and is topped with a white crenellated parapet. The window panes are outlined in black and are surrounded with white mouldings. The roof is washed with blue. A line of crenellations, as on the top of the tower, has been added above the windows along the roof line. Otherwise it is from the same moulds as the one to the right. 223mm high.
Courtesy Sotheby's.

Model of a Gothick Chapel c.1820 *below right*
The greyish walls are incised to represent brickwork. The windows and doors are picked out with black and the model rests on a mossy green base. 267mm high. *Courtesy Sotheby's.*

Model of a church c.1820
In this moulded, rather rough creamware model of a church; the walls are marked out in ochre to simulate stones. The roof is incised in imitation of tiles and coloured a deep blue. The door surround is orange and there is a thick yellow line round the base. The tower (ending in a chimney pot) which has been moulded separately is blotched on the side with patches of green. 230mm high. *Courtesy Jonathan Horne.*

Gothic cottages money-box c.1815
Money-box in the form of semi-detached gothic cottages with blue tiled roof, ochre windows and doors outlined in black and spotted in blue. The base is speckled in ochre and black. 153mm high. *Huntly House Museum, Edinburgh. HH 2353.16.62.*

54. A group of three cottages c.1810

Left: a gothic cottage 130mm high. This model was one of the ones reissued by the Kents of Burslem and is illustrated in their 1955 Catalogue. It was called 'Campbell Cottage' No. 189. William Kent founded his business in 1878 'for making old Staffordshire pottery in the traditional way'.

Centre: a circular toll-house money-box. 120mm high.
Right: a blue-tiled cottage with a flowering tree at one end and a classical female emptying a cornucopia in relief on the other. On the base is the mark shown on the opposite page. 115mm high. *Private Collection.*

55. Sailor pipe c.1805
A pipe in the form of a sailor sitting astride a barrel. 162mm high. *Courtesy Leonard Russell.*

56. Fantastic pipe c.1800
This strange conceit is made up of a woman's head and a cornucopia. The stem of the pipe is in the form of a serpent. 127mm high. *Courtesy Leonard Russell.*

254

Cottage money-box c.1810
A similar cottage to the one on the right opposite, flanked with disproportionately large figures of a standing girl and a seated child. 115mm high. *The Royal Pavilion Art Gallery and Museums, Brighton. HW 703.*

The indecipherable mark from the base of the cottage on the right illustrated in colour opposite.

Reproduction cottage c.1950
This is illustrated in Kent of Burslem's booklet 'The Story of Old Staffordshire Pottery'. It is called 'Man Cottage No.450'. Compared to the original old cottages, it is very heavy. The green is a pale emerald and the ochre a more anaemic colour than used on the old ones. Only the blue is approximately right. It could not be mistaken for an early nineteenth century piece. The Kents ceased production in 1962. 120mm high. *Private Collection.*

16. Figures and animals

By tradition, the two Ralph Woods, father (1715-72) and son (1748-95) were said to be the most prolific manufacturers of coloured glazed earthenware figures and Toby jugs in the last part of the eighteenth century. In fact there is no evidence that the elder Ralph Wood ever made any figures. He worked for most of his life as a modeller and mould maker for saltglazed useful stonewares for John and Thomas Wedgwood. The figures however were made by the potteries of the younger Ralph Wood and his brother John who became far more successful than Ralph (who had endless money troubles).

The earliest documentary reference to these figures is in John Wood's Sales Ledger of 1783, where are listed sets of Faith, Hope and Charity, shepherds, gardeners, stags and hinds and various others.

All the Wood figures were well modelled with distinctive features; clearly defined slightly bulging eyes and rather large hands. Though some of the colour glazed or china glazed figures were impressed either R. WOOD or Ra. WOOD or even Ra. Wood Burslem, we have never seen an *underglaze* coloured figure with any of the Wood marks.

In the section dealing with the Woods in the Schreiber Collection Catalogue[1] one of the authors writes:

> 'Towards the end of the eighteenth century a change is observable in the figures made at the Wood factory, even where the same moulds continued to be used. A well-marked category shows patterns – borders of costumes or sprigs on dresses in pigments amongst which a thick brownish yellow is conspicuous – painted under a colourless glaze; useful wares and plaques as well as figures occur with painting of this kind...'

At least a couple of dozen figures decorated with underglaze colouring were taken from moulds based on Ralph Wood designs. Such as a set of the Seasons, some were probably made at the Wood factories, but many of these were made by other potters. Because of the vitality of their colouring they make quite a different impact from the somewhat pallid coloured glaze originals.

An underglaze coloured St. George and the Dragon that was sold at Sotheby's in the 1970s was in many ways more appealing than the original model. It had shed its sophistication and taken on a naïve quality that is one of the attractions of this type of ware, as of much of English and Scottish pottery, from the early salt-glazed pew groups to mid-nineteenth century flat-backed mantelpiece ornaments.

Among other Wood inspired underglaze coloured figures are a shepherd carrying a lamb on his back, known as The Lost Sheep, a pair symbolising Old Age, a couple known as Simon and Iphigenia, another couple of musicians

1. *Catalogue of the Schreiber Collection, Vol. 2 Earthenware,* London, 1930. This volume of the catalogue was prepared not only by Bernard Rackham, Keeper of the Department of Ceramics at the Victoria and Albert Museum, but also by Herbert Read and W.B. Honey, both of the Ceramic Department.

The Seasons

Four classical female figures mounted on tapered square bases decorated with upright stiff leaves, based on models by Ralph Wood. Spring is holding an upturned cornucopia full of flowers, 'Summer' is clasping fruits and a small cornucopia, 'Autumn' is pressing a sheaf of corn and a sickle to her breast and 'Winter' is wrapped in an orange coloured robe with a brazier at her feet. Average height 237mm. *Private Collection.*

These figures are in no way a matching set. Spring is the best modelled and is subtly coloured in washes of manganese, blue, yellow and a mossy green. The figure and base are hollow and unglazed inside. Summer is more crudely coloured and is mounted on a square base with a solid top (except for a small circular perforation). Autumn is the odd one out, being very

light in weight and cream coloured; such additional colouring as she has is confined to manganese and pale blue. The figure and base are hollow and unglazed. Winter has a similar base to Summer.

In the original Wood version of the series, the figures decorated with coloured glazes are mounted on high square socles with medallions on each face. A figure of 'Winter' wrapped in a blue and ochre spotted cloak edged with brown and mounted on a green base on the top of the white socle which has a dotted pattern of blue and yellow round the top can be seen in the Royal Scottish Museum *1890.3.* This is rather a crude and heavy figure, but not unattractive and obviously deriving from a Wood model, possibly made at one of the East Coast potteries.

with hurdy-gurdys, Charity and Roman Charity and a huntsman with a dog.

To give some idea of the original value of such figures and of their coloured glaze predecessors, in 1783 Ralph Wood was selling single figures to Josiah and Thomas Wedgwood for ninepence each. At the same time six dozen unclassified small figures were invoiced to the Wedgwoods at nine shillings![2]

Apart from the Wood productions, innumerable figures often in the form of primitive little ornaments, are of unknown origin. Towards the end of the eighteenth century and in the early nineteenth, in the lists of potters given in various Directories, many are listed as earthenware manufacturers, but some specifically as toy or figure makers. There must have been dozens of small 'pot banks' turning out anonymous small figures by the thousands.

---

2. Frank Falkner, *The Wood Family of Burslem*, London, 1912.

St. George and the Dragon c.1810
A vividly coloured group painted in burnt orange, blue and black on a mottled and sponged base. St George is spearing the recumbent dragon. This piece is from the Ralph Wood mould No.23. 265mm high. *Courtesy Sotheby's.*
Similar groups are to be found with different combinations of colour.

Toy ornaments c.1780-90
A group of 'toy' ornaments showing the arbitrary way the blobs of colour were applied. The colours are limited to a manganese brown and ochre. The centre and right hand figures, which appear in colour in the group opposite have manganese washed hair and green washed bases. 112mm, 117mm and 100mm high. *Private Collection.*

57. St George and the Dragon c.1820
A most unusual group consisting of a
standing figure of St George dressed in
a manganese coloured tunic with a blue
and orange helmet. The dragon at his
feet and the rocky base upon which the
figures are mounted is also washed in
manganese. Two classical ladies in
Empire-style gowns and long flowing
draperies of yellow and orange flank the
main figure. They are perhaps meant
to represent Ceres and Cybele. 254mm
high. *Collection Mrs Constance Stobo.*

58. Toy figures c.1785-1800
A group of small underglaze coloured
figures. Three of them show the
arbitrary painting with blobs of ochre
and manganese 95mm-130mm high.
Private Collection.

Autumn c.1790
The girl is wearing a yellow overdress spotted in dark blue with an underskirt of white dotted with ochre and blue spots. She carries a yellow sheaf of corn and a brown sickle. Her hair is manganese brown and she stands on a green washed mound mounted on a high tapered square base with chamfered corners, decorated with a border of stiff leaves in relief. The whole base is sponged in blue and ochre. 219mm high. *Private Collection.*

Autumn c.1790
A creamware figure of a girl wearing a spotted blue and orange robe with a white underskirt dotted with blue. Her hair and features are coloured brown. She carries a yellow sheaf of corn and a brown sickle and stands on a green mound with vegetation. The whole is mounted on a high tapered square base patterned with acanthus leaves in uncoloured relief and a brown line below them. Another variation of the Ralph Wood Autumn. 220mm high. *Royal Ontario Museum, Toronto, Canada. 941.16.*

Charity c.1790 *opposite at top of page*
The front and back views of this crude but attractive group decorated in ochre, brown and blue. The figures are mounted on a square, tapered base with relief moulded stiff leaves coloured green. 235mm high. *Art Gallery and Museum, Glasgow. 38.10.jb.*

There is another Charity in the Huntly House Museum, Edinburgh *HH 2353.6.62,* attributed to Portobello.

Hope c.1790 *opposite left*
Figure from a set of Faith, Hope and Charity, coloured under the glaze with manganese and yellow stripes. There is a pattern of relief moulded stiff leaves round the tapered square base, washed in green. The back of the figure has been left uncoloured. 215mm high. *Private Collection.*

Faith c.1790 *opposite right*
A figure of Faith, standing with outstretched hand (because of this, she is rarely found with her arm intact). She has manganese brown hair and her gown is splashed with orange, blue and yellow, very much in the manner of the ones at Liverpool attributed to the Herculaneum Pottery. 215mm high. *Courtesy Leonard Russell.*

261

60. The Hurdy-Gurdy Player c.1790
A figure of a man holding an orange coloured hurdy-gurdy. He stands on a green washed mound, mounted on a stepped square base banded with brown and orange. 241mm high. *Courtesy Peter Manheim Ltd., London.*

59. Man with a pannier c.1790 *top left*
A standing figure of a man with a pannier at his side, from which peer two rabbits. He is mounted on a green mound on top of a tapered square base decorated with stiff green leaves. 223mm high. *The Royal Pavilion Art Gallery and Museums, Brighton. HW 1288.*

61. Girl in a mob cap c.1790
A well-modelled figure of a young girl wearing a mob cap, mounted on a stepped square base, decorated on the front with yellow, ochre, manganese and blue strokes of colour. The hollow underneath of the base is unglazed. 165mm high. *Private Collection.* This figure with its large hands has marked Ralph Wood characteristics.

Female Hurdy-Gurdy Player c.1790
The lady stands on a rocky green mound decorated with applied flowers. She holds an orange coloured hurdy-gurdy in her hands. The base is mounted on a brown lined square base. The colouring is limited to orange, yellow, green and brown. 230mm high. *Crown Copyright, Victoria and Albert Museum. C.48.1947.*

There is a similar pair of figures in the Royal Pavilion Art Gallery and Museums, Brighton. *HW 896 & a.*

Old Age and The Lost Sheep *top right*
After the models by Ralph Wood. The old man is wearing a blue coat with a brown collar, ochre breeches and a green washed hat. He stands on a green and blue mottled mound decorated with large flowers on top of a square brown-banded base. The figure has been attributed to either the Rawmarsh or Kilnhurst potteries. 222mm high *173.81.* The shepherd is wearing a pale manganese hat, ochre coat and breeches, his waistcoat is patterned with brown dots. He stands on a mottled mound, mounted on a brown-banded square base with a relief pattern of green stiff leaves between the bands. 214mm high. *87.80.* It is interesting to see how very different this figure is to the one marked HAWLEY (see page 73). *Museum and Art Gallery, Doncaster.*

Rural Musicians c.1790
A woman with a lute and a man with a wind instrument stand in front of a bocage on a green-washed mound, mounted on a high tapered square base decorated with flowers. Coloured in ochre, orange, yellow and blue. 209mm high. *Courtesy Brook-Hart Collection.*

Piping Shepherd spill vase group c.1790

The figure of a shepherd leans against the three-part vase, in the form of a brown and green washed tree trunk with branches. He is playing a yellow pipe and is dressed in a brown hat, blue jacket and yellow breeches. At his feet are a ram, a ewe and a lamb reclining. On the branches of the tree are three yellow birds, one sitting on its nest. The general colouring in its darkness of tone is very similar to pieces marked HAWLEY, but this group is unmarked. 203mm high. *Yorkshire Museum.*

Shepherdess c.1800

A standing figure of a girl, holding a basket and with a lamb standing by her side. Her bonnet and blouse are coloured in yellow and orange and she is wearing a blue apron. The rocky base is dappled in streaks of blue, orange and green. 203mm high. *Fitzwilliam Museum, Cambridge.*

Resting shepherd spill vase c.1790

A small figure of a tired shepherd boy dressed in an orange coat and yellow breeches with a brown hat, rests at the foot of a tree trunk with four branches, which forms a spill vase. With the shepherd are two lambs blobbed with orange. The base and the tree stump are coloured with mingled manganese, ochre and copper oxide colours reminiscent of Whieldon's coloured glazes. 133mm high. *Courtesy Leonard Russell.*

Girl with a basket of fruit c.1795
A simply modelled standing figure of a girl wearing a yellow apron. Her dress is blotched in manganese and orange and she stands on a green-washed base. 130mm high. *Private Collection.*

Boy holding a rabbit c.1785-90 *above centre*
The colouring is applied in washes of manganese and green, giving the appearance of coloured glazes. 120mm high. *Private Collection.*

Seated boy c.1790
A figure of a boy, probably by Ralph Wood. He is seated with one elbow resting on a barrel, wearing a brown hat, manganese waistcoat and the back of his coat is washed in green. The barrel has horizontal brown stripes. 114mm high. *Courtesy Sotheby's.*

Seated woman with a cat c.1790-1800
A crudely moulded figure of a woman seated in a large white chair, holding a cat on her lap. She has brown hair and black eyes and is wearing a yellow dress trimmed with blue round the neck and brown shoes. The cat has black eyes and is dotted with blue. 88mm high. *Colonial Williamsburg Foundation. 1963-494.* This figure was formerly in the C.B.Kidd Collection (No. 1183).

Seated woman with a dog c.1800-10
A creamware figure of a woman holding a bowl of fruit in her lap, with a dog at her side, resting his head on her arm. Her high-waisted dress is spotted with orange. She is supported at the back by bushes, sponged in orange. The group rests on a green-washed base. 88mm high. *Colonial Williamsburg Foundation. 1963-507.* The figure was formerly in the C.B.Kidd Collection.

A pair of ladies holding fans c.1795
Both figures are wearing brown shawls over brown and blue spotted white dresses, they hold blue fans. The figures stand on green moulded mound bases. 132mm high. *Royal Ontario Museum, Toronto, Canada. 966. 265.2 a&b.*

Mr Peter Kaellgren of the European Department of the Royal Ontario Museum suggests that these figures may represent women at the time of the French Revolution as they are wearing 'Liberty' caps and one has bands of blue and brown at the edge, suggesting the French tricolour. If this supposition is correct, they might have been made for the French export market.

Iphigenia c.1790 *top left*
The lady is dressed in a yellow bodice and flower-patterned skirt and is holding up an apron full of fruit. She stands on a green mound on a tapering high, square base decorated with stiff green leaves in relief. 241mm high. *Private Collection.* She is usually partnered with a young man known as Cymon. These figures are based on characters from Boccaccio's *Decameron*.

There is another example of this figure in the ceramic collection at Colonial Williamsburg *1963.580.* This was once in the C.B.Kidd Collection.

A standing woman with a parasol c.1790
A figure of a woman wearing a brown hat and a white dress spotted in blue, orange and manganese. She holds a folded parasol in her right hand with a long orange handle, and she stands on a green-washed base with a pricked pattern, mounted on a square base banded in brown. 135mm high. Marked on the front 'B I' and on the back 'P O W'. *Colonial Williamsburg Foundation. 1963-286.* This figure was formerly in the C.B.Kidd Collection (No. 1195).

62. Girl with cat and boy with dog c.1800
A pair of figures opaquely coloured, the girl with a
brown bonnet, dark blue jacket and deep yellow
skirt; the boy is wearing a brown hat, dark blue
coat, orange waistcoat and yellow breeches. She
holds an orange coloured cat in her hand and he has
an orange coloured dog at his feet. Both figures
stand on dark green mound bases mounted on
square plinths. 197 and 192mm high. *Courtesy Elias
Clark Collection.* From the nature of the colouring,
these figures might well have been made by Hawley
at Kilnhurst or Rawmarsh.

63. 'Summer' and 'Autumn' c.1800
A pair of figures from a set of the Seasons after
models by Ralph Wood. The small figure of the girl
is perched on a green-washed tree stump wearing a
brown hat with a ribbon tied under her chin and a
white dress, sprigged and trimmed with ochre. She
holds a basket of fruit close to her bosom. She is
mounted on a stepped square base with a brown
line running round the lower edge. 125mm high.
The figure of the boy is perched on a green and
ochre rococo mound, wearing a white hat and a
white coat spotted with ochre dots, yellow breeches
and holding a sheaf of yellow corn and a manganese
brown sickle; his hair is the same colour. The figure
is mounted on a stepped square base with an ochre
line round it. 123mm high. *Private Collection.*

Tavern wench with a bottle c.1790

This is a very unusual figure of a girl in a beribboned mob cap and décolleté dress, carrying a brown bottle in her left arm. Her dress is spotted with orange, patterned with blue, edged with yellow and elaborately looped up and fastened behind, exposing a white underskirt with a blue flounce at the hem. The bottom of the figure is edged with stiff triangular leaves alternately coloured blue and green. This pearlware figure is surprisingly heavy, but when examined, the skirt is seen to be hollow, revealing her naked to the waist, realistically modelled, with a pair of shapely legs and feet in neat brown shoes. 191mm high. *Reproduced by courtesy of the Trustees of the British Museum. 1981.1-1.451.*

Tavern wench with a bottle c.1790 *top left*

A similar, but not identical figure to the one on the right. She is wearing a yellow overdress trimmed with blue and an orange and green tiered underskirt. She carries a blue bottle and is also naked to the waist. 191mm high.
Colonial Williamsburg Foundation. 1963-309.

A similar figure but modestly placed on a square orange and black mottled base (216mm high) can be seen in the Royal Pavilion Art Gallery and Museums, Brighton. *HW 1474.*

Woman and child group c.1785

A small early group of a woman holding a child by the hand. She wears a grey-green dress and an orange overdress and is holding up her white apron full of fruit or flowers. The child is dressed in an orange robe. The two stand on a mound splashed with orange and dark green on top of a square base, the sides of which are washed with a dark grey-green. 140mm high. *Courtesy Peter Manheim Ltd., London.*

Three female figures c.1790-1800
Left: a girl with a bird in a cage coloured in manganese, yellow and blue on a green-washed mound mounted on a brown-banded square base. 137mm high. *1963-280.*
Centre: a girl with a bundle and a bird coloured in brown, blue and yellow mounted on a rockybase sponged in orange, green and brown. 179mm high. *1963-578.*
Right: a girl with a basket of fruit coloured in yellow, green and manganese on a square base. 146mm high. *1963-717. Colonial Williamsburg Foundation.* Formerly in the C.B.Kidd Collection.

Three male figures c.1790-1800
Left: a boy with a basket of eggs, coloured in brown, blue and yellow on a green-washed mound above a square brown-banded base. 133mm high *1963-279.*
Centre: a bearded man with an orange and green coat, orange striped breeches and blue dotted waistcoat and stockings, on a square blue marbled base. 130mm high. *1963-287.*

Right: a Scottish shepherd holding a yellow thistle and coloured in brown, yellow and blue on a green, brown and orange mottled mound above a brown-banded base. 157mm high. *1963-570.* Formerly in the C.B.Kidd Collection. *Colonial Williamsburg Foundation.* Compare to a salt-glazed group *II 88* in Victoria and Albert Museum and see Mackintosh's book for a similar group with tortoiseshell glazes.

Sportsman with a dog c.1810 *left*

A standing figure of a sportsman holding a gun to his side and wearing a manganese brown cap and boots, a yellow ochre jacket and white breeches, by his side an ochre spotted dog is pawing his left leg. This nicely modelled group rests on a green mound. 178mm high. *The Royal Pavilion Art Gallery and Museums, Brighton. HW 1085.*

Farmer c.1800 *centre*

A small press-moulded figure of a farmer, a similar figure to that illustrated on page 259 in the group of small figures. 98mm high. *The Royal Pavilion Art Gallery and Museums, Brighton. HW 1138.*

Sailor c.1810 *right*

A figure of a sailor wearing a brown hat, blue coat, yellow neckerchief, patterned blue trousers, black shoes with yellow buckles standing on a rocky base smeared in green, brown and orange. He is leaning on the stock of an anchor. 196mm high. *The Royal Pavilion Art Gallery and Museums, Brighton. HW 289.*

Sportsman with a gun c.1800

The figure of a sportsman with a gun dressed in an ochre jacket, but otherwise patterned in an arbitrary manner with green, blue and ochre dashes. The square base is decorated with a green border of small acanthus leaves. 198mm high. *Crown Copyright, Victoria and Albert Museum. C.80.1952.*

Farmer's wife c.1790

A small press moulded figure of a woman, a partner to the farmer illustrated above. Her hat is washed in manganese and her dress is decorated with brown and yellow blobs. She holds a cockerel in her lap. 98mm high. *Private Collection.*

London Cryers c.1790-1800
The figure of a girl in a yellow skirt spotted with black, the rest of her dress spotted with brown and grey. She holds a basket of fruit and stands on a rocky green mound with, in impressed capitals, LONDON CRYERS round the front of the base. 142mm high. *Crown Copyright, Victoria and Albert Museum. CIRC. 458.1967.*

This may be one of a series, but so far none of the other Cries of London have been found by us. The bowl which the girl holds is identical with one at the base of a watch stand and also a tall clock money-box from the pottery that used the large impressed crown mark (see pages 88 and 91).

The Umbrella Courtship c.1810
Two figures blending into each other as they kiss, stand under a brown umbrella. The man is wearing a black hat, blue frock coat and white trousers, both edged with ochre. The girl has a bonnet trimmed with puce and a white dress spotted with blue and puce. They stand on a green-washed base edged with a relief pattern of grasses. 140mm high. *Private Collection.*

A similar group decorated with enamel colours can be seen in the Royal Pavilion Art Gallery and Museums, Brighton. *HW 1679.* The green-washed mound with its pricked surface and moulded leaf pattern is very similar to that under 'London Cryers'. Also, the blue spots surrounded by puce circles on the girl's dress are identical to those on the dress worn by the woman in the 'Wesley' cow group on page 83.

Bowl of fruit c.1800-20
This is a detail from the watchstand group illustrated in colour on page 88. It is from a similar mould to the container carried by the 'London Cryer' figure, shown in the picture above. The bowl is 22mm high.

It seems possible from the evidence of this bowl and from other details illustrated on the figures above that these figures may have been made by the pottery that used the large impressed crown mark.

271

Flora and Apollo c.1790
A pair of small figures standing on green-washed mounds mounted on stepped brown-banded square bases. The figures are blobbed in burnt orange and brown and carry a yellow cornucopia and a yellow lyre respectively. Their hair is brown. 140 and 135mm high. *Private Collection.*

Flora was the Roman goddess of flowering plants, hence her doing duty for the classical figure of Spring, in various sets of the Seasons. She is usually depicting clasping a cornucopia to her bosom, or standing with one at her side.

Apollo, the son of Zeus and Leto was the patron of youth and athletic prowess and also the god of agriculture, known as the protector of corn, the preventer of blight and the destroyer of locusts. His most usual attributes were the lyre and the bow. He was represented more than any other deity in ancient art, most famously in the Apollo Belvedere, most typically in a statue also in Rome that shows him standing naked and holding a lyre in his left hand.

Pair of figures under a tree c.1790
A most unusual and rather primitive little group; the man is dressed in a long blue surcoat and yellow breeches. The lady is wearing a yellow blouse with an orange scarf and a white skirt spotted with blue. The tree is moulded in three pieces with flowers and fruit in abundance, coloured blue, yellow, orange and green. They are mounted on a pale green rocky mound. 120mm high. *Courtesy Jonathan Horne.*

Summer or Plenty c.1795
A figure of a woman wearing an ochre tiara and reclining against a dark green bocage. She is holding a large green cornucopia full of flowers and fruits. The figure is mounted on a green mounded base on top of an ochre sided rectangular base, the top of which is washed in green and decorated with a row of large applied flowers alternately coloured blue and ochre. 150mm high. *Courtesy Jonathan Horne.*

Two figures of Amphitrite and the dolphin c.1800
Two small rather crude press-moulded figures of the goddess, each with a green-washed dolphin at her side. One is draped in a white robe, spotted in brown and ochre, she has manganese washed hair and stands on a small square base. The other is mounted on a larger square base, which is banded in manganese. She has a circlet round her head and her modestly draped robe is coloured with yellow, burnt orange and blue. 145 and 149mm high. *Private Collection.*

Amphitrite was the wife of Poseidon, king of the sea. These figures are very like early sixteenth century terracotta bas relief figures by Giovanna da Bologna.

They are sometimes referred to as Venus and the Dolphin. Venus or Aphrodite (the Greek goddess of Love) was also worshipped as a goddess of the sea, hence her association with seahorses, shells, fish and dolphins. She was also made in salt-glazed stoneware.

Amphitrite and the dolphin c.1800 *top right*
A graceful, but rather crude figure of the goddess with a dolphin at her side, the dolphin is coloured green except for its head which is uncoloured but picked out with manganese. Amphitrite wears an orange cloak draped over one shoulder and a circlet of green leaves round her loins. The group is mounted on a stepped rectangular white base with chamfered corners and a blue pencilled line at the top. 157mm high. *Royal Scottish Museum. 190.482.*

There is a figure very similar to this one, but on a different base marked 'John Pattison 1825', pencilled in brown on the base. There does not seem to be a record of this potter.[1]

1. R.G.Haggar, 'Pattison of Lane End and Notes on Tittensor', *Apollo,* Vol.51, 1950.

Hermes or Mercury, the winged messenger c.1800
The young god is wearing a manganese and ochre coloured winged helmet. His right hand holds despatches to his forehead and his left holds a caduceus, which he is pressing to his breast. His short white tunic is spotted with ochre and brown and he stands against a green-washed support. The figure is mounted on a square base. 190mm high. *Private Collection.* This figure is inspired by an early sixteenth century terracotta figure by Giovanna da Bologna.

Pomona c.1795
A lightly coloured figure in a blue spotted dress with a yellow sash. She is lifting up her apron to hold some fruit in its folds. She stands on a waisted socle mounted on a tapering square base, which is banded in blue. Her hair is manganese washed and her dress is feathered blue at the foot. 200mm high. *City Museum and Art Gallery, Stoke-on-Trent. 250.P.49.*

Ceres c.1795 *top right*
A companion figure to Pomona, standing on a similar socle only in this case coloured green and the square base is lined with brown. She has manganese coloured hair and is holding a yellow corn sheaf. She is wearing a white tunic striped and spotted with ochre, with a green belt over a long yellow underskirt. She has a long yellow scarf over her shoulder. 197mm high. *Private Collection.*

Figure with obelisk c.1800
A classical female figure leaning on an obelisk is dressed in a blue washed robe, patterned in a darker blue and an ochre coloured cloak spotted in brown. The obelisk and stepped plinth are both marbled in blue and the top of the plinth is washed in orange. 150mm high. *Royal Scottish Museum, Edinburgh. 1898.305.*

Roman Charity c.1790

This group, of which there are coloured glaze, uncoloured, enamel coloured and underglaze coloured versions was originally made by the elder Ralph Wood, for some examples are to be found marked R.WOOD. The earlier (and perhaps less attractive) groups are not mounted on square bases. This sparingly underglaze coloured piece is beautifully modelled and painted with a little orange, yellow, green and brown. It shows the prisoner Cimon, who was sustained by the milk of his daughter, sitting by her and her clamouring children. 210mm high. *Courtesy Leonard Russell.*

Lucretia c.1790
The nude figure of Lucretia lies on a couch, whether before or
after the rape by Tarquinius is hard to say. Her head and arm
rest on a dark blue pillow with ochre tassels, the yellow scroll
ends of the couch are moulded with the mask of a man's face.
280mm long. *Courtesy Sotheby's.*

65. Standing horse c.1800 *opposite*
The horse stands four square on a shaped green-washed base
plate. It is decorated with patches of ochre and sponged in
manganese. 165mm high. *Courtesy Sotheby's.*

Sleeping child c.1800
The figure of a sleeping child with his head on a basket of fruit.
The green cushion on which he is lying is mounted on a
rectangular base with a painted border of flowers in ochre,
green, yellow and brown. 128mm long. *Crown Copyright, Victoria
and Albert Museum. C.450.1928.*

This is after a black basaltes figure marked WEDGWOOD
c.1780. An example of this can be seen in the Wedgwood
Museum at Barlaston.

65. Circus elephant with passengers 1800-20 *opposite*
A white bodied elephant, stiffly moulded with a curled trunk and
upright ochre tusks, and ochre feet. The body is sponged with
patches of black and there are dotted black eyebrows. It is being
ridden by a man in a blue jacket, yellow breeches and orange
topped boots. Behind the man is a figure of a monkey and a
small recumbent lion. 197mm high. *Courtesy Sotheby's.*

64. Philip Astley and the Dancing Horse c.1800-20

A circus act of a skewbald horse patched with manganese and burnt orange, rearing up on its hind legs, while its daring rider lies on his back below the animal's forelegs. 152mm high. *Courtesy Sotheby's.*

A similar group can be seen in the Museum at Newcastle under Lyme and another with an orange horse with a dark brown mane and tail and a white face with the man in a blue coat and orange breeches, mounted on a different kind of base decorated with stiff leaves in relief, can be seen in the Art Gallery and Museum, Glasgow, *E49.113.199.*

64. Standing horse c.1800 *centre*

A stiffly standing horse has its body sponged in manganese. It has white hocks and black hooves. On its back is a blue checked saddle-cloth with an ochre girth strap. The beast is mounted on a waisted, thin, green-washed base plate with brown sides. 165mm high. *Courtesy Sotheby's.*

64. Mounted horseman c.1810 *to the right*

A rider astride a black and white piebald horse is wearing a black top hat and black boots with ochre tops and a puce coat trimmed with ochre. His ochre saddle rests on a blue saddle-cloth trimmed with ochre. The horse stands on a base with rounded corners and a green-washed top, the sloping sides are speckled in orange, blue and black. The horse has eyebrows dotted in exactly the same manner as the Toby jug from the pottery that used the large impressed crown mark. 235mm high. *Courtesy Sotheby's.*

Philip Astley was born in 1742 at Newcastle under Lyme, the son of a cabinetmaker. At the age of 17 he joined General Eliott's Light Horse, attaining the rank of sergeant-major. He became famous as a breaker-in and trainer of horses, eventually opening a circus at Westminster in 1770. In 1798 he opened Astley's Royal Amphitheatre in London which was destroyed by fire in 1802 but rebuilt two years later. He died in Paris in 1814.

Horse with two riders c.1790 *opposite*
A dappled grey horse with a grey mane carries two riders, a man in a blue coat, manganese hat and boots with ochre tops. The lady riding pillion is raising her hat. This is the same figure that appears as a shepherdess on one of the 'large crown' sheep groups and also on one of the cow groups, but this otherwise bears little resemblance to the other pieces from that pottery. It is mounted on a rectangular stand, green-washed on top and with the sides sponged in grey, green and yellow. *Leeds Art Galleries, Temple Newsam House. 28.47/41.*

Racehorses c.1800
A pair of racehorses standing on flat green base plates. One is coloured smoothly with ochre and wears a blue and white saddle cloth, the other animal is sponged with ochre and wears a blue saddle cloth with a yellow girth strap. 152mm high. *The Royal Pavilion Art Gallery and Museums, Brighton. HW 1055.*

Animals

Animals in underglaze colouring range from the very large pearlware horses from the Leeds Pottery, to smaller models of racehorses and Suffolk punches decorated with sponged colours and standing foursquare on flat green washed bases, or to cow creamers, down to little toys – sheep, monkeys, dogs or deer only three or four inches high, usually decorated with blobs of manganese or ochre. There were also large brightly coloured cockerels, melancholy lions resting a paw on a ball, circus elephants mounted by monkeys, and pigs bestraddled by drunken Irishmen.

Groups of cows and calves and large sheep with attendants from the pottery that used the large crown mark are most distinctive. Numerous versions of a bull-baiting group that originated from the Wood pottery also appeared in underglaze colours, as did various other animals from the same factory. Animals are very rarely marked.

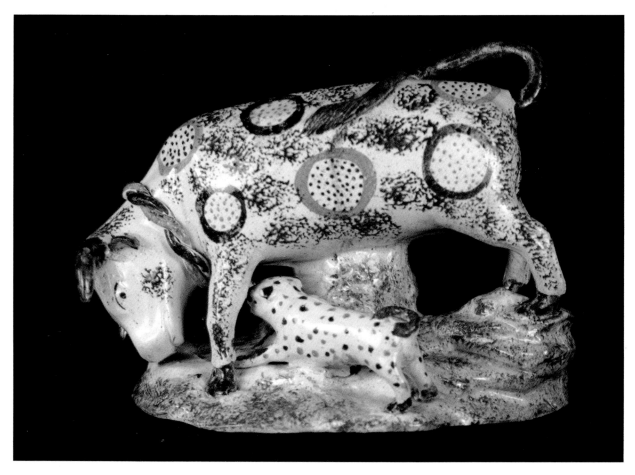

66. Bull-baiting group c.1790
This Ralph wood group in underglaze colouring shows a bull tethered to a tree stump and a bull terrier on a green sponged rocky base. The bull is sponged in manganese, with manganese brown and burnt orange circles on his back and flanks, his horns and tail are also brown. The dog is spotted in brown and orange. 203mm high. *Private Collection.*

This revolting sport was finally prohibited by an Act of Parliament in 1835.

67. Standing lion c.1795
A lion with a brown spotted yellow body, brown and burnt orange face has an amusing if melancholy expression. It stands on a rectangular plinth, moulded with stiff leaves, alternately coloured green and orange with a yellow bottom rim. The top of the stand is sponged in orange and green. The creature's forepaw rests on an orange ball. 183mm high. *Courtesy Sotheby's.*

Standing lion c.1790
A lion with a burnt orange coloured body, face and tail spotted in blue, orange and black, and with black paws. He stands on a rectangular base with sloping sides, decorated with freely drawn trailing pattern of flowers and foliage. His eyes are heavily outlined and he has an agreeable expression. 140mm high. *City Art Gallery and Museum, Stoke-on-Trent.*

Recumbent lion c.1790
A small figure of a recumbent lion, wearing a haughty expression, coloured lightly in orange and brown, and lying on a hollow green mounded base. 89mm high. *Courtesy Leonard Russell.*

Cow creamer c.1810
Cow cream jug, sponged in black and burnt orange, with black horns. It is mounted on a shaped flat stand with a projection for the milkmaid, which is washed in green. The very small milkmaid has black hair and is wearing a green dress. 134mm high. *Private Collection.* A comparable figure to some in the City Museum and Art Gallery, Stoke-on-Trent which bear the mark of St Anthony's Pottery, Sunderland.

Cow creamers c.1790 *opposite*
A pair of lively cow creamers, modelled with some spirit and standing four square on canted rectangular bases with rounded corners, edged with vertical blue repeating patterns. The cows are dappled in black, ochre and burnt orange. Each cow is being milked by a ridiculously small milkmaid (or milkman), wearing a manganese-washed hat and burnt ochre jacket. 138mm high. *Private Collection.*

Cow creamer 1800-20
A white bodied cow with a slightly crackled glaze decorated with yellow patches outlined in black, with black speckles. The ears, horns and hooves are also decorated with black. There is a little lid with a mushroom shaped knob in the centre of the cow's back. It is mounted on a moulded oval base decorated with black and mauve sponging. 159mm high. *Courtesy Leonard Russell.*

Stag at lodge c.1790
The seated stag has a white body, decorated with large black patches. The antlers are speckled with black and the eyebrows are dotted with black. The stag rests on a green-washed mound decorated with grasses in relief, in front of a green bocage with yellow flowers with puce centres. 153mm high. *Private Collection.*

Sheep with two lambs c.1800
A well-modelled little group set on a serpentine fronted blue sided base. The animals are touched with ochre and the sheep has brown horns. 121mm high. *City Art Gallery and Museum, Stoke-on-Trent. 2944.*

Cockerel c.1790
A cockerel after a model by Ralph Wood. It has a detachable
head and stands in an alert attitude. It is strongly coloured in
yellow, burnt orange and blue and stands on a green mound
above a rectangular base with a blue top and brown and yellow
edges. 230mm high. *Courtesy Elias Clark Collection.*

Rearing horse with thrown rider c.1790
The whole group is sponged in light olive green, grey and yellow under the glaze, even the oval base. 203mm high. *The Royal Pavilion Art Gallery and Museums, Brighton. HW 1057.*

Horse 1800-20
A figure of a horse made in putty coloured clay and decorated with mauve patches surrounded in black, the body is spotted with black, with a black mane and hooves and dotted black eyebrows. The base is sponged in black and mauve and is oval in form with sloping sides. 150mm high. *Courtesy Elias Clark Collection.*

Irishman and pig c.1790
A group consisting of an intoxicated Irishman astride a pig. The base is decorated with thin green threads of clay to simulate grass. The man wears a brown hat, burnt orange jacket and blue breeches. 172mm high. *The Royal Pavilion Art Gallery and Museums, Brighton. HW 1260.*

Not least among the many attractions of Pratt ware is humour, a quality that keeps cropping up in English pottery, whether it is on slipware chargers, salt-glazed pew groups or the witty conceits of some modern potters. The drunken Irishman seemed to us a happy note with which to end our book.

17. Afterthoughts

In the half a dozen years or so that have passed since the first edition of this book was published, various pots that we have not seen before have appeared. These include five marked pieces, one of a Newcastle upon Tyne cow creamer. We had shown a comparable piece in the book but this is worth showing here because of the extreme rarity of such pieces. Two jugs had the familiar WEDGWOOD mark, but the other two were quite new to us. One of these was a cornucopia mug with the mark BECKETT on the base. This mark refers to the Staffordshire potters John and Robert Beckett, who worked at Longton at the beginning of the nineteenth century. The other was a teapot that passed through the London Sale Rooms in November 1989. This was decorated in a typical Pratt palette with a lion finial on the lid. Inside the lid C. GRESLEY was impressed in small capital letters, the same mark appeared in a faint impression on the base of the pot. This mark must refer to one of the Church Gresley potteries in Derbyshire.

Church Gresley

The potteries in this district in the late eighteenth century were known to have made rough domestic wares, but in *The Staffordshire Advertiser* of 17 March 1798 a factory at Church Gresley in Derbyshire was advertised for sale as a going concern with a list of contents showing that it would have been possible to have made good quality earthenware there.[1]

Sir Nigel Gresley is said to have founded a factory at Church Gresley in 1794. In 1800 this pottery was purchased by W. Nadin, a colliery proprietor, who ran it until 1808 when it was finally closed.[2] Whether it was this pottery that made the Pratt ware teapot it is impossible to say. There are at the moment four other known pieces with variations of the spelling. One is a blue printed plate, another a creamware tureen, the third a caneware jug and the fourth a tea canister dated 1772.

Llewellynn Jewitt mentions several potteries in Church Gresley, one established about 1790 by a Mr Leedham for making coarse pancheon ware which was bought by W. Bourne about 1816, who made 'Derbyshire ironstone caneware, Rockingham, mottled, black lustre, buff and other wares.' Also the Hill Top Pottery was established in Church Gresley in 1810 by John Cooper, who made similar ware.[3]

These marked pieces help to spread the net a little wider and bring the total of Pratt ware pieces that we have seen with different marks up to thirty-three.

The clock money box shown in the photograph opposite is comparable to those on pages 88-91, but is flanked by two soldiers which are larger than the usual little civilians and their bases almost overlap the stand. This money box must have been made by the same factory as the other ones illustrated earlier in the book.

1. The Northern Ceramic Society's *Newsletter No 67* September 1987, article by Clarice and Harold Blakey.
2. *The Concise Encyclopedia of English Pottery and Porcelain* by W. Mankowitz and R.G. Haggar. 1957.
3. *The Ceramic Art of Great Britain,* L. Jewitt 1883.

68. Teapot c.1800 and Clock Money Box 1800-20.
Straight sided teapot, decorated on both sides with the same relief figures of ladies, churning butter, sitting at a table pouring tea and carrying a basket. Stiff leaf decoration round the top and an orange coloured lion finial on the lid. Sparsely coloured with the usual Pratt palette. Impressed under the lid and on the base C. GRESLEY. 140mm high.

A moneybox in the form of a long case clock, flanked by an officer and a soldier mounted on typical sponged base with a green top, with a spaniel resting at the foot of the clock. 230mm high. *Courtesy Jonathan Horne.*

The figures of the soldiers, unusual to find on a clock money box, are much larger than the usual little civilians, their bases almost overlap the stand.

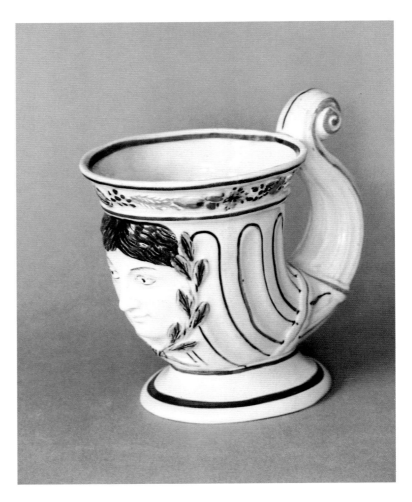

69. Cornucopia mug c.1802
Pearl ware mug banded in brown at top and bottom, with the addition of blue and orange lining.
The relief head with brown hair is framed with green leaves. A border of fruit in relief round
the top is painted in yellow, orange, green and brown. Impressed under the base BECKETT.
in Capital letters. 120mm high. *Photograph courtesy Leonard Russell*

A similar specimen is now in the City Museum and Art Gallery, Stoke-on-Trent. Another
unmarked cornucopia mug is shown on page 209.

John and Robert Beckett

John and Robert Beckett were in business in Longton from 1802-04. Their
partnership was actually dissolved on 28 December 1803. Robert Beckett was
gazetted Ensign in the Lane End Volunteers in 1803 and was still listed as an
earthenware manufacturer in Holden's Directory of 1805. This corncupia mug
appears to be the first recorded marked piece from the Beckett pottery.[1]

---

1. This information has been supplied by Rodney Hampson MA and comes from an appendix
to his Thesis on Longton.

70. Cow creamer with Milkmaid c.1810
White earthenware cow sponged in ochre and manganese with a milkmaid wearing a brown blouse and a yellow skirt, mounted on a shaped flat green base, edged with manganese. Impressed $_{\mathrm{SEWELL}}^{7}$ under the base. Made at the St. Anthony's Pottery, Newcastle upon Tyne. 130mm high. *Private Collection.* For a similar cow impressed SEWELL see page 100.

Cow Creamers

At the City Museum and Art Gallery, Stoke-on-Trent there are over 700 cow creamers, which were bequeathed to the Museum by Mrs Keiller. Of these only three are marked, one with the word SEWELL. The cow creamer illustrated on this page is also impressed SEWELL, but unlike the Stoke-on-Trent creamer has an accompanying milkmaid. These Sewell cow creamers are deeper in the body than most other ones and their horns point forwards.

71. Coffee pot c.1790
A pearlware pot decorated with two ionic shaped columns on each side, ovoid in section and coloured in cobalt, mossy green, ochre and Naples yellow, very similar to the teapot marked ASTBURY. Lid missing. Similar lids have a swan finial. 190mm high. *Private Collection.*

292

72 and 73. Birds and Windmill jug c.1800-10
A most unusual pearl ware jug, unmarked, with scenes of birds feeding nestlings on one side and a landscape with a windmill and cottage on the other. There is a leaf and floral border round the neck and an upright vineleaf border at the bottom. In usual Pratt palette with green and Naples yellow predominating. The shape of the jug, particularly the handle, is similar to an unmarked stag hunting jug in the Wolverhampton Museum. (See page 174.) 155mm high. *Courtesy Elias Clark.*

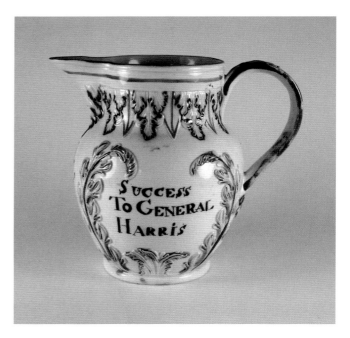

74. Brougham and Denman jug 1820
A small pearlware jug with a splayed foot and a scalloped rim
has a spout decorated with a horned satyr's head with horns and
beard coloured in manganese, otherwise decorated with cobalt
blue and burnt orange. 107mm high. *Private Collection.*

75. General Harris jug c.1797
Pearlware jug sparsely coloured in cobalt, ochre, pale green and
brown and inscribed in dark brown on one side 'Success to
General Harris'. Under the spout is a fouled anchor in brown
and on the verso a brown strawberry leaf. Impressed
WEDGWOOD in small capitals on the base. 140mm high. *Private
Collection.*

Major General George Harris, First Baron Harris, was in
command of the army in Madras and in 1797 he captured the
fortress of Seringapatam from the notorious Tipoo Sahib.

Commemorative pieces

The most interesting commemorative jug to have come to light recently is the
small Brougham and Denman jug which is very similar to the enamel coloured
jug shown on page 137. It is the only underglaze coloured version of this jug
that we have seen.

The handsome Duke of Wellington jug shown on the opposite page is in
some ways comparable to the Waterloo jug shown on page 172, though that
jug has trophies of war on the verso.

The crudely lettered General Harris jug may be a unique example, for jugs
of this design without any inscription can be found in various sizes.

The portrait bust of Admiral Earl St Vincent is after a stoneware bust made
by the Herculaneum Pottery, an example of which is in the Merseyside County
Museum, Liverpool.

The Apotheosis of Nelson jug has relief designs including Nelson in a chariot
drawn by sea horses. These designs also appear on a smear-glazed white
stoneware jug and on a similar mug marked T & J Hollins.

76. Duke of Wellington jug c.1815

A pearlware jug, with the figure of the Duke of Wellington astride a charger, with a cutlass in his outstretched right hand. 'DUKE' and 'WELLINGTON' are impressed on yellow scrolls on either side of the horseman. The bottom part of the jug is fluted and the top decorated with a repeat pattern in orange and blue. 162mm high. *Courtesy Terence Lockett.*

Admiral Jervis bust c.1798

A portrait bust of Admiral Earl St Vincent, wearing an ochre jacket with yellow frogging and a blue sash. 200mm high. *Courtesy Phillips, Son and Neale.*

From the manner of painting and particularly the treatment of the eyes, this bust may have been made by the Hawley's at Rawmarsh. It does not seem to be a very good likeness of the Admiral.

Apotheosis of Nelson c.1805

Sparsely coloured, green and blue feathered border and an encircling pattern of orange flowers enclosed in manganese ovals. Acanthus leaves outlined in brown and yellow surround the lower part. Below the spout there is a relief of Nelson sitting in a chariot drawn by seahorses. Nelson is being crowned by Neptune. The other reliefs include Britannia and a lion, Clio the Muse of History and figures depicting Hope and Plenty. 155mm high. *Private Collection.*

295

77. Loyal Volunteers jugs c.1803 and 1888-1957
Two creamware versions of the L1 Volunteers jug; the one on the left showing three soldiers with their rifles in the firing position is decorated in underglaze colours. This jug is unmarked but was probably made at the Leeds Pottery. The jug on the right with the soldiers presenting arms is a much later version with a very pale cream body and over-glaze enamel colours. Made by the Seniors at their pottery at Hunslet in Leeds and impressed on the base LEEDS POTTERY. 155mm and 148mm high. *Private Collection.*
(See pages 67-70).

Reproductions

The photograph of two Loyal Volunteer jugs shows quite clearly the difference between the original underglaze coloured jug, made c.1803 and the overglaze coloured jug made by the Seniors at Leeds at any time between 1888 when they opened and 1957 when they finally closed their Hunslet pottery.

78. Loyal Volunteers plaque c.1803
A cream coloured earthenware plaque showing the same three soldiers presenting arms, as appear on the L1 Volunteers jugs. 145mm high. *Courtesy Jonathan Horne.*

79. Teapot with classical design and painted floral decoration, c.1800
A fine quality teapot, decorated on one side with a seated figure of Mercury and on the other of another classical figure, each set in oval medallions, flanked with incised yellow panels and painted floral decorations. The lid is surmounted with a swan finial. Coloured in the usual Pratt palette. 160mm high. *Private Collection.*

80. Dolphin sauceboat c.1800
Underglaze coloured in green and ochre with black eyes. There is a manganese band round the oval base. 110mm high. *Private Collection.*

82. Scent Bottle c.1810.
A small scent bottle, underglaze coloured in blue, yellow and mulberry. 70mm high. *A. and H. Thomas Collection.*

81. Pepperpot c.1800-20
A pearlware pepperpot in the form of the bust of a woman, draped in blue, yellow and orange and wearing a black hat with a wide brim and a perforated crown. Mounted on a waisted socle moulded with acanthus leaves and sponged in orange and blue. From the nature of the colouring it may have been made by the pottery that used the large impressed crown mark. 105mm high. *Private Collection.*

83. Love token c.1800
The creamware heart shaped token is decorated with embracing figures and is coloured in blue, green and manganese. The token itself is pierced and sewn to a small heart shaped cushion. 65mm high. *Courtesy Jonathan Horne.*

84. Raised oval patterned jug c.1800
Jug decorated with a pattern of raised ovals, coloured in yellow, manganese and cobalt blue. The lower part of the jug is fluted and there is a painted pattern of flowers and leaves around the neck. The handle incorporating a circle is quite unique in Pratt ware. 120mm high. *Private Collection.*

Puzzle jugs

Earlier versions of these jugs were made in earthenware, stoneware or Delft ware. The one shown here is very untypical, for these jugs usually had full globular bodies and pierced cylindrical necks. The joke was that it was almost impossible to pour or drink from these jugs without spilling the contents.

Puzzle jug 1791
This unusual pearlware piece is sparingly coloured in blue, green and manganese. There are friezes of moulded classical figures set against an orange peel textured background and similar figures interspersed with acanthus leaves round the lower part of the jug. Round the middle of the jug is a line of incised lettering infilled with brown: 'If we slip as sure the best may err were still supported by Almighty care 1791'. The handle is hollow and modelled in the form of an angel with outstretched wings, blowing a trumpet, which forms the sucking spout. 185mm high. *Courtesy Sothebys.*

85. Sir Francis Burdett jug c.1810
An unusual oval creamware jug. The fully moulded portrait has the impressed name below. A seated figure of Liberty decorates the other side. Sparely coloured in burnt orange, brown, green and yellow. 145mm high. *Private Collection.*

86. Sir Francis Burdett jug c.1810
This creamware jug, covered with a green glaze, comes from the same mould as the Prattware example. 145mm high. *Private Collection.*
See page 142 for details of Sir Francis Burdett's career.

Repeats of Pratt ware designs in other bodies

In chapter two we mentioned the fact that the same relief designs that appear on Pratt ware can also be found on fine white smear glazed stoneware and black basalt ware. Since we wrote that we have found a jug in cream coloured earthenware, covered in a green glaze; this was the 'Sir Francis Burdett' jug. We have also found a 'Toper and Smoker' jug in a very crisp brown stoneware body, almost identical in form to the 'Toper and Smoker' Pratt jug shown on page 195 and finally an 'American Eagle' jug (see page 208) in a drab body with pink lustre decorations.

In addition to the 'Mischievous Sport' design on smear glazed stoneware (see page 61) the same design appears on a black basalt sucrier. Various Pratt ware teapots were also made in black basalt.

Black basalt sucrier, c.1795
A sucrier with the scenes of 'Mischievous Sport' on one side and 'Sportive Innocence' on the other. Both set in heart-shaped frames, similar to the designs on various Pratt ware pieces. (See page 188). 105mm high. *Clarice and Harold Blakey Collection.*

300

87. Brown stoneware jug c.1800-10
This very crisply modelled stoneware jug with on one side the scene of a horseman reclining and smoking and on the other a toper. Almost identical to the Pratt ware jug on page 195. This stoneware jug may have been made at Brampton in Derbyshire, but it is unmarked. 145mm high. *Private Collection.*

88. American Eagle jug c.1815
This jug is in a drab ware body, decorated in relief with leaves and flowers and on one side the American Eagle, coloured with pink lustre with underlying washes of pink. There is also a repeating pattern of uncoloured stiff leaves. This jug is identical in design, even to the handle, to the Pratt ware jug shown in colour on page 208. 150mm high. *Private Collection.*

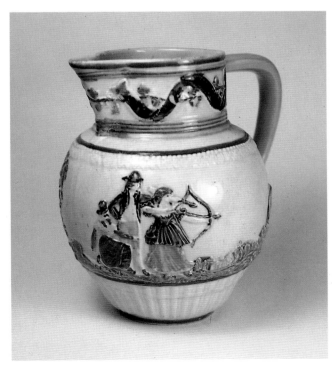

89. The Archery Lesson jug c.1795
A small full bellied jug with a drab putty coloured body, brown banded and decorated in the usual underglaze colours. On the reverse side are two lovers standing between trees. 136mm high. *Private Collection.*

The archery scene is from a Turner mould (see page 27), and appears on a very similar stoneware jug dated 1794. The subject may have been inspired by a popular print called 'Archery at Hatfield House'. This jug was originally in the Bruce George Collection.

301

90. Girl in a mob cap c.1790

A figure very similar to that illustrated on page 262, but wearing a cobalt blue dress and standing on a brown mound, mounted on a flared, floral swagged base, coloured in brown, green and blue. 172mm high. *Private Collection.*

Similar bases can be found on a small group of figures, usually decorated with coloured glazes, though some are found in both underglaze and over glaze colours.

A number of figures on this type of base can be seen in Pat Halfpenny's *English Earthenware Figures 1740-1840.*

92. Figures of gardener and toper c.1795

The gardener is dressed in an ochre coloured coat, Naples yellow breeches and manganese hat and shoes. He stands on a green washed mound, on a square white base. The toper has a manganese hat, ochre coloured coat and blue breeches. He is seated on a white support and leans on a white barrel striped in manganese. 135mm and 115mm high. *Private Collection.*

91. Spill vase with sheep and lamb c.1800

One of a pair, the sheep sparsely coloured with yellow blobs, standing in front of a greeny-grey washed spill vase in the form of a tree trunk. Mounted on a green base with a lamb resting at her feet. There is a small green bocage on either side of the tree trunk. 135mm high. *Private Collection.*

A ram, which is a pair to this sheep, is illustrated in Herbert Read's *Staffordshire Pottery Figures.*

93-95. Mug with sprigged decorations c.1800
This unusual mug has a background of pale blue slip with a vine border and is decorated with classical figures on either side and on the front with a primitive group of the Lion and Unicorn flanking a frame topped with a crown and encircling the Prince of Wales feathers. These decorations are sprigged on the blue background. 85mm. high. *Private Collection.*

There is also a small jug with similar pale blue slip and sprigged decorations in the Sheffield Museum at Weston Park.

Bottle c.1800
A bottle decorated in the usual Pratt palette with different scenes of putti representing the seasons. On the base is a mark with a large letter G impressed with a + mark on either side. 120mm high. *Castle Museum, Nottingham.*
We have so far been unable to identify this mark.

Sprigged mug

It is most unusual to find Pratt ware jugs, mugs etc with sprigged decorations. Nearly always the decorations were sprigged onto the master block and moulds were taken from these; from these the ware was pressed. The mug shown here is untypical of Pratt ware in that it is banded with a blue slip and the decorations were then sprigged on over that.

There is also a small jug with similar pale blue slip and sprigged decoration in the Sheffield Museum at Weston Park.

The bottle from the Castle Museum, Nottingham, is included here because it has a curious unidentified mark.

Appendix I

Will of William Pratt: dated November 13th 1794

The last Will and Testament of me William Pratt of Lane Delf in the County of Stafford Potter. First I will that all my just debts be paid and with the payment of them and of my funeral expenses and probate of this my Will I charge and make liable all my real and personal estate. Also, I give devise and bequeath all and singular my real and personal estates and effects whatsoever and wheresoever unto my dear and loving wife Ellen Pratt and unto James Caird of Newcastle under Lyme in the said County Gentleman, and Charles Simpson of Lane End in the said County Gentleman their heirs and assigns for ever upon Special Trust and Confidences to sell and dispose of the same and turn them into money in the most convenient time they can or at separate times before my youngest child shall attain her age of twenty-one years or in case she shall happen to die, then before my youngest surviving child shall attain that age. And the money thereby arising and from my debts to put and place at interest at the discretion of my Executors hereinafter named and the interest thereby arising and from the rents and profits of my said Real and Personal Estates in the meantime and until the same shall be sold as aforesaid to permit and suffer my said Wife to have and take and employ in and for the maintenance and education bringing up and support of herself and my children until the youngest of them shall attain his or her age of twenty-one years as aforesaid or so much thereof as shall be sufficient and necessary for those purposes. And in case my said Trustees shall think it advisable to borrow and take up at interest any sum or sums of money at interest on mortgate or otherwise on my said Estates for the purposes of paying any of my debts, I do hereby authorize then to do the same as they shall think most proper, provided always and it is my will that none of my household goods shall be sold and disposed of until after my youngest surviving child shall attain the Age of Twenty-one years without the special consent of my said Wife unless she shall happen to marry again provided also that if at any time my said Wife and the said James Caird shall think proper and that it will be for the benefit of any of my children to advance any of them any sum of money not exceeding one hundred pounds in part of their respective portions in my said property it shall be in their power and discretion so to do. And I will that immediately on my said youngest surviving child attaining the age of twenty-one years a division shall immediately take place and be made of all and singular the money arising from my said estate and effects as aforesaid in manner following that is to say the interest of the sum of six hundred pounds I give to my Wife for and during the term of her natural life and also so many of my household goods as shall be necessary to furnish a convenient dwelling house to dwell in and such as she shall choose, the remainder thereof to be then sold and the money therefrom coming as also all other my said property I will shall be divided and paid unto and amongst all my children equally share and share alike without any preference whatsoever. But in case my said Wife shall happen to marry again, then I will that the several trusts hereinbefore reposed in her shall cease and determine and devolve unto my said other trustees and in that case I also will that from and after that event she shall not have any share or interest in the rents profits or interest on my real and Personal Estates nor of the said six hundred pounds, nor the said household goods. But instead thereof I give and

bequeath to her the sum of three hundred pounds to be paid to her within twelve months next after her said marriage and in case of remaining my widow and enjoying the interest of the said sum of six hundred pounds during her life. Then after her decease I will that one half part thereof shall be divided amongst my children as the other part of my estate and effects is directed to be divided and paid and the other half part thereof I will shall be at the disposal of my said Wife by Will or otherwise at her death. And I do declare that the said Legacies so given to my Wife are in full satisfaction and discharge of all power and thirds which she may have or claim from my said Real and personal Estate and Effects. Lastly I nominate and appoint my said Wife the said James Caird and Charles Simpson Executrix and Executors of this my last Will and Testament hereby revoking all other Wills by me made. In witness whereof I have hereunto set my hand and seal the thirteenth day of November in the year of Our Lord One thousand seven hundred and ninetyfour.
Signed   W. Pratt

Signed sealed published and declared by the said William Pratt the Testator as and for his last Will and Testament the interlineations being first made namely the words (and the said James Caird) and also the words (it shall be in their power and discretion so to do) as and for his last Will and Testament in the presence of us who at his request and in his presence have subscribed our names as witnesses.
Signed   J. Heath
         W. Edwards
         S. Solon

William Pratt's Will and Probate dated 1799 with the document of same date Renouncing the Trust and Executorship of James Caird and Charles Simpson are lodged at the Joint Record Office, Lichfield, Staffordshire. The transcript of Probate Records B/C/11 in the Lichfield Joint Record Office appear by courtesy of the Staffordshire County Archivist.

Appendix II

Will of Ellen Pratt dated December 28th 1814

In the name of God Amen I Ellen Pratt of Lane Delph in the Parish of Stoke upon Trent in the County of Stafford Widow do make and ordain this to be my last Will and Testament in manner following   First I direct that all my just debts and my funeral and Testamentary expenses shall be paid and discharged as soon as conveniently maybe after my decease by my Executors hereinafter named out of my Personal Estate Whereas William Pratt late of Lane Delph aforesaid Potter my late Husband deceased by his last Will and Testament bearing date on or about the 13th day of November One Thousand Seven Hundred and Ninety four after directing his Debts and Funeral expenses to be paid and his real Estates to be sold Gave the Interest of the sum of six hundred pounds to me during my life and after my decease he willed that one half thereof should be divided amongst his children and the other half thereof he willed should be at my disposal by Will or otherwise at my death Now I do hereby give bequeath and dispose of the sum of three hundred pounds being one half of the said sum of six hundred pounds together with all my Household Goods and Furniture Plate Linen China and all other my Personal Estate and Effects whatsoever and wheresoever and of what nature or kind soever in manner following that is to say I will and direct that so much thereof as may be necessary shall be applied in payment of all my just Debts and of my funeral and Testamentary expenses and I give and bequeath the sum of one hundred pounds other part thereof unto my daughter Mary Heath Pratt and I direct the same to be paid to her at the expiration of Twelve Calendar Months after my decease and as to all the rest and residue of the said sum of three hundred pounds and of my said other Personalty I give and bequeath the same unto and amongst all my children namely William Pratt, Felix Pratt, John Pratt, Samuel Pratt, Richard Pratt, Myra the Wife of Thomas Harley and the said Mary Heath Pratt equally between them share and share alike And it is my Mind and Will that in case my Personalty shall not be sufficient after payment of my said Debts and general and Testamentary expenses to pay the said legacy or Sum of One hundred Pounds hereinbefore by me given to my said Daughter Mary Heath Pratt then and in such case I do hereby charge and make liable my real Estate hereinafter mentioned with the payment of the said Legacy of One hundred Pounds to my said Daughter Mary Heath Pratt and subject thereto I Give and devise all those my Dwelling houses with the Gardens and Crofts thereto adjoining called Bryons Croft and the Brick House Croft situate and being at or near Lane End in the said Parish of Stoke upon Trent and County of Stafford And also all that my one undivided moiety or equal half part or share of and in All those Potworks Buildings Hereditaments and premises situate and being at Lane Delph aforesaid as the same are now in the occupation of my son John Pratt and also all other my real Estate situate in Lane Delph or elsewhere in the County of Stafford and all my right estate and interest therein or thereto unto the said William Pratt, Felix Pratt, John Pratt, Samuel Pratt, Richard Pratt, Myra the Wife of the said Thomas Harley and Mary Heath Pratt Their heirs and Assigns to hold To them the said William Pratt, Felix Pratt, John Pratt, Samuel Pratt, Richard Pratt, Myra the Wife of the said Thomas Harley and Mary Heath Pratt Their heirs and Assigns for ever equally between them share and share alike as Tenants in Common and not as joint Tenants And it is my Mind and Will that in case any one or more of my said Children shall happen to die before me leaving lawful issue him her or them surviving and then I Give devise and bequeath the part or share or parts or shares of him her or them so dying and leaving issue unto and amongst such issue his her or their Heirs or Assigns for ever in equal shares as Tenants in Common and not as joint Tenants but in case any of them my said Children shall happen to die before me without Issue then I Give devise and bequeath the part or share or parts or shares of him her or them so dying without issue unto the survivors and then my said Children their Heirs and Assigns for ever in equal shares as Tenants in Common and not as joint Tenants And Lastly I do hereby nominate constitute and appoint my said Son Richard Pratt and my Son in Law the said Thomas Harley Executors of this my Will hereby revoking and making void all former and other Will and Wills by me at any time heretofore made In Testimony whereof I have hereunto set my hand and seal

this twenty eighth day of December in the Year of Our Lord one thousand
eight hundred and fourteen.
Signed Sealed published and Declared
by the said Ellen Pratt the Testatrix
as and for her last Will and Testament
in the presence of us who at her   Ellen Pratt
request and in her presence and in
that of each other have hereunto
subscribed our names as Witnesses
   Wm Clarke
   Anthony Forrister
   Daniel Bridgwood

Ellen Pratt's Will and Probate thereof dated July 24th 1815. Transcripts of
Probate Records B/C/ 11 in the Lichfield Joint Record Office appear by
courtesy of The Staffordshire County Archivist.

Appendix III

Extracts from the Will of Felix Pratt of Fenton and Probate dated March 9th 1860

Felix Pratt had three sons, Felix Edwards, Thomas Heath and Matthew Pratt
and three daughters Mary, (wife of John Arnott, potter of Fenton), Alicia
Sarah and Myra Elizabeth Hayes. In his Will he wrote:
'...I give and devise unto the said Felix Edwards Pratt, Thomas Heath Pratt
and Matthew Pratt...my messuages and tenements with the outbuildings,
gardens and appurtenances belonging situate in Pratt Street in Fenton and
now in occupation of John Arnott also a small piece of ground now in the
occupation of Messrs Pratt & Company and used by them as a Marl Bank, also
my messuages etc in High Street Fenton, and my three messuages in Park
Street in Fenton (lately called Lane Delph) and my messuages and tenements
and shop with outbuildings, gardens and appurtenances thereto belonging
situate near the Bridge in Wharf Street to my three sons.' (He lists the various
occupiers)

He left his messuages or tenements and the shop with outbuildings and
appurtenances being near the Cross Keys at Fenton (lately called Lane Delph)
in the Parish of Stoke-on-Trent and miscellaneous shares to include his co-
partner Richard Pratt, who shared all the stock in trade and utensils with his
three sons and three daughters. He left an unspecified number of shares in the
Stoke, Fenton and Longton Gas Works, the Manchester and Liverpool
Banking Co., the Gas Works at Newcastle-under-Lyme and the Staffordshire
Potteries Water Works, as well as a mortgage on a dwelling house and
premises in Burslem let to a Mr. Thomas Lord, boot and shoe maker.

He also left 'two undivided ninety-nine parts or shares of and in the Market
House Stalls, effects and premises belonging to the company of Proprietors of
the Market held at Stoke-on-Trent aforesaid and of and in the Tolls due and
profit arising therefrom unto my son Matthew Pratt.'

The Probate concludes with the statement that his effects were under

£10,000, which shows they must have been in a fair way of business. These extracts are lodged in the Stafford Record Office, Stafford. D 3272/5/20/419 and appear here by courtesy of the Staffordshire County Archivist.

Appendix IV

Recipes for bodies suitable for pressing and casting from Taylor's *Complete Practical Potter*, Shelton, 1847.

No 16 Pearl White Body

150 lbs of Cornish Stone

120 lbs of Blue Clay
110 lbs of China Clay
110 lbs of Flint
(This one is suitable for casting, containing as it does non-plastic ingredients).

No 229 Good body for pressed ware

30 gallons of Blue Clay slip
   24oz to the pint
4 gallons of China Clay slip 26oz to ditto
6½ gallons of Flint Slop (sic) 32oz to ditto
   Add a little stain
(Contains 3:1 plastic to non-plastic
   ingredients).

Although this book is later than the Pratt ware period, the recipes for bodies suitable for casting and pressing are those used earlier in the century.

Appendix V

Extract from M.J.A.Chaptal, *Chemistry applied to the Arts and Manufactures*, London, 1807, Vol.II Cobalt.

The word Cobalt comes from the German word Kobald meaning 'an evil being'. Cobalt was found in the state of oxide combined with sulphur, arsenic and the arsenical acid. . .Arsenic is almost inseparable from this metal (cobalt). The arsenic was removed in a reverberatory furnace terminating in a long chimney. The oxide of arsenic volatized and attached itself to the sides of the chimney. With a rough sense of justice 'it was only allowed to be taken off by men who had been condemned to death for crimes they had committed'. Cobalt deprived of arsenic is known as zaffre. 'It was mixed with one half or three quarters of sand and one part good potash to form glass, which when stamped, sifted and pounded form to the blue of smalts.'

Appendix VI

Extract from M.J.A.Chaptal, *Chemistry applied to the Arts and Manufactures*, London, 1807, Vol.III Prussic Acid

'Animal substances have been the only ones hitherto employed for extracting Prussic acid used in the arts; and although the distillation of blood and the action of nitric acid upon animal albumen, gluten and fibres produce it, it has been chiefly by presenting to it an alkaline base that it has been hitherto extracted; and it is afterwards from these combinations that we liberate it, when we wish to have it pure, or to make it act upon other bases.

First Potash, mixed with an equal quantity of Bullock's blood and calcined until the mixture no longer yields any flame, and is converted in to a red charcoal, seizes upon the prussic acid and forms a prussiate of potash, soluble in water, and which we may clear from all other substances which make it salt, by throwing the red charcoal out of the crucible in to water and afterwards separating the deposit of the liquid in order to have a very pure prussiate of potash. This solution which was for a long time called phlogisticated alkali, and colouring liquid of Prussian Blue is susceptible of furnishing crystals of prussiate if concentrated by evaporation.'

A note about the production of Prussian Blue from Bullock's Blood by Edward Smyth, FRCS.

Cobalt of course is a metallic element and its pigment is quite different from Prussian Blue which is in fact ferric ferrocyanide. As soon as blood (animal or human) begins to break down, it quickly changes from being alkaline to becoming acid as carbonic acid asserts itself, deriving from the bicarbonate salt. This decay of animal blood (no doubt accelerated by some other chemical agent such as a potassium salt) was the basis of Prussian Blue. The decaying blood contained considerable quantities of sulphur which was quickly changed into sulphuretted hydrogen and hence the smell of rotten eggs that so distressed Anthony Hilcote's neighbours on the banks of the Firth of Forth.'

Appendix VII

Notes from *Chemical Essays* by Samuel Parkes, London 1806-1815

Parkes gives brief notes about underglaze colours but does not state precise quantities. In his text he writes: 'The metallic preparations which are commonly used, are the oxides and their combinations with acids. Cobalt yields a blue; antimony and silver give yellows and oranges;...copper for greens; and the reds, browns and blacks are derived from iron'. And then in a series of footnotes he elaborates on this brief statement: 'The oxide of cobalt is usually prepared from zaffre, which is an expensive article imported from Saxony. A few years ago very fine oxide of cobalt was prepared from a mineral found in Cornwall; but the quantity was small, and the vein is now exhausted.

For preparing these yellows, the antimony is first calcined with four times its weight of nitre, and is then mixed with a certain proportion of vitrified lead.

Copper has usually been taken in the state of a precipitate; but some potters have found an article of more value in the pure oxide of copper, which they procure by placing sheets of copper in the ovens in which the ware is glazed. It has lately been discovered that a small proportion of copper mixed with the iron very much increases the intensity of the blacks on earthenware. Iron is capable of giving a great variety of colours, according to the way in which it is managed. For instance, the black oxide produced by heated air only, will be a very different article from an oxide prepared by other means...'

No mention here of manganese, which both Thomas Lakin and Joseph Tomkinson give in their recipes for an underglaze brown.

Samuel Parkes (1761-1825) who was born at Stourbridge in Worcestershire went to a Dame's school in Stourbridge where Mrs. Siddons (then Sarah Kemble) was a fellow pupil. In 1793 he moved to Stoke-on-Trent where he spent about ten years running a soap-boiling business, also becoming familiar with the pottery industry some years before writing his *Essays*.

He had business dealings with Wedgwood and Byerley, and in 1814 sent his manuscript on pottery to Josiah Wedgwood II to check what he had to say about the Etruria firm. Wedgwood replied making numerous amendments in reference to Wedgwoods and Etruria. These corrections were published by Parkes in Volume V. He asked if he could use Josiah Wedgwood's name in his *Essays*. To this Wedgwood would not agree as he said he had not had enough time to give the manuscript his full attention.[1] In 1803 Parkes established himself as a manufacturing chemist in Goswell Street, London. The first edition of his *Chemical Essays* was issued in 1806 and continued to appear until 1815. As a result of this, he achieved considerable fame and received honours from various learned societies.

1. Notes and material supplied by Rodney Hampson.

Appendix VIII

Colours under the glaze

No 1   Painting green   run down
        6 lbs yellow under the glaze   glost oven
        6 lbs ground glass   afterwards to be ground
        ¾ (lb) or 16 ounces of blue calx

No 2   Brown under the glaze
        3 litharge   to be calcined at the top of the
        2 Antimony & 1 Manganese   biscuit oven under the chimney
                                                          – not to be covered
        Add to the above when sent to the mill; to every 10 lbs of the above add
        2 lbs Zaffre and ½ lb Blue Calx

No 3   Yellow under the glaze
        4 lbs Tin Ash. 1 lb Antimony i litharge
        pounded fine and well mixed together and fired over a flinted hiller one
        inch thick and not to be covered

No 4   Orange under the glaze
        4 Antimony   4 litharge   2 Tinashes   2 Colcotha[1]
        or
        3 litharge   2 Antimony   1¼ Crocus Martis
        All the above to be fired according to directions in No 2.

1. According to the Oxford English Dictionary 'Colcothar' is also called 'Crocus Martis', though apparently the Rileys thought there was a difference.

From John and Richard Riley's notebook c.1824 lodged in the City Museum and Art Gallery Stoke-on-Trent.

John and Richard Riley were manufacturers of earthenware and china in Burslem and elsewhere from 1802 to 1824.

Appendix IX

Extracts from *The Valuable Receipts of the late Mr. Thomas Lakin. Leeds 1824*

To make a Naples yellow underglaze

Take 12 parts of white lead, 2 parts of Diaphoretic Antimony, 1 part of Crude Sal Amonic (sic) ½ part of Alum
It is requisite that the ingredients for this colour be finely mixed up together, and calcined in a crucible, over a slow fire, for the space of three hours, stirring it nearly the whole of the time, when the mass will be found of a beautiful yellow or gold colour.

To make a lining brown underglaze

Take 7 parts of glass of Antimony, 3 parts of raw litharge, 2½ parts of manganese, 1 part of nitre and 1 part of blue calx.

To make a painting brown underglaze

Take 5 parts of glass of Antimony, 5 parts of litharge and ½ a part of blue calx.

To make an orange under the glaze

Take 6 parts of raw litharge, 4 parts of Crude Antimony, 2 parts of Crocus Martis and one part of oxide of tin.

To make a yellow under the glaze

Take 4 parts of raw litharge, 3 parts of Crude Antimony and 1½ parts of oxide of tin.

To make a green underglaze

Take 12 parts of oxide of yellow, 4 parts of white enamel, 2 parts of frit and 1¼ parts of blue calx.
The ingredients for the preceding colours underglaze, with the exception of green, should be mixed together and calcined in a reverberatory furnace or glazing oven, in seggar (sic) hillers, or dishes lined with flint; Then spread on the mixture about an inch in thickness, observing that the hiller or dish have a sufficient access of air allowed to prevent the metals from reviving again in their metallic state; the green ingredients only require grinding.

To procure the regulus of zaffre

This is the first process towards making blue calx and is called running down, but more properly smelting. 112 parts zaffre
57 parts potash
18½ parts charcoal

The charcoal being pulverized and all the materials mixed up together afterwards put into crucibles capable of holding 3 or 4 quarts and filled quite full. Then placed in a reverberatory furnace commencing with a slow fire, but as soon as it is heated will require a considerably stronger fire before cohesion between different particles is sufficiently destroyed. Will take about ten hours. The weight of the regulus being 31-33 lbs; on examining the scoria if there remains with it small pieces of metal like small shot, or when pounded the scoria has a bluish cast, the fire has not been strong enough. At the bottom of each cake of regulus there will be bismuth slightly adhering, which is easily separated without the application of any great degree of heat, by placing the cakes upon an iron plate or pan which will soon bring the bismuth into a state of liquifaction and separated from the regulus.

To refine the Regulus of Zaffre

Take 50 parts of regulus, 6 parts of potash and 3 parts of sand. Put in smaller crucibles holding about 1½ lb each (repeat firing instructions as above for about 8 hours) Another course of refining may be necessary.

To procure blue calx from refined regulus of zaffre

Take 30 parts of refined regulus, 1 part of plaster and ½ part of borax.

To make a superior cream coloured body

1½ parts Blue Clay, 1½ parts Brown Clay
1 part Black Clay, 1 part Cornish Clay
1 part of flint, ¼ part Cornish stone

To make a white earthenware glaze

35 parts of Cornish stone 20 parts Borax 10 parts Crystal of Soda ⅛ part of Blue Calx.
Calcined, pulverized coarsely and ground with 20 lbs white lead 10 lbs Cornish Stone 5 lbs flint to produce a fine white glaze.

Appendix X
The mining of cobalt

The first discovery of cobalt in the British Isles was in Scotland. A vein of silver had been discovered in the Ochil Hills in 1711. For a short while it proved very profitable, but was soon exhausted and the mine was closed. In 1759 the mine was reopened and in a further and unsuccessful search for silver, a large deposit of cobalt ore was discovered, which proved of great value to the Scottish potteries. The English potters continued to rely on supplies from Saxony, until the Napoleonic wars caused them to look elsewhere.

It was not until the early years of the nineteenth century that adequate supplies of cobalt were found in Cornwall and Cheshire. The largest supplies in Cornwall came from the Wheal Sparnon mine, Redruth, a large and flourishing copper mine which was abandoned in 1768, and was reopened in 1808, soon producing copper and tin. Cobalt appears to have been recognised there at least as early as 1808; in July 1817 the *West Briton* reported that about £4,000 worth of cobalt oxide had been sold to the potters in the previous twelve

312

months.[1] The refining was done in Staffordshire by the British Cobalt Smelting Company at Hanley.[2]

Cobalt ore was also found in 1806 at the Alderley Edge copper and lead mines in Cheshire, which had been leased to the Alderley Mine Company by Sir John Stanley in the previous year. Samples of this cobalt ore were sent to Josiah Wedgwood II, but met with little favour.[3] However, a couple of years later, supplies of cobalt ore from the Alderley mines were leased to John Plowes of the Ferrybridge Pottery (which made Pratt ware), for £2,000 per annum plus a royalty to Lord Stanley. Deliveries of this cobalt ore to Ferrybridge began in 1808; within a year the lease was terminated, maybe because of cash flow problems from which the Ferrybridge partners were suffering.

The Alderley Mine Company continued to produce cobalt ore which was taken to a treatment works at Wallasey; this works closed in 1817, no doubt due to competition, resulting from the revival of imports of what was possibly a superior cobalt ore from the Continent.[4]

Cobalt was in fact for a while used rather sparingly on most Pratt ware, probably because it was in short supply during the Napoleonic Wars.

---

1. Dr. A.K. Hamilton Jenkin, *Mines and Miners of Cornwall*, III, Around Redruth, Bracknell, 1979.
2. Bernard Watney, *English Blue and White Porcelain of the Eighteenth Century*, London, 1973.
3. Wedgwood Ms. 269-2. Keele University Library.
4. G. Warrington, B.Sc., Ph.D., F.G.S., 'The Copper Mines of Alderley Edge and Mottram St. Andrew, Cheshire', *Journal of the Chester Archaeological Society*, Vol. 64, 1981.

Bibliography

1. *Staffordshire Potters from the Rate Books 1807-1859,* transcribed by Alfred Meigh, Keele University Library, 1940.
   Simeon Shaw, *History of the Staffordshire Potteries,* Hanley, 1829. Reprinted 1970 by David & Charles, Newton Abbot, and S.R. Publications Ltd., Wakefield.
   William Chaffers, *Marks and Monograms on Pottery and Porcelain,* Reeves and Turner, London, 13th edn., 1912.
   G. Woolliscroft Rhead, *The Earthenware Collector,* Herbert Jenkins, London, 1920.

2. M.J.A. Chaptal, *Chemistry Applied to the Arts and Manufactures,* London, 1807.
   Samuel Parkes, F.L.S., *Chemical Essays,* London, 1815.
   The Valuable Receipts of the late Mr. Thomas Lakin, Leeds, 1824.
   Simeon Shaw, *The Chemistry of Pottery,* London, 1837.
   Taylor's Complete Practical Potter, Shelton, 1847.
   Dr. Ure's Dictionary of Arts, Manufactures and Mines, Ed. Robert Hunt, F.R.S., London, 7th Edn., 1875.
   E.J.D. Warrilow, *A Sociological History of Stoke-on-Trent,* Etruscan Publications, 1960.
   Donald Towner, *Creamware,* Faber and Faber, London, 1978.

3. John Ward, *The History of the Borough of Stoke-on-Trent,* 1843, reprinted by David & Charles, Newton Abbot, and S.R. Publications Ltd., Wakefield, 1970.
   Eliza Meteyard, *The Life of Josiah Wedgwood,* Hurst and Blackett, London, 1875.
   Josiah C. Wedgwood, *A History of the Wedgwood Family,* London, 1908.
   Josiah C. Wedgwood, *Staffordshire Pottery and its History,* Samson Low Marston & Co., London, 1913.
   The Selected Letters of Josiah Wedgwood, Ed. Ann Finer and George Savage, Cory, Adams and Mackay, London, 1965.

4. J.R. & F. Kidson, *Historical Notices of the Old Leeds Pottery,* pub. by J.R. Kidson, Leeds, 1892.
   Donald Towner, *The Leeds Pottery,* Cory, Adams and Mackay, London, 1963.
   Oxley Grabham, *Yorkshire Potteries, Pots and Potters,* York, 1916, reprinted S.R. Publications, Wakefield, 1971.
   Heather Lawrence, *Yorkshire Pots and Potteries,* David & Charles, Newton Abbot, 1974.
   Peter Walton, *Creamware and other English Pottery at Temple Newsam House, Leeds,* Manningham Press, Bradford, 1976.
   Diana Edwards Roussel, *The Castleford Pottery 1790-1821,* Wakefield, 1982.

5. H. Boswell Lancaster, *Liverpool and her Potters,* Jones & Co., Liverpool, 1936.
   Alan Smith, *The Illustrated Guide to Liverpool Herculaneum Pottery 1796-1840,* Barrie & Jenkins, London, 1970.

6.   R.C. Bell, *Tyneside Pottery,* Studio Vista, London, 1971.
      J.T. Shaw, *Sunderland Ware: the Potteries of Wearside,* Sunderland, 1973.

7.   J. Arnold Fleming, *Scottish Pottery,* Maclehose, Jackson & Co., Glasgow, 1923.
      Patrick McVeigh, *Scottish East Coast Potteries 1750-1840,* John Donald, Edinburgh, 1979.

9 and 10.   John Hall, *Staffordshire Portrait Figures,* Charles Letts & Co. Ltd., London, 1972.
      John and Jennifer May, *Commemorative Pottery 1780-1900,* Heinemann, London, 1972.
      Robin Reilly and George Savage, *Wedgwood: the Portrait Medallions,* Barrie & Jenkins, London, 1973.

11.   Arthur Hayden, *Spode and his Successors,* Cassell & Co., London, 1925.
      Reginald G. Haggar, *English Country Pottery,* London, 1950.
      Bevis Hillier, *The Turners of Lane End,* Cory, Adams and Mackay, London, 1965.
      Leonard Whiter, *Spode,* Barrie & Jenkins, London, 1970.

12.   Wedgwood, *Early Wedgwood Pottery,* Barlaston, 1951.
      Wedgwood, *The Book of Wedgwood Bas-Reliefs,* Barlaston, 1982.

13.   R.K. Price, *Astbury, Whieldon and Ralph Wood Figures and Toby Jugs,* John Lane, London, 1922.
      Sir Harold Mackintosh, Bt., *Early English Figure Pottery,* Chapman and Hall, London, 1938.

16.   G.W. & F.A. Rhead, *Staffordshire Pots and Potters,* Hutchinson & Co., London, 1906.
      Frank Falkner, *The Wood Family of Burslem,* London, 1912, reprinted by E.P. Publishing Ltd., Wakefield, 1972.
      Cyril Earle, *The Earle Collection of Early Staffordshire Pottery,* A. Brown & Sons, London and New York, 1915.
      Herbert Read, *Staffordshire Pottery Figures,* Duckworth, London, 1929.
      Reginald G. Haggar, *Staffordshire Chimney Ornaments,* London, 1955.

Catalogues and Encyclopedias

Henry Willett, *Catalogue of a Collection of Pottery and Porcelain illustrating Popular British History,* H.M.S.O., 1899. (This catalogue was compiled for an exhibition at the Bethnal Green branch of the Victoria and Albert Museum. The remains of the collection are housed at the Royal Pavilion Art Gallery and Museums, Brighton.)
Bernard Rackham, *Catalogue of the Schreiber Collection, Vol. 2 Earthenware, Victoria and Albert Museum, 1930.*
Bernard Rackham, *Catalogue of the Glaisher Collection of Pottery and Porcelain in the Fitzwilliam Museum, Cambridge,* Cambridge, 1934.

W. Mankowitz and R.G. Haggar, *The Concise Encyclopedia of English Pottery and Porcelain,* André Deutsch, London, 1957.

Geoffrey A. Godden, *Encyclopedia of British Pottery and Porcelain Marks,* Herbert Jenkins, London, 1964.

Geoffrey A. Godden, *An Illustrated Encyclopedia of British Pottery and Porcelain,* Herbert Jenkins, 1966.

Ross E. Taggart, *The Frank P. and Harriet C. Burnap Collection of English Pottery,* Nelson Gallery-Atkins Museum, Kansas City, Missouri, 1967.

Jo Draper, *Jugs in the Northampton Museum,* Northampton Borough Council, 1978.

The Delhom Gallery Guide: Pottery, Mint Museum, Charlotte, North Carolina, 1982.

A. Hurst, *Catalogue of the Boynton Collection of Yorkshire Pottery,* 1922.

Articles referred to in: *Northern Ceramic Society's Journals, English Ceramic Circle's Transactions, Scottish Pottery Historical Review, Apollo, The Connoisseur, American Antiques Collector, Antiques Magazine, The American Wedgwoodian.*

Index to Chapter 17 Afterthoughts

Index